CHURCH, STATE, AND THE CRISIS
IN AMERICAN SECULARISM

Church, State, and the Crisis in American Secularism

BRUCE LEDEWITZ

INDIANA UNIVERSITY PRESS

Bloomington & Indianapolis

This book is a publication of

Indiana University Press
601 North Morton Street
Bloomington, Indiana 47404-3797 USA

iupress.indiana.edu

Telephone orders   800-842-6796
Fax orders   812-855-7931
Orders by e-mail   iuporder@indiana.edu

⊚ The paper used in this publication
meets the minimum requirements of
the American National Standard for
Information Sciences—Permanence
of Paper for Printed Library
Materials, ANSI Z39.48-1992.

Manufactured in the United
States of America

Library of Congress Cataloging-
in-Publication Data

Ledewitz, Bruce [date]
  Church, state, and the crisis in American
secularism / Bruce Ledewitz.
    p. cm.
  Includes bibliographical
references and index.
  ISBN 978-0-253-35634-5 (hardcover
: alk. paper) 1. Church and state—
United States. 2. Ecclesiastical
law—United States. 3. Freedom of
religion—United States. I. Title.
  KF4865.L43 2011
  342.7308'52—dc22

                          2010054366

1 2 3 4 5   16 15 14 13 12 11

To Charles L. Black, Jr., who made the People live

If you believe in magic, come along with me

The Lovin' Spoonful

CONTENTS

PREFACE

This book is the third in a series. The other two books are *American Religious Democracy: Coming to Terms with the End of Secular Politics* (2007) and *Hallowed Secularism: Theory, Belief, Practice* (2009). Although each book stands on its own, I owe my readers a statement of the context out of which this book arises and an overview of what I have been trying to accomplish with all three.

The 2004 presidential election demonstrated to me that American politics and law were not consistent with reality. In politics, while we were giving lip service to the idea that we had a secular government, anyone could see that our elections were characterized by religiously oriented voting. In law, the doctrine of government neutrality toward religion dominated judicial opinions, but the actual outcomes of cases were inconsistent with any such rule. And in many ways we were emphasizing a divide between religion and secularism while the concerns and commitments of religious and non-religious people actually overlapped. It seemed to me that we needed to reorganize our thinking in these related areas.

I began with politics in *American Religious Democracy*. I argued there that the 2004 election, with its very clear delineation of religious voting patterns—the more often you went to church, the more likely you were to vote for George W. Bush—rendered talk of "secular" politics ridiculous. Nor did the 2004 election result in "theocracy"—it was democracy in action.

Religious democracy was more than just a fact of political reality. I argued that the whole notion of secular politics is empty; that religion, which many secularists had been trying to banish from public life, was on the whole a beneficial and even necessary aspect of politics. I suggested that secularists take another look at religious values, language, and traditions in what one reviewer called a "secular sermon."

Of course, by the time the book came out, we were in the early stages of the 2008 presidential campaign, which turned out to be even more religiously oriented than the 2004 race had been. So, in that sense, my thesis about religious democracy was vindicated.

But, in another sense, a more secular reality was already dawning. During the period 2004–2007, a new phenomenon emerged—a fully popular atheism that became known as the New Atheism. The list of the New Atheists is well known: Sam Harris, Daniel Dennett, Richard Dawkins, Victor Stenger, and of course Christopher Hitchens. These writers made it possible, almost respectable, for large numbers of people to openly despise religion. There were more secularists than ever before, many of them were young, and some of these young people were ignorant about religion and were learning about it from those New Atheist books.

I viewed this trend with dread, for there could be nothing worse for secularists than to be drawn into this anti-religionism. I feared it especially for the young who had little contact with intelligent religion of any kind and did not even know the Bible. They were mostly unfamiliar with the positive aspects of religion. I thought they might take a Christopher-Hitchens fantasy of God and believers for the real thing. And then what would they have? None of these New Atheists offered a positive alternative philosophy for living.

In this spirit I wrote *Hallowed Secularism,* with a little help from E. L. Doctorow, from whose novel, *City of God,* I took the central image. I hoped in this book to offer a different secular world to those who, like myself, could not believe in all the doctrines of any of Our Religions, but who might be drawn to them all the same. I am one who admires Our Religions from afar, so to speak, believing that many of the religions' particulars are wrong, but somehow that their overall thrust is the closest thing to 'right' there is. The original title of the book was, "A Guide for the Non-Believer," as I intended it to serve as a guidebook.

After those two books, it became obvious to me that American constitutional law stood in the way of any serious engagement of secularism with religion. We could not have a politics open to religion if we were required by law to have secular politics. We could not have holiness in our personal lives and divine justice in our social lives if everything was framed as having a secular purpose and secular meant without the holy. We needed a new law of church and state.

The tricky part of this change was that we were going to get a new law of church and state no matter what I or anyone else wrote. Once Chief Justice John Roberts and Associate Justice Samuel Alito were added to the Supreme Court, it was just a matter of time before the government neutrality cases were overruled, either expressly or practically. So it wasn't necessary to argue for changing the outcomes of cases. Rather, I wanted the law of church and state to change in a different way. I wanted not just more room for religion, but a new understanding of the relationship among religion, secularism, and national life. I didn't want the religious people to win cases, and I didn't want secularists to lose them. I wanted all of us to win. How could that be accomplished?

Given demographic changes in America, there is something clearly right about the nonreligious State. You cannot just ignore millions of secularists. And there is also something clearly right about rejecting any government-sponsored, normative claims by the majority's monotheistic religion. You cannot just ignore millions of religious believers who reject the Creator–God of the Bible. What was needed was a constitutional interpretation that proclaimed some kind of common ground among monotheistic believers, non-monotheistic believers, and nonbelievers. That common ground would also exclude people, of course, but it would not do so along religious and anti-religious lines.

I believe that the tradition of higher law, broadly conceived as the theory of objective value, accomplishes just such a common ground. With it, we could have a religious politics or a secular politics, or both, without infringing on anyone's beliefs. With higher law as a foundation, one could foresee the emergence of a secular way of life genuinely open to the meaning of religion. The secularist could be hallowed without embracing any religious dogma.

That was my hope in writing this book. I have tried here to describe a legal regime that would support the politics and theology I had already set forth in the two earlier books. Whether this attempt succeeded, only the reader can judge.

ACKNOWLEDGMENTS

In the two books that preceded this one, I thanked my friends and family and acknowledged my intellectual debts. None of that needs to be repeated, with one exception: I must once again thank my friend and colleague of thirty years, Robert Taylor. Robert and I have studied together throughout most of that time. Like Socrates, Robert does not like to write and, again like Socrates, he succeeds in imparting the wisdom of how little we know.

There are several other persons, whom I wish to thank here, who have had an important relationship to this book. First and foremost I owe a debt to Robert Sloan, Editorial Director of Indiana University Press. Bob believed in this book from the start and took a chance on a novel thesis from a relatively unknown author at an out-of-the-way school. I also want to thank the staff at Indiana University Press for their hard work in preparing the book. Next, I would like to thank the Duquesne Law School Summer Writing Program, which in 2008 and 2009 allowed me to prepare two law review articles that formed the foundation of this book. The first article, "Could Government Speech Endorsing a Higher Law Resolve the Establishment Crisis?" *St. Mary's Law Journal* 41 (2009): 41, provided the skeleton for parts 1 and 2; and the second, "The New New Secularism and the End of the Law of Separation of Church and State," *Buffalo Public Interest Law Journal* 28 (2010): 1, forms the basis of part 3. The editors of these two journals have kindly granted permission for the use of those articles here. My current research assistant, Melissa Derby, and former research assistant, Kaitlynd Kruger, provided inestimable help in preparing the manuscript and supplementary materials. Bridget Praskovich, a crackerjack proofreader, and Amy Lovell at Duquesne Law School figured out everything needed for the actual publication of the book, and then put it in final form, while my administrative assistant, Kathy Koehler, kept track of everything else. I thank them all.

I also want to acknowledge Charles Black, to whom this book is dedicated. I knew Professor Black at Yale Law School, where he was my teacher. I learned three lessons from him. First, I learned that justice is real and enduring—a lesson I should not have needed to learn, for it was something I already believed. But it was a lesson that suffered many attacks from other quarters in law school. I also learned that the People are the intended beneficiaries of all that a lawyer does. We must keep the People in our minds at all times and not imagine a nation of merely individual interests. Finally, I learned that law is an art. It is the art of serving the welfare of the People, and though law has many technical aspects, it has no technical function.

Finally, my deep love and thanks to my wife, Patt, who saved me once and continues to save me every day.

INTRODUCTION

There are two church/state crises today in America. The first is a crisis in the law of the Establishment Clause, which states that "Congress shall make no law respecting an establishment of religion." Although the United States Supreme Court has promised government neutrality toward religion, America continues to have a very religiously oriented, indeed a monotheistically oriented, public square. In over a half century since *Everson v. Board of Education*[1] first introduced the norms of government neutrality and the wall of separation between church and state, there is still no broad consensus among the American people concerning the proper role of religion in the public square. Nor is there basic agreement among the justices on the United States Supreme Court as to the permissible role of religion. There are details that are shared, such as the anti-coercion principle, but there is not agreement as to foundations. The key question—whether we are to have a genuinely secular government—has not been answered. The gap between the Court's pronouncements, on the one hand, and social reality, on the other, is perhaps best symbolized by the words "under God" in the Pledge of Allegiance, which a lower federal court, in 2003, found to be an unconstitutional establishment of religion, before the United States Supreme Court reversed the decision on standing grounds. Many observers of the legal landscape expect a change either in what we do or in what we say about what we do. Most expect the Court to disclaim neutrality.

The second crisis is as yet barely visible to most people. Secularism is growing in America. Perhaps 15 percent of the population has no institutional religion and this number will likely increase. Secularism is now popular enough that one may consider it a social phenomenon in its own right. Secularism is no longer a simple description of the consequence of loss of belief; to many, it represents an alternative way of life that should be satisfying in its own right.

The crisis in secularism is in its relationship to religion. American secularism has been reflexively anti-religion. This distancing has cut secularism off from the sources of wisdom that religion has traditionally represented. New voices in secularism are calling for a reevaluation of the available sources of meaning for human life, which might lead to a rapprochement with religion. At this point, no one can foresee the direction in which secularism in America will go. Will it continue in its current direction toward relativism and postmodern humanism or will it seek common ground with our religious traditions?

These two crises—in the interpretation of the Establishment Clause and within secularism—are related. It is not too dramatic to say that strict separation of church and state is currently American secularism's official constitutional position. The concept of constitutionalized separation of church and state provides the normative foundation for secularism's general attempt to distance itself from religion and to treat religion as a merely personal and private matter. A movement in secularism toward engagement with religious sources is, therefore, almost inconceivable without an accompanying reconsideration of the meaning of the Establishment Clause.

What is needed to resolve both crises is a common ground between religion and secularism. If it could be shown that many believers and nonbelievers share certain commitments, those commitments could then be expressed in the public square, even by government, without any violation of the separation of church and state. And perhaps, although this is a more controversial assertion, religious imagery, language, and symbols could be used to illustrate these shared commitments.

I believe that the higher law tradition can represent just such common ground. Let me demonstrate in a story just how this common ground might work. At a 2008 symposium entitled "Is There a Higher Law? Does it Matter?" Pepperdine law professor Robert Cochran discussed his law-student days at the University of Virginia. In the story, Cochran's professor of jurisprudence—Calvin Woodward—illustrated through the architecture of the University of Virginia a kind of moral thinking that was disappearing in the twentieth century:

> Above the columns at the entrance to Clark Hall . . . carved in stone was the statement: "That those alone may be servants of the law who labor with learning, courage, and devotion to preserve liberty and promote justice."
> From the front, we walked into a massive entry hall, adorned on either side with murals. On one side was Moses presenting the Ten Commandments to the Israelites. On the other was what appeared to be a debate in a Greek public square. As we gazed up at the larger-than-life figures, they seemed to represent the higher aspirations of the law.[2]

The key to the story for Professor Cochran was the word "justice" in the inscription. Once, all or most American lawyers would have agreed that justice is an objective value—something built into the fabric of existence. Thus assertions about justice could be regarded as true or false in some sense, and law could be measured against that objective standard as either just or unjust. One name for this understanding of reality is the doctrine of higher law, of which the best known exemplar is natural law. This was the point of the story in terms of the symposium topic. According to the jurisprudence professor, this kind of higher law thinking was in decline and was being replaced by various forms of moral and legal relativism. Cochran was taught that this trend toward relativism was the major jurisprudential shift of the twentieth century.

In terms of the Establishment Clause, there are two important implications of this story. First, the University of Virginia, a public university—hence the government—was supporting one side in this modern controversy over the nature of morality. The government, in the guise of the university, was asserting, symbolically but quite definitively, that justice is real. That was the government's message in the inscription and in the murals. Second, the government was using a traditional religious image—the giving of the Ten Commandments to Israel—along with a nonreligious image—Greek philosophers—to illustrate this government message about the nature of morality. So, in essence, the government was taking a controversial metaphysical position and was using religion in part to support and represent it.

There would probably be widespread agreement that these murals displayed at a public university do not violate the constitutional prohibition against the establishment of religion. For some people, including Justice Stephen Breyer, the fact that the architecture had been there for a while, and without controversy, would itself eliminate any Establishment Clause problem.[3] But I think many people, including many nonbelievers, would feel that there was no violation even if the university were to put the images up anew.

The reason that this display of the Ten Commandments would probably not raise an establishment-of-religion objection is the presence of Greek philosophical debate as part of the display. That reference to Athens demonstrates that the government was using a religious symbol along with a nonreligious symbol to make a moral claim that transcends the particular message of either symbol. The government was asserting the importance of justice, not that God gave the law. The use of the murals suggests that both the Hebrews and the Greek philosophers believed that justice is real and that we observers should believe it, too.

The monotheistic religious believer—Christian, Jew, Muslim, or other—who encounters this architectural display would understand that it is asserting that justice is real. Such a believer agrees with that position. But she would also believe that the Greek philosophers were mistaken in imagining that human reason alone could reveal ultimate justice. In other words, the believer's acceptance of the government's nonreligious message is enhanced, but only to a degree, by the use of a traditional religious symbol.

A higher law secularist would have a different reaction to the display. This secularist would agree that justice is real, but would believe that religion is mistaken in promoting the notion of a supernatural revelation of justice. Instead, she holds that either reason, history, nature, or some combination thereof, are adequate explanations of the source of our concept of justice and of what justice ultimately requires. This nonreligious foundation for the government's message is represented by the Greek philosophers.

Thus, for both the religious and the nonreligious observer, the display may be understood to present a purportedly universal message transcending any one religious tradition, and, at the same time, to present religiously sectarian meanings, about which the observers would disagree. Both observers would understand the display along these lines.

Now imagine a skeptical secular observer. Many modern thinkers, especially among the nonreligious, dispute the assertion that justice is real as either a false, or even a meaningless, claim. Such a person, looking at this architectural display, would insist that both the Ten Commandments and the conclusions of Greek philosophy represent thought systems that were highly culturally conditioned (for example, in their view of women). None of the assertions in the Bible or in Greek philosophy are eternally and objectively valid. The government message in the display is thus false.

Yet, despite this profound disagreement with the message of the display, it would be difficult to argue that this secular relativist has a legal right to prevent the government from making the claim that justice is real. The government constantly makes assertions that many people dispute, but such assertions do not violate anyone's constitutional rights. That authority has a name in constitutional jurisprudence. It is called the doctrine of government speech.

This book suggests that there might be in Professor Cochran's simple story a resolution of both the Establishment Clause crisis and the crisis in secularism. The doctrine of government speech may justifiably permit many seemingly religious government messages. These religious messages might be constitutionally permitted as plausible assertions of the existence of higher law.

As we will see, justices on the United States Supreme Court have already suggested that when the government is using religious symbols in a way that can be understood as supporting interests that transcend religion, or is using public resources to promote such interests, the government is not violating the Establishment Clause. Thus, for example, the government was permitted in the *Everson* case to bus students to all schools, including religious ones, in the interests of the nonreligious value of public safety.

But the justices have not yet transferred this kind of government discretion to government assertions about the nature of reality. The unwillingness of the justices to engage with philosophical and religious ideas on a deeper level has led to an odd discrepancy. Public religious displays and imagery are routinely upheld by the courts, but without any convincing explanation. This book aims to provide that explanation and to do so through the concept of higher law.

Sometimes displays such as the one at the University of Virginia, public prayer, or other such forms of religious expression, are referred to dismissively as "ceremonial deism" or "civil religion." In effect, they are said not to be religious at all. But the claims that justice is real, that rights are inherent, that the universe is meaningful, or even that there is a desire among human beings for absolute meaning, are not banal or simplistic. They are at the heart of a fundamental cultural dispute in the early twenty-first century. We will return to this dispute in the chapters that follow.

Usually arguments like the one I am making, that welcome religion into the public square, would be made by a religious believer and would then be opposed by nonbelievers. But a change in the cultural status of secularism has occurred that has altered this context. I am proposing a new law of church and state as a secularist, in the interests of a healthy secularism.

Secularists I will discuss in this book, notably Austin Dacey, Chet Raymo, and André Comte-Sponville, among others, are thinking about secularism in a new way, including its commitments to truth and to spirituality. Although these thinkers disagree profoundly among themselves on many topics, they probably would all assent to the idea that it is not sufficient for secularism to just be anti-religion. A secular civilization needs to assert more than that to be healthy.

As a secularist myself, I have been part of this recent secular ferment. Assuming that one day there will be a genuinely autonomous secular culture in America, I have been wondering what that culture will be like. I have noticed that among some legal thinkers who champion the separation of church and state, there is an assumption that moral relativism is part and parcel of a secular public square. Steven Gey is a good example of this tendency because he is aware of, and open about, his assumptions.

I fear that the secular commitment to the separation of church and state will slide into other commitments, such as an instinctive rejection of the notion of the objective existence of values.

So what is at stake in reconceptualizing church and state in order to permit government to endorse a common core of values often associated with religion is to keep a cultural space open for perspectives other than relativism, materialism, and humanism. It is an attempt to simultaneously expand and sharpen the debate that is going on today within secularism. Without this cultural space, a secular society might find itself enmeshed in relativism and even nihilism without ever actually consciously choosing that path.

Pope Benedict XVI recently said something that is very close to the sentiment in this book. The Pope visited the United States in April 2008. Reflecting later on that visit, he was quoted as saying that "in its multicultural plurality . . . founded on the basis of a 'happy marriage' of religious principles [and] political rights" the United States "is an example of healthy secularism."[4]

These words by the Pope reflect an acknowledgment that America is secular now in important ways. The Pope was not criticizing that or seeking to change it. He was suggesting, however, that American life is currently as healthy as it is—as hopeful, as truthful, and as open—in part because of America's religious heritage. Unspoken by the Pope, but nevertheless to be feared, is the possibility that if that religious heritage fades from public consciousness, American life may come to express a different kind of secularism, one that is not so healthy. This book argues for a vibrant and religiously open secularism. It is an attempt to refute a narrow secular state position and to support instead a state supportive of deep and enriching spiritual life.

In addition to my fears for secularism, there is another reason to propose a new understanding of the relationship of church and state at this time. The current composition of the United States Supreme Court is quite supportive of the public expression of religion. The current Court is not going to remove the words "under God" from the Pledge of Allegiance or limit public subsidies for school voucher programs or do anything else along those lines. Litigants supporting religious expression in the public square do not need this book to succeed in the courts.

And that will remain true for a long time, even though the Democrats captured the White House and retained control of Congress in the 2008 election.

But, while it might appear that I agree with the Court majority in these areas, the reader will see that my understanding of religious imagery and its role in public life is much more inclusive than that of the current Court majority. That majority may be willing to embrace Jews, Christians, and, to a lesser extent, Muslims, but at the expense not only of nonbelievers, but of Buddhists, Hindus, and other minority religious believers. And that Court majority seems poised to do this in the name of a false and restrictive version of American history. The Court thus seems to be positioning itself to control matters that should be left open to further cultural and political development, and to be doing so on the basis of cultural winners and losers.

I would like to substitute a different understanding of the relationship among majority believers, minority believers, and nonbelievers. This book aims to free both secularism and religion from our current wooden categories so that transcendent reality, which is a part of higher law, broadly conceived, will no longer be used as a weapon in political and legal contests. I hope that we will soon be using the word "God," and other religious symbols, not to support a sectarian program, but to evoke commitments that are actually widely shared among believers and nonbelievers.

The legal theorist Ronald Dworkin observed in his book *Is Democracy Possible Here?*[5] that America is divided over the role religion should play in politics and public life. He suggests that debate about these matters must "end in a debate about competing ideals" rather than about particular practices.[6] Dworkin then offers two models to illustrate the choices before us:

> Americans agree on one crucially important principle: our government must be tolerant of all peaceful religious faiths and also of people of no faith. But from what base should our tolerance spring? Should we be a religious nation, collectively committed to values of faith and worship, but with tolerance for religious minorities including nonbelievers? Or should we be a nation committed to thoroughly secular government but with tolerance and accommodation for people of religious faith? A religious nation that tolerates nonbelief? Or a secular nation that tolerates religion?[7]

If I had to choose between these two models, I would choose the secular state, for reasons that Dworkin presents. But it is my hope that we can avoid this kind of either/or decision. If we have to choose between these models, the outcome of every election will be influenced by voting along the religion-or-secular-state line. Every election will be something of a referendum on God's role in the public square. This scenario would be unfortunate for America in many ways, and I notice that the Democratic Party seems anxious to avoid that kind of continuing electoral divide.

This book suggests instead that there can be a connection between religion and at least certain forms of secularism that blurs the distinction Dworkin is sharpening. This is not a matter of political compromise, but of seeing real connections. Religious imagery in the public square turns out to contain myriad meanings that transcend religion and may thus bridge the religious divisions that exist among us.

This book proceeds along a simple framework. Part 1 sets forth the Establishment Clause crisis and recounts how efforts to resolve it have failed. Part 2 proposes government speech endorsing higher law and using religious imagery to do so, at least in part, as a solution to the crisis. Part 3 argues that secularism itself is at a crossroads and that the acceptance of a higher law orientation would be the beginning of a reformation within secularism.

The relationship between parts 2 and 3 is key. As the third book in the trilogy, a higher law Establishment Clause is the constitutional theory behind a certain kind of secularism. That constitutional theory and that secularism must go together.

PART ONE

The Establishment Clause Crisis

ONE

What We Say: The Supreme Court's Promise of Government Neutrality toward Religion

The crisis in interpreting the Establishment Clause lies in the gap between what the United States Supreme Court has written that the Constitution demands—what we say—and what American society actually does. The Court has promised government neutrality toward religion; but our practices suggest something quite different. Neutrality has a variety of meanings, as we shall see, but all of its meanings require that the government not endorse religion as a preferred status for the citizenry. The endorsement of religion, however, is precisely what government does today in many ways. Indeed the majority of Americans may believe that government ought to endorse religion. Therein lies the crisis. In this chapter, I will set forth in broad outline the Court's promise of government neutrality. In the next chapter, I will discuss some of our non-neutral government practices.

In 1947, in *Everson v. Board of Education*,[1] the United States Supreme Court upheld, 5–4, the public reimbursement of parents for the cost of transporting children to any primary or secondary school, including private, religious schools. It was a subsidy meant to keep children from dangerous pedestrian routes. Justice Hugo Black wrote the majority opinion upholding the subsidy. Justice Wiley Rutledge wrote the principal dissent.

The *Everson* majority opinion is entitled to more weight in the movement toward establishing government neutrality toward religion than a close, 5–4 decision would normally be accorded. Despite upholding the bus subsidy that was at issue in the case, Justice Black's majority opinion basically agreed with the dissenters about the constitutional values controlling the relationship between church and state. Insofar as the majority opinion limited the role of religion in public life, it spoke for the dissenters too, who wanted to go even further in separating church and state. Thus *Everson* represented, in effect, a manifesto by a unanimous Supreme Court on behalf of a neutral government that could not aid religion.

Justice Black's language of separation between government and religion was uncompromising. The people of the new American nation, he wrote, concluded that

> individual religious liberty could be achieved best under a government which was stripped of all power to tax, to support, or otherwise to assist any or all religions.[2]

Justice Black strongly identified Thomas Jefferson's and James Madison's opposition to a proposed Virginia tax in support "of the established church"—actually the proposal would have supported any Christian denomination—as the beginning of the anti-establishment tradition that culminated in the two religion clauses in the First Amendment: the prohibition against any law respecting an establishment of religion and the protection of the free exercise of religion. Although the Court had previously referred to the well-known letter by Jefferson to the Danbury Baptist Association,[3] it was in *Everson* that Jefferson became a pivotal figure in interpreting the Establishment Clause and in which his famous image of the "wall of separation" between church and state came to dominate all of the justices' views of the proper place of religion in American public life.

Justice Black's opinion included a well-known description of the reach of the Establishment Clause. This description probably represented the view of the entire Court:

> Neither a state nor the Federal Government can set up a church. Neither can pass laws which aid one religion, aid all religions, or prefer one religion over another. Neither can force nor influence a person to go to or to remain away from church against his will or force him to profess a belief or disbelief in any religion. No person can be punished for entertaining or professing religious beliefs or disbeliefs, for church attendance or non-attendance. No tax in any amount, large

or small, can be levied to support any religious activities or institutions, whatever they may be called, or whatever form they may adopt to teach or practice religion. Neither a state nor the Federal Government can, openly or secretly, participate in the affairs of any religious organizations or groups and vice versa.

The State was to be "neutral in its relations with groups of religious believers and non-believers...."[4]

The disagreement between the majority and the dissenters in *Everson* was not about whether there was a wall of separation between church and state—Justice Black agreed with the dissenters that the "wall must be kept high and impregnable" and that there must not be "the slightest breach." The disagreement was only over whether a "general program" of transportation that did not exclude religious schools was constitutional. Five justices thought the program was constitutional; four thought not.

The basic, legally binding elements of government neutrality toward religion emerged full blown in the *Everson* opinion, even though there had been little litigation previously over such matters. The opinion rejected the approach of nonpreferentialism—that government might aid all religions on a nondiscriminatory basis. For Justice Black, it was not enough for government not to discriminate among religious groups. The government was not to be permitted to "aid all religions" either. Thus Justice Black anticipated the question that arises today: whether religion itself may be preferred by the government over irreligion. Black's answer, for the whole Court on this point, was that government must be neutral between believers and nonbelievers.

Yet *Everson* did not reach the issue of symbolic expression of belief in the public square. The case concerned government neutrality in terms of material aid to religious institutions, such as private religious schools. It was a case about tax money and subsidies. *Everson* might thus tell us nothing about symbolic government use of religion, such as the words "under God" in the Pledge of Allegiance or the presence of a Ten Commandments display in a county courthouse. For issues like that we must look elsewhere in the case law.

The non-material cases that really brought the Establishment Clause to the attention of the public—what we might call government religious expression cases—were *Engel v. Vitale*[5] in 1962 and *School District of Abington Township v. Schempp*[6] in 1963, which prohibited prayer and

Bible reading, respectively, in the public schools. These cases moved the wall of separation between church and state out of the musty realm of taxes and subsidies into the highly charged and emotional arena of prayer and confession. These cases are the ancestors of today's dispute about the words "under God" in the Pledge of Allegiance.

In *Engel*, Justice Black's majority opinion—7–1 on the main issue—struck down the New York State Board of Regents's nondenominational daily prayer, which was voluntary in the sense that no student was required to participate. The prayer itself was banal, having more to do with obedience to parents and teachers, it seemed, than with any genuine religious sentiment: "Almighty God, we acknowledge our dependence upon Thee, and we beg Thy blessings upon us, our parents, our teachers, and our Country."

Because the prayer had actually been written by government officials, the Court could strike down this practice of praying on the narrow ground that the government could not "compose official prayers." A practice like that was too close to what official establishments of religion in Europe had done. The narrowness of that ground meant that it might perhaps be constitutional for a public school, for example, to host different members of the clergy, each offering his or her own prayers for the students each day.

Notwithstanding the narrow ground of the holding, Justice Black's majority opinion reiterated his view in *Everson* that religion and government were constitutionally required to occupy separate and distinct realms. The opinion interpreted the purpose of the Establishment Clause to prevent a "union" of government and religion, and he attributed to the framers of the Constitution the view that "religion is too personal, too sacred, too holy, to permit its 'unhallowed perversion' by a civil magistrate."[7]

In contrast to the narrow context in *Engel*, *Schempp* raised the issue of the relationship of government and religious belief in a more general setting. As described in Justice Tom Clark's opinion for a 7–1 majority, every morning in senior high school, at the beginning of the school day, a student's reading of ten verses from any version of the Old or New Testament was broadcast into each homeroom. There was no preface to these readings, nor any discussion. After the reading, the students stood and were led, similarly by student broadcast, in the recitation of the Lord's Prayer. Any student who wished to abstain could absent himself or herself from the classroom or simply refrain from the reading and recitation.

The Court struck down these practices. Justice Clark's opinion revisited Justice Rutledge's dissent in *Everson* and quoted its description of the reach and purpose of the Establishment Clause:

> The (First) Amendment's purpose was not to strike merely at the official establishment of a single sect, creed or religion, outlawing only a formal relation such as had prevailed in England and some of the colonies. Necessarily it was to uproot all such relationships. But the object was broader than separating church and state in this narrow sense. It was to create a complete and permanent separation of the spheres of religious activity and civil authority by comprehensively forbidding every form of public aid or support for religion.[8]

Justice Clark also quoted from Justice Robert Jackson's dissent in *Everson* concerning the nature of the relationship between religious and secular education in general. The public schools, Justice Clark quoted Jackson as having written, "are organized 'on the premise that secular education can be isolated from all religious teaching. . . .'"[9]

Justice Jackson's observation is obviously debatable. It is not clear that education can be easily divided into religious and secular components. Such a conclusion depends on what religion is taken to include. For example, in the *Schempp* case, the Pennsylvania Superintendent of Public Instruction testified that Bible reading constitutes "a strong contradiction to the materialistic trends of our time."[10] Already, therefore, in 1963, the question of the government's view of materialism was felt by some to be relevant to Establishment Clause analysis. Such attitudes toward materialism are a significant matter in terms of the higher law discussed later in this book. I'm not sure anyone can say how Justice Jackson might have responded to the question of whether anti-materialism is a "religious teaching."

Of course love of, and service to, others can be taught in ways other than reading the Bible. My point is that the education of the whole person necessarily involves matters that religion also addresses—for example, the meaning and purpose of life and the nature of a good life.

Schempp did more than outlaw Bible reading in the public schools. Justice Clark's opinion delineated a "test" to evaluate future Establishment Clause challenges in the name of the "wholesome 'neutrality'" that government must evince toward religion. Such tests are important in constitutional law because they allow lower courts to act in an area with more confidence. Only when judges in the lower courts think they understand how the next case should be decided are constitutional provisions readily applied. Justice Clark even called his formulation a "test." Because the Establishment Clause "withdrew all legislative power respecting religious belief or the expression thereof," the test would require nonreligious grounds for government action:

> The test may be stated as follows: what are the purpose and the primary effect of the enactment? If either is the advancement or inhibition of religion then the enactment exceeds the scope of legislative power as circumscribed by the Constitution. That is to say that to withstand the strictures of the Establishment Clause there must be a secular legislative purpose and a primary effect that neither advances nor inhibits religion.[11]

Even under this formulation, the Court in *Schempp* could have concluded that Bible reading was a permissible religious means to a secular end—the goal of educating students to become decent people—but that would have contradicted the opinion's starting point. You could not separate church and state—religion and government—the way the Court wished to do if blatantly religious means were permitted in order to accomplish *any* governmental ends. Bible reading as a permitted means to good citizenship would have blurred the religious/secular boundary that Justice Clark meant to sharpen. As far as the majority was concerned, after *Schempp,* school authorities, and indeed all government officials, would be prohibited from concern about the religious or spiritual well being of the citizenry. Any such concern would be considered "religious" and hence unconstitutional.

The "test" described in *Schempp* was expanded in 1971 in *Lemon v. Kurtzman.*[12] The decision in *Lemon* struck down programs of aid to private schools, including religious schools, in Rhode Island and Pennsylvania. Under the Pennsylvania statute, tax money was paid for the cost of teachers' salaries, textbooks, and other material in certain specified secular subjects. In Rhode Island, the state paid a supplement—15 percent of the annual salaries—to teachers in private elementary schools who taught only certain secular subjects. Chief Justice Warren Burger's majority opinion restated the purpose and effect categories of the Establishment Clause test, but added a prohibition on "entanglement" between government and religious institutions. To survive a challenge under the Establishment Clause, he held, government action must satisfy three criteria:

> First, the statute must have a secular legislative purpose; second, its principal or primary effect must be one that neither advances nor inhibits religion; finally, the statute must not foster "an excessive government entanglement with religion."[13]

The entanglement criterion was taken from *Walz v. Tax Commission*.[14] In 1970, *Walz* had upheld state tax exemption for real property owned by religious institutions that was used for actual religious worship under a broad tax exemption covering property devoted to religious, educational, or charitable purposes. *Walz* illustrates that the neutrality principle was never absolute, a point I will return to below.

The Lemon test, as it came to be known, dominated constitutional decisions from its inception in 1971 into the 1980s. Even today it is the closest thing we have to a doctrine of the constitutional law of church and state. As originally intended and interpreted, the Lemon test represented a strong commitment to government neutrality and separation of church and state. A respected textbook states that the "high water mark" of the Lemon test interpreted to prohibit any government aid to religious institutions occurred in 1985,[15] in a pair of cases decided the same day— July 1—and both subsequently overruled, at least in part: *School District of Grand Rapids v. Ball*[16] and *Aguilar v. Felton*.[17]

Ball and *Aguilar* both involved material aid to religious institutions. In both cases, government employees provided services to school children on the grounds of religious schools. Probably not coincidentally, 1985 also witnessed the Court's strongest statement in favor of the required indifference by government to the religious interests and desires of the citizenry. That case was *Wallace v. Jaffree*.[18]

Alabama had enacted in 1978 a statute authorizing a one-minute period of silence in all public schools "for meditation." In 1981, Alabama enacted a successor statute that authorized a period of silence "for meditation or voluntary prayer." It was the successor statute that the Court struck down in *Jaffree*.

Justice John Paul Stevens's opinion for five justices—Justice Sandra Day O'Connor only concurred in the Court's result—found that the 1981 Alabama statute violated the first requirement of the Lemon test. The amendment adding the words "or voluntary prayer" represented an "effort to return voluntary prayer" to the public schools, in the plain words of the bill's sponsor. Justice Stevens read the record to show that Alabama's only purpose was to advance religion: "the statute had *no* secular purpose."[19] In Stevens's view, the promotion of prayer is not a secular goal.

One can quibble with Justice Stevens about whether the record in the case had to be read that way. The State had argued that it was merely protecting the right of students to pray if they wished to do so, as Justice Stevens's opinion affirmed students had a constitutional right to do.

But for our purposes, Justice Stevens's view represents a strong legal manifestation of the requirement of government neutrality toward religion. The Alabama statute was unconstitutional because the legislative majority that enacted it wanted school children to pray to God as a good thing in and of itself. They wanted to encourage children to be religious, and that is precisely why the statute failed the Lemon test. The government must be neutral about religion in the sense that government officials are expected to be indifferent about whether religion is practiced or not practiced among the citizenry. As Justice Stevens wrote, no doubt correctly describing the majority of the Alabama legislature, "the State intended to characterize prayer as a favored activity."[20]

As the context in *Jaffree* made clear, inquiry into religious purpose is not aimed at the private or subconscious hopes of individual legislators. Purpose in the case was manifest in a public sense by the addition of legislative language encouraging prayer.

Concurring in the result, rather than joining Justice Stevens's opinion, Justice O'Connor applied a differently phrased test for Establishment Clause cases—the endorsement test. Justice O'Connor had proposed this test the term before *Jaffree* was decided, in her concurrence in *Lynch v. Donnelly*,[21] a case that upheld inclusion of a nativity scene in a municipality's Christmas display. Endorsement was not intended by Justice O'Connor to replace the Lemon test, but to serve as a refinement of it. In a sense, Justice O'Connor amplified the Lemon test by giving it context and by combining the inquiry into purpose and effect through examination of what message the government intended to convey and what it did convey. Justice O'Connor described the underlying rationale of the endorsement test as follows in *Lynch:*

> The Establishment Clause prohibits government from making adherence to a religion relevant in any way to a person's standing in the political community. Government can run afoul of that prohibition in two principal ways. One is excessive entanglement with religious institutions. . . . The second and more direct infringement is government endorsement or disapproval of religion. Endorsement sends a message to nonadherents that they are outsiders, not full members of the political community, and an accompanying message to adherents that they are insiders, favored members of the political community.[22]

For purposes of government neutrality, the endorsement test, like the Lemon test as originally interpreted, prohibits government officials from wanting schoolchildren or other citizens to be religious and from acting pursuant to such a goal. As Justice O'Connor wrote in *Jaffree,* the Establishment Clause prevents the government "from conveying or attempting to convey a message that religion . . . is favored or preferred."[23] Since the Alabama legislature plainly and publicly expressed their desire to encourage children to pray, the statute was unconstitutional. Thus, in *Jaffree,* the Lemon test by itself, and as supplemented by the endorsement test, prohibited government from sponsoring prayer. As recently as 2000, in *Santa Fe Independent School District v. Doe,*[24] the Court invoked the endorsement test along these same lines and struck down, 6–3, a public high school policy of student "invocation" at football games as a state purpose to preserve and promote a religious practice.

Although government neutrality was the dominant theme in Establishment Clause decisions through *Jaffree,* there were, of course, dissents from this approach as well. Justice William Rehnquist's dissent in *Jaffree,* for example (he was not chief justice at the time this case was decided) took issue with the majority at precisely this point—that it was unconstitutional for the government to encourage prayer and thus religion:

> It would come as much of a shock to those who drafted the Bill of Rights as it will to a large number of thoughtful Americans today to learn that the Constitution, as construed by the majority, prohibits the Alabama Legislature from "endorsing" prayer.[25]

In Rehnquist's view, James Madison proposed the Establishment Clause not to require government neutrality between religion and irreligion, but to prevent the creation of a national religion and, perhaps as well, to prevent discrimination among religious sects.[26]

We will return to Rehnquist's view in chapter 4, among the alternatives to government neutrality. I mention him here to show that the neutrality to which he objected was the dominant paradigm in 1985.

The Lemon test has had its ups and downs since 1985, both in terms of criticism of the test, including calls to overrule it, and in changing interpretations of the test. However in two recent well-known instances, the public display of the Ten Commandments in county courthouses and a statement in a Pennsylvania high school's biology curriculum, the Lemon test was used in something like its original meaning of ensuring government neutrality toward religion.

In 2005, the Supreme Court decided on the same day two cases challenging public settings for the Ten Commandments. The two cases split the Court essentially down the middle, 5–4 in one case to allow the display and 5–4 not to, in the other case. In *Van Orden v. Perry*,[27] the Court upheld the placement of a monument inscribed with the Ten Commandments on the grounds of the Texas state capital. In *McCreary County v. American Civil Liberties Union of Kentucky*,[28] the Court struck down Ten Commandment displays at two county courthouses. The differing outcomes turned on the changed vote of one justice, Stephen Breyer. In other words, eight of the nine justices thought the cases should be decided the same way.

In the case upholding the Ten Commandments display, *Van Orden*, Chief Justice Rehnquist, writing a plurality opinion for Justices Anthony Kennedy, Antonin Scalia, and Clarence Thomas, expressly avoided applying the Lemon test. Instead, he emphasized the history of official acknowledgment of the role of religion in America, a theme we will return to in chapter 3.

Justice Breyer contributed the necessary fifth vote to uphold the display—Justices O'Connor, Stevens, Souter, and Ginsburg dissented. Justice Breyer characterized the case as "borderline" and opined that there could be "no test-related substitute for the exercise of legal judgment."[29] Based on a variety of fact-specific evidence, Justice Breyer concluded that prohibiting the display would lead to more religious divisiveness than permitting it.

Given his anguished indecision and refusal to apply any test in *Van Orden*, it is surprising that Justice Breyer rather easily joined Justice Souter's majority opinion in *McCreary County*, striking down the courthouse displays.[30] The majority in *McCreary County* was composed of the four dissenters in *Van Orden*, plus Justice Breyer. Justice Souter's opinion expressly reaffirmed the requirement under the Lemon test of a secular purpose in order to uphold governmental action challenged under the Establishment Clause, though he noted that an illegitimate government purpose had been dispositive in only four cases since *Lemon* itself was decided. The majority refused to abandon the purpose inquiry and found "a predominantly religious purpose" behind the display in *McCreary*, based largely upon the express religious intentions that had been manifest in earlier, but recent, Ten Commandments displays and legislative pronouncements. Justice Souter specifically noted that "at the ceremony for posting the framed Commandments in Pulaski County, the county executive was accompanied by his pastor, who testified to the certainty of the existence of God."[31]

Thus unconstitutionality was linked by the majority to the failure of the government to express neutrality toward religion. Souter was criticizing the government for being too closely associated with the claim that God exists. That was a violation of government neutrality.

The other recent religious purpose and endorsement inquiry to achieve national attention occurred in the Dover, Pennsylvania, litigation over a disclaimer the local school board required to be read to ninth-grade biology students before the beginning of the portion of the course teaching evolution. In *Kitzmiller v. Dover Area School District*,[32] Federal District Judge John E. Jones III held, after a highly publicized, five-week trial in fall 2005, that the statement violated the Establishment Clause and an analogous provision in the Pennsylvania Constitution.

The disclaimer that the School Board adopted did not mention religion per se:

> The Pennsylvania Academic Standards require students to learn about Darwin's Theory of Evolution and eventually to take a standardized test of which evolution is a part.

Because Darwin's Theory is a theory, it continues to be tested as new evidence is discovered. The Theory is not a fact. Gaps in the Theory exist for which there is no evidence. A theory is defined as a well-tested explanation that unifies a broad range of observations.

Intelligent Design is an explanation of the origin of life that differs from Darwin's view. The reference book, Of Pandas and People, is available for students who might be interested in gaining an understanding of what Intelligent Design actually involves.

With respect to any theory, students are encouraged to keep an open mind. The school leaves the discussion of the Origins of Life to individual students and their families. As a Standards-driven district, class instruction focuses upon preparing students to achieve proficiency on Standards-based assessments.

Judge Jones held that a "reasonable, objective observer" would understand the religious foundations of the intelligent-design movement and that the corresponding objective student and Dover citizen, given the Board's public actions, would perceive the disclaimer as an endorsement of religion. In addition, Judge Jones found "outright lies under oath" by members of the school board and expressions of a desire to bring "faith and prayer back into the schools." The judge concluded that the school board members "consciously chose to change Dover's biology curriculum to advance religion."[33]

The voters in Dover were apparently unhappy with this controversy. Just a few days after the trial ended, and before the opinion was issued, all eight incumbent school board members on the ballot lost their bids for reelection. Consequently Judge Jones's decision was not appealed.

We can conclude from all of the above that the government neutrality principle has been the dominant interpretation of the Establishment Clause and continues to this day to be highly influential in constitutional law. In the next chapter, we will examine the growing challenge to neutrality.

Before proceeding, however, we must first look at approaches to church and state in the case law that might have raised a challenge to neutrality but for different reasons have not been viewed as doing so. One way that the courts have avoided direct challenge to the neutrality doctrine is by treating speech that might well be considered the responsibility of the government as if it were private speech. So, while speech by a student was found to constitute government action in the *Santa Fe* case, students have been treated as private speakers and have given graduation speeches praising Jesus since *Lee v. Weisman*[34] invalidated official high school graduation prayers. If a school district allows student graduation speakers to invoke religious themes and images in the name of the rights of students to free speech, government neutrality toward religion is often held not to be violated.[35]

Another way that neutrality can be satisfied when the government is actually aiding religion is through the different meanings that neutrality can have. Depending on the definition of neutrality, there can be a great deal of government financial aid going to religion, and quite a lot of other types of government assistance to religion, without necessarily violating the concept.

Professor Douglas Laycock has delineated two important distinctions in Establishment Clause analysis: neutrality versus separation and formal neutrality versus substantive neutrality.[36] Although the justices tend to use the terms separation and neutrality interchangeably, the result in *Everson* itself, in which aid that benefited religious schools was permitted, demonstrates the difference between them. The program at issue in *Everson* was both formally and substantively neutral. Formal neutrality requires the absence of religious categories in public policy, while substantive neutrality refers to the tendency of the government policy at issue to encourage, whether by incentives or otherwise, religious belief and affiliation or nonbelief and nonaffiliation. Busing in *Everson* was available for any school and did not encourage parents to choose any particular kind of school. Thus the busing was neutral in both senses.

But the busing program did channel public support to religious schools. Thus the program, while perhaps manifesting neutrality, did not manifest strict separation between church and state.

The Cleveland school voucher program upheld in *Zelman v. Simmons-Harris*[37] is an even better example than *Everson* of the help that government can provide to religious institutions without violating neutrality, again, at least in the view of some. In *Zelman*, almost all the government voucher money ended up going to private religious schools. And there is no reason to doubt that the availability of the funding helped keep some of these religious schools afloat. Clearly the voucher program was formally neutral in the sense that it did not contain religious categories and might be considered substantively neutral as well, as long as one viewed the voucher program against the ongoing subsidy for secular public education. As far as Chief Justice Rehnquist's majority opinion was concerned, the decision by parents to spend voucher money at a particular religious school was insulated from Establishment Clause challenge, much as was the GI Bill when government funds were used to prepare a veteran for the ministry. Rehnquist called the voucher program one of "true private choice."[38]

The point is not whether *Zelman* was properly decided, but that the majority in *Zelman* did not deepen the current crisis in neutrality doctrine and thus did not necessitate a new conceptual approach to the Establishment Clause. Chief Justice Rehnquist while not reaffirming government neutrality did not challenge it either. In fact, the opinion claimed that the voucher program was "neutral in all respects toward religion."[39]

A third way in which government assistance to religion has been permitted despite the concept of government neutrality is that the Supreme Court has always viewed accommodation of religion as a constitutionally permissible governmental goal. This was the reason why the original Alabama statute in *Jaffree* setting aside a "period of silence" "for meditation" was acknowledged by Justice Stevens to have been constitutional even though some students would use that moment for prayer: students had a right to engage in voluntary prayer, and a moment of silence during the school day was an appropriate means to protect that right.

But of course, as everyone knew, Alabama legislators did not care about meditation when they enacted the original moment-of-silence law. They obviously wanted students to pray, but feared expressly saying so in case of a lawsuit. Their purely religious motivation did not violate the Establishment Clause because this motivation was expressed in a way that allowed religion to flourish rather than be mandated. So the meditation law, notwithstanding the religious motivation behind it, was considered to be neutral toward religion.

Accommodation of religion is common in our society, but the concept is fraught with distinctions and perhaps even contradictions. The term "accommodation" is used very loosely in judicial opinions. It has been applied to religious displays on public property and access by believers and religious institutions to government resources on an equal basis with nonreligious entities. Such broad usage turns accommodation into a substitute for acknowledgment of religion and for fair treatment of religion. I am using the term, instead, in a narrower sense to refer to changes in law that are aimed at rendering religious practices less onerous than they would otherwise be.

There are two ways in which government accommodates religious practice in this narrow sense. In the first, a government policy, though not aimed at religion as such, creates a difficulty for religious practice, which is then lessened by exempting religion from the requirements of law in order to assuage that difficulty. The classic example of such accommodation was the exemption during Prohibition of wine for sacramental purposes from the general ban on intoxicating liquor. Another example was the World War II recognition of a draft exemption for individual, religiously based conscientious objection. More controversially, the Civil Rights Act of 1964 exempts religious organizations from the prohibition against discrimination in employment on the basis of religion. This exemption was upheld by the Court in 1987.[40]

In the second type of accommodation, government changes the law to ease religious practice, even though the government did not itself create any difficulty for religious believers in the first place. One of the early debates in American history, for example, was whether the mail would be delivered on Sundays. Undoubtedly, some opponents of Sunday delivery simply wanted to protect the Lord's Day—a purely religious motivation. Others, however, did not wish to force postal employees to work on a day that many of these workers wished to set aside for religious reasons. Accommodating that desire would today be regarded by the courts as a secular purpose.

Another example of this kind of accommodation is the creation of a national holiday for Christmas. Not making Christmas a national holiday would not itself have burdened believers. Without a national holiday, their celebration of Christmas would be hindered simply by having to work. It is obvious that most Christians would have to work if Christmas were not a national holiday because Christians make up such a large portion of the national workforce. But the economic realities that would create the problem for religious practice would not be the fault of the government nor attributable to it. If Christmas were not a national holiday, its celebration would be a patchwork of legal statuses, as is the case today for the celebration of Yom Kippur in areas where Jews make up a significant portion of the population. Some cities or states would declare Christmas a holiday, many union contracts would recognize it, some public schools would close and so forth. Making Christmas a national holiday is a good idea, but it is an accommodation for religious believers in a situation in which government did not create the difficulty for religious practice.

Obviously the distinction between these two types of accommodations cannot be pushed very hard because it is, to a certain extent, arbitrary. Whether government would be considered to be imposing a burden by insisting on work on Sundays or Christmas, or would be considered not to be imposing a burden by simply treating these as normal workdays, is a matter of perspective. Fortunately the concept of neutrality can be applied however the distinction is worked out.

In terms of current law, the Supreme Court has tended to uphold accommodations for religious practice, especially when the accommodation is aimed at what the Court views as assuaging a government-imposed burden on religion. Thus the accommodation of wine during Prohibition would not be unconstitutional under Establishment Clause case law today. However when the exemption from law seems simply to favor religion over nonreligion, the results are more uncertain. So, in *Texas Monthly, Inc. v. Bullock*,[41] the Court, without a majority opinion, struck down a tax exemption that was limited to religious books. This decision would seem to be consistent with the general Establishment Clause principle of government neutrality between religion and nonreligion.

Accommodation that might be upheld if modest in scope can also be found unconstitutional if the benefit to religion is deemed to be onerous to some people. In *Thornton v. Caldor Inc.*,[42] the Court held that a Connecticut law granting what Chief Justice Warren Burger's majority opinion characterized as "an absolute and unqualified right not to work on their chosen Sabbath" violated the Establishment Clause. The statute provided that "No person who states that a particular day of the week is observed as his Sabbath may be required by his employer to work on

such day. An employee's refusal to work on his Sabbath shall not constitute grounds for his dismissal." Chief Justice Burger's opinion objected
that the statute granted the right not to work "no matter what burden or
inconvenience this imposes on the employer or fellow workers."[43] This
constituted a primary effect that advanced a religious practice and thus
violated the Establishment Clause as defined by the Lemon test. A more
modest Sabbath exemption would certainly have been upheld.

Accommodation must also be neutral among different religions in
order to be upheld. In *Board of Education of Kiryas Joel v. Grumet*,[44] the
Supreme Court prohibited New York from constituting a village composed entirely of extremely Orthodox Jews—Satmar Hasidim—as a
separate school district so that handicapped Orthodox Jewish children
could receive special education without having to attend public schools
in the larger school district outside the village. Not surprisingly, when
the children from such a sheltered religious background had attended
secular schools, the result had been panic, fear, and trauma.

Justice Souter's ground for striking down this new school district
was not convincing. He wrote that this government action represented
discrimination against some other, future religious group that might not
receive the same treatment: "we have no assurance that the next similarly
situated group seeking a school district of its own will receive one...."[45]
But there was no reason to think the legislature would not respond to
some future religious need in a positive way. In addition, as Justice Anthony Kennedy observed, that future group, if refused relief, could go
to court with precisely this argument of discrimination and presumably
prevail. Though Justice Kennedy concurred in striking down the school
district, he did so on the much more defensible ground that government
should not be drawing jurisdictional boundaries based on religion.

While the Court views accommodation as generally constitutionally
permissible, the question for our purposes is whether accommodation
of religion is consistent with government neutrality toward religion. Accommodations like the religious exemption from Prohibition cannot
be understood apart from an obvious positive government regard for
religion. If the government really did not care whether or not people
practiced their religions, why would the government create such exemp-
tions? After all, the underlying government policy in regard to some-

thing like Prohibition was not adopted in order to harm religion. So the exemption was not undoing a harm to religion in that sense. A neutral government policy toward religion might be one that adopted policies without regard to their effects upon religious practice. That was true of Prohibition. Exempting religion from generally applicable law is thus not really neutral. It is intended to, and does, aid adherents to religion over and against everyone else, who must comply with the ban. This is why Chicago law professor Philip Kurland, in his classic 1961 article, "Of Church and State and the Supreme Court,"[46] opposed using religion as a standard in legislation or other government actions even "to confer a benefit" to religion.[47]

Nor can one any longer maintain that accommodation of religious practices is permissible under a regime of neutrality because such accommodation promotes an independent constitutional value, the free exercise of religion. Prior to 1990, the Supreme Court had permitted accommodation under the shadow, as it were, of the Free Exercise Clause: "[G]overnment may (and sometimes must) accommodate religious practices and . . . may do so without violating the Establishment Clause."[48] But just three years after Justice William Brennan wrote that defense of accommodation, the Court in *Employment Division v. Smith*,[49] refused to apply the compelling state interest test in a case in which claimants who were dismissed from employment by a drug rehabilitation organization were then denied unemployment benefits because their illegal use of peyote in a religious ceremony was the reason for their dismissal. Justice Antonin Scalia's 5–4 majority opinion used the occasion to reexamine the meaning of the Free Exercise Clause. The result was that the Free Exercise Clause was held to never protect a religious practice from the requirements of a generally applicable law. Therefore no religious exemption was required from the criminal prohibition against the use of peyote. The prior employment compensation cases were distinguished on the ground that unemployment compensation claims are usually evaluated individually in order to ascertain why employment was terminated. In the context of individual evaluation, in which many factors will be taken into account, religious motivations may not be disregarded. But, in a context in which government has determined that certain conduct is always unacceptable, the Free Exercise Clause never requires an accommodation for the burdened religious practice.

As Professor Laycock points out, Prohibition without a religious exemption satisfies formal neutrality even though it directly outlaws core religious practices. On the other hand, exempting religious practices from Prohibition without the justification of complying with the Free Exercise Clause violates formal neutrality. This hypothetical result is why he proposes substantive neutrality as an alternative to formal neutrality and why he opposes the result in *Smith*.

The accommodation experience shows why definitions of government neutrality toward religion are tricky. As we have seen, even apparent favoritism toward religion can be argued to be neutral. Yet there does appear to be a core meaning of neutrality. The government cannot take active steps that suggest that religion is better than irreligion.

That standard still allows favorable government treatment of religion. When the government recognizes that religion is important to many of its citizens and tries to minimize interference with that interest, the government is only doing what it does for many activities—for example, making the first day of hunting season a school holiday. Thus, when the government merely recognizes that some of the citizenry are already religious and tries to ensure that their interests are taken into account in government decision making, it does no more than accommodate religion in the same way it often accommodates other "private" interests. This is another sense of neutrality, one in which religious believers are treated as simply another important interest group.

Under neutrality, however, there must be a limit to permissible favoritism. The question in the next chapter concerns expressions of government approval for the underlying activity of religious belief and practice beyond recognition of the simple fact that some Americans engage in religious activities. When the government affirms that we are a "Nation under God," the government is not simply subsidizing an activity (like hunting) but is treating the activity as something positive, as something, so to speak, that the non-hunter should take up.

We can see the difference between acknowledgment and promotion, and the consequent challenge to the neutrality principle, in the released time cases. In 1948, just a year after the recognition of neutrality as the fundamental Establishment Clause value in *Everson*, Justice Black wrote the majority opinion in *McCollum v. Board of Education*,[50] striking down a released time program in which, for part of the school day, participating students attended privately provided religious instruction in the public school building, while non-participating students pursued secular studies in another part of the school. Protestant, Catholic, and Jewish teachers taught religious classes in public school once a week at the end of the school day. The teachers were paid by the local ecumenical religious council. Parents either signed their children up for one of these classes, or the children attended what was effectively a study hall. Justice Black wrote the majority opinion and repeated his language from *Everson* concerning the wall of separation. Here, he wrote, the tax-supported public schools were aiding religious groups "to spread their faith."[51]

McCollum is not a surprising opinion from the perspective of neutrality. As Justice Black wrote, not only were the students being instructed in religion in "public school buildings," but also, the state was rounding the students up through its "compulsory public school machinery."[52] The state was not neutral toward religion.

The surprise came four years later, in *Zorach v. Clauson*,[53] in which a released time program was upheld, despite *McCollum*, on the ground that in *Zorach*, religious instruction during the school day took place in church buildings, while non-participating students stayed behind in the public school building. Justice Black dissented, pointing out that "the *McCollum* decision would have been the same if the religious classes had not been held in the school buildings."[54]

Justice William Douglas, who wrote the majority opinion in *Zorach*, had been on the Court in 1947, and had joined Justice Black's majority opinion in *Everson* with its separation and neutrality language, and had also joined the majority in *McCollum*. Thus Justice Douglas could not have been considered particularly pro-religion.

The *Zorach* opinion takes a very different view of the relationship between church and state, and it is not one that can be considered neutral:

> The nullification of this law would have wide and profound effects. A catholic student applies to his teacher for permission to leave the school during hours on a Holy Day of Obligation to attend a mass. A Jewish student asks his teacher for permission to be excused for Yom Kippur. A Protestant wants the afternoon off for a family baptismal ceremony. In each case the teacher requires parental consent in writing. In each case the teacher, in order to make sure the student is not a truant, goes further and requires a report from the priest, the rabbi, or the minister. The teacher in other words cooperates in a religious program to

the extent of making it possible for her students to participate in it. Whether she does it occasionally for a few students, regularly for one, or pursuant to a systematized program designed to further the religious needs of all the students, does not alter the character of the act.

As we will see in the next chapter, Justice Douglas referred to the "religious nature of our people" as a justification for released time programs. This phrase suggests that the Court was taking a side between the two models that Professor Dworkin offers. America is not a secular nation that tolerates religion but a religious nation that tolerates nonbelief. And Justice Douglas seems to treat that choice as very much an either/or.

We have now come to the limit of the doctrine of government neutrality toward religion. At the crucial point in the opinion, Justice Douglas did not look at precedent but at social practice, at the central place of religion in our national life. He did not look at what we say, but at what we do. And, looking at what we do, he did not find neutrality. We now turn in the same direction as Justice Douglas, toward the American practice of public religious expression.

TWO

What We Do: The Failure of the Supreme Court to Redeem the Promise of Government Neutrality

Three years before *Everson* was decided, there was a dramatic manifestation of a nation in an open relationship to religion in the public sphere. On June 6, 1944, President Franklin Delano Roosevelt addressed the nation on the occasion of the D-Day landings in Normandy. He spoke for only a few minutes. He asked the nation to join him in prayer.

> Almighty God: Our sons, pride of our Nation, this day have set upon a mighty endeavor, a struggle to preserve our Republic, our religion, and our civilization, and to set free a suffering humanity.
>
> Some will never return. Embrace these, Father, and receive them, Thy heroic servants, into Thy kingdom.

FDR explained why he had not called for a National Day of Prayer:

> [B]ecause the road is long and the desire is great, I ask that our people devote themselves in a continuance of prayer. As we rise to each new day, and again when each day is spent, let words of prayer be on our lips, invoking Thy help to our efforts.

And this is how he ended his prayer and his remarks:

> With Thy blessing, we shall prevail over the unholy forces of our enemy. Help us to conquer the apostles of greed and racial arrogances. Lead us to the saving of our country, and with our sister Nations into a world unity that will spell a sure peace—a peace invulnerable to the schemings of unworthy men. And a peace that will let all of men live in freedom, reaping the just rewards of their honest toil.
>
> Thy will be done, Almighty God.
>
> Amen.

In order to understand the tension between FDR's address and the concept of government neutrality toward religion, we must first ask, what did FDR's prayer mean in terms of church and state? The reader should note that the God to whom FDR addressed this prayer is a God of history. Like Abraham Lincoln—and Thomas Jefferson for that matter—FDR apparently had a sense that God had something to do with the great affairs of state. FDR was certain that God was on our side in the struggle against the evil of Nazism.

This idea of the God of history has consequences as we begin to consider the proper relationship of church and state. Obviously, if religion has something to do with the way things happen in the world—if religion does not turn out to be simply a personal matter—the call for government neutrality toward religion will be undermined. In fact, if religion is about something in the world, government neutrality toward it will in some sense be impossible.

Second, we must note that this address by FDR really was a prayer to God. This radio address was not merely a formal matter, like the word "God" inserted in an otherwise secular presidential inaugural speech. It probably did not occur to FDR that this act of public piety might be inappropriate. At a time of needed national unity, FDR was not pushing any envelope or making any symbolic point. He was not showing up any political or ideological opponent. We must conclude that, as of 1944, it was not considered improper, by the public at large at any rate, for a president to publicly address God. America was at this time, in 1944, at home with genuinely pious public prayer.

Finally, since FDR speaks of "our religion" and of God's welcoming the dead into his "kingdom," we must ask just how inclusive FDR was being here. Is this a Christian prayer?

Today we might assume that FDR was speaking of a specifically Christian God and that he was excluding nonbelievers and minority believers. After all, this prayer predated Will Herberg's book, *Protestant, Catholic, Jew,*[1] by ten years, and so "our religion" implicitly excludes Jews, let alone Buddhists, Muslims, Hindus, and nonbelievers. And, of course, the Kingdom of God is a very particular Christian symbol.

Nevertheless, FDR spoke of "our religion" in the same sense that he invoked "our civilization." I doubt that he meant to exclude any American from the umbrella of the war effort.

The FDR D-Day public prayer exemplifies a nation completely infused with religion. When the Court, a short time later in *Everson,* and then repeatedly after that, promised a government neutral toward religion, the justices were undertaking a monumental social task.

Probably everyone would agree that this task—the judicial promise of neutrality—has not been accomplished, at least not yet. For example, before Barack Obama was inaugurated as president, a group of atheists and agnostics sued to prevent the addition of the words "So help me God" to the presidential oath of office and to prevent two ministers, the Revs. Joseph Lowery and Rick Warren, from offering prayers at the inaugural ceremony. The requested injunction was denied,[2] and the phrase and the prayers went forward. This example illustrates the fact that what we do as a society is in no sense neutral toward religion.

I have been calling the failure of the justices to enforce neutrality, or to provide as a substitute any interpretation of the Establishment Clause other than neutrality, the crisis of the Establishment Clause. In this chapter I will show, primarily through the instances of the Pledge of Allegiance and displays of the Ten Commandments, some ways in which government neutrality has been breached. After that, I will take up a second question; assuming the Court has retreated from its commitment to government neutrality without acknowledging the change, why should this be considered a crisis?

The tension between government neutrality and common American religious practices was obvious in the case law from the beginning of the neutrality era. The year after *Everson* was decided, the Court in *McCollum v. Board of Education*[3] began the process of trying to remake our religious democracy into a secular democracy by overturning a released time program in public school.

Justice Stanley Reed dissented in *McCollum.* He wrote about the many ways in which religion and American public life were currently intertwined. This was not primarily an excursion into history, but into ordinary life, especially in the public schools. Reed had joined the majority in *Everson,* and he did not repudiate the language in that opinion, but now he was sounding a note of warning: "This Court cannot be too cautious in upsetting practices embedded in our society by many years of experience."[4]

This dissent marks the first judicial acknowledgment of the gap between the doctrine of government neutrality toward religion and American social practice.

As we saw in chapter 1, four years after *McCollum*, the Supreme Court upheld a released time program in *Zorach v. Clauson*.[5] The program in question was different from the one in *McCollum* in the sense that the students involved left public school during the school day for the religious activities. So the religious instruction was not on public school property. Yet the differences between the two programs were otherwise not that great.

The tone of Justice Douglas's majority opinion implied that he was much more cognizant of the social setting and role of religion in American society than the Court had been in *McCollum*. He wrote:

> We are a religious people whose institutions presuppose a Supreme Being.... When the state encourages religious instruction or cooperates with religious authorities by adjusting the schedule of public events to sectarian needs, it follows the best of our traditions. For it then respects the religious nature of our people and accommodates the public service to their spiritual needs. To hold that it may not would be to find in the Constitution a requirement that the government show a callous indifference to religious groups. That would be preferring those who believe in no religion over those who do believe.... [W]e find no constitutional requirement which makes it necessary for government to be hostile to religion and to throw its weight against efforts to widen the effective scope of religious influence.[6]

This is obviously not government neutrality toward religion. The state is here, Justice Douglas noted, "encourag[ing] religious instruction." And it is doing so because that is what a religious people would want their government to do. Otherwise,

> the state and religion would be aliens to each other—hostile, suspicious, and even unfriendly. Churches could not be required to pay even property taxes. Municipalities would not be permitted to render police or fire protection to religious groups. Policemen who helped parishioners into their places of worship would violate the Constitution. Prayers in our legislative halls; the appeals to the Almighty in the messages of the Chief Executive; the proclamations making Thanksgiving Day a holiday; "so help me God" in our courtroom oaths—these

and all other references to the Almighty that run through our laws, our public rituals, our ceremonies would be flouting the First Amendment. A fastidious atheist or agnostic could even object to the supplication with which the Court opens each session: "God save the United States and this Honorable Court."[7]

Justice Douglas was prescient both in the sense that there would later be Establishment Clause challenges to these sorts of historic public religious expressions and, also, that these examples of traditional religious expressions would come to be argued as evidence against the principle of government religious neutrality. Justice Douglas considered these national practices to be religious in some generalized sense, but found them to be constitutionally acceptable all the same. Thus the majority limited neutrality in the name of social practice.

Ten years later, Justice Black's majority opinion in *Engel v. Vitale,* which struck down prayer in the public schools, also referred to these sorts of public religious practices but seemed to regard them as not genuinely religious at all:

> There is of course nothing in the decision reached here that is inconsistent with the fact that school children and others are officially encouraged to express love for our country by reciting historical documents such as the Declaration of Independence which contain references to the Deity or by singing officially espoused anthems which include the composer's professions of faith in a Supreme Being, or with the fact that there are many manifestations in our public life of belief in God. Such patriotic or ceremonial occasions bear no true resemblance to the unquestioned religious exercise that the State of New York has sponsored in this instance.[8]

According to Justice Black, these practices are merely part of ceremonial or patriotic occasions, so that the religious expressions included may also be considered merely ceremonial or patriotic. Justice Black was suggesting that these traditional expressions are not violations of the Establishment Clause because they are not really religious. It would therefore follow, if these traditional expressions are not genuinely religious, that they are not supportive of any new religious expressions in the public realm, especially if such future expressions were seriously meant to be religious, as opposed to pro forma. The requirement of the Establishment Clause, argued Justice Black, is that government may not promote religion. Justice Black was here explaining how that requirement of government religious neutrality is consistent with a practice of making apparently religious references in American public life.

Engel marks the true beginning of the struggle on the Supreme Court over American religious practices. Prayer in the schools had more emotional and political resonance than did released time programs. Justice Black's treatment of these religious practices was challenged in *Engel* by Justice Potter Stewart's dissent. Then, a year later, in *Schempp*, Justice Brennan responded in the kind of debate that presaged the divisions on the Court today over neutrality.

Justice Stewart began his dissent in *Engel* by referring to the "spiritual heritage of our nation." The word "spiritual" here probably was intended by Justice Stewart to suggest that these traditional religious practices, such as opening Supreme Court sessions with the phrase "God save the United States and this honorable court," are nonsectarian. The use of the word "spiritual" may prove even more appropriate in the current age of religious seeking than it was in 1962, when Justice Stewart invoked it. Many people today can accept practices deemed spiritual, whereas they might balk at anything labeled religious.

Then Justice Stewart provided a list of official and public invocations of the protections of God, from the Court's own opening ceremony to presidential statements, to paid chaplains, to one of the stanzas in our national anthem, to the Pledge of Allegiance, to our National Day of Prayer, to our national motto, "In God We Trust," to the Declaration of Independence. Justice Stewart's point was that since these practices are not unconstitutional, which he was assuming, neither is New York State's school prayer in *Engel*.

Justice Brennan's response in defense of neutrality in his concurrence in *Schempp* began with the wording of the Establishment Clause itself against the background of the struggle over disestablishment in Virginia. The point of the wording of the clause—no establishment of "religion"—was not merely to prevent the establishment, in a formal sense, of one sect, but a prohibition on establishing religion itself. This was a strong endorsement of government neutrality. Justice Brennan concluded this section sweepingly:

> In sum, the history which our prior decisions have summoned to aid interpreta-
> tion of the Establishment Clause permits little doubt that its prohibition was
> designed comprehensively to prevent those official involvements of religion
> which would tend to foster or discourage religious worship or belief.[9]

But Justice Brennan regarded history as only a source of general themes, not as a solution to particular constitutional questions. The framers would not have given consideration to the specific question at issue in *Schempp,* he wrote,[10] because, among other differences, national public schooling was a modern invention.

Justice Brennan also discussed the Court's free exercise cases and the issue, which would later return in opinions by Justice Clarence Thomas, of whether non-establishment was a principle that restricted only the federal government and not the states. In that context, Justice Brennan suggested that the views of the mid-nineteenth century might be relevant to the reach of the Establishment Clause since the extension of the Establishment Clause to the states was a product of the Fourteenth Amendment.[11] We will return to that issue in chapter 4.

Justice Brennan considered the history of the particular practices at issue in *Schempp*—Bible reading and religious exercises in schools. Although such practices have long existed in many places, "almost from the beginning, Bible reading and daily prayer in the schools have been the subject of debate, criticism by educators and other public officials and proscription by courts and legislative councils."[12]

Justice Brennan quoted some of these objections, some of which raised constitutional or quasi-constitutional arguments. Ironically, to-ward the end of his concurrence, Justice Brennan mentioned legisla-tive invocation prayers as probably constitutional, a position he later repudiated.[13]

Finally, Justice Brennan referred to the kinds of public religious practices Justice Stewart had referenced in *Engel:* the motto, "In God We Trust," which is constitutional because it is "simply interwoven . . . so deeply into the fabric of our civil polity" and "patriotic exercises" that "recognize the historical fact that our Nation was believed to have been founded 'under God.'"[14] Despite these apparently religious practices, concluded Justice Brennan, the goal of the framers was to have, in the words of the nineteenth-century jurist and United States Attorney Gen-eral, Jeremiah S. Black, "a State without religion."

So the early response of the Court to the gap between what we say—government religious neutrality—and what we do—invoking religious expression ubiquitously—was to dismiss American religious practices as not genuinely religious and thus to allow them to continue despite the neutrality principle.

This strategy of pretense has also been employed with regard to the words "under God" in the Pledge of Allegiance. When that issue came to the Court in *Elk Grove Unified School District v. Newdow* in 2004,[15] the Court reversed the Ninth Circuit Court of Appeals, which had ruled the words "under God" in the Pledge of Allegiance to be unconstitutional.[16] Given Supreme Court precedent requiring religious neutrality, the Ninth Circuit was surely right that putting the words "under God" in the Pledge of Allegiance in 1954 was a religious act, was not justified by long historical practice, and was not religiously insignificant. Yet, when the Ninth Circuit held that "under God" was unconstitutional, everyone knew that the decision would be reversed by the Supreme Court.

Imagine the political fallout there would have been if the Court had affirmed the Ninth Circuit. An Associated Press poll in March 2004 reported that 87 percent of Americans supported retaining the words "under God" in the Pledge of Allegiance.[17] As Steven Shiffrin put it, "one need not have been a constitutional lawyer to predict that the Court would find a way to overturn the Ninth Circuit...."[18] A decision upholding the Ninth Circuit would have led to a serious, and possibly successful, effort to amend the Constitution, with an amendment of uncertain scope. It was not likely that the Court would invite such a struggle, if for no other reason than what Justice Scalia called in a related context, the Court's "instinct for self preservation."[19]

The Supreme Court reversed the Ninth Circuit decision on the ground that the plaintiff lacked standing to raise the issue rather than ruling on the merits of the case. Thus a rather strained interpretation of standing kept the Court from provoking a political firestorm in which the Court would have had few allies.

Is the "under God" language in the Pledge of Allegiance so unimportant that removing it is not worth the fight? As Steven Gey has persuasively argued, the language of the Pledge is not trivial in its own right and is also a marker of the overall place of government-sponsored religion.[20] I will argue later in this book that the words "under God" can be understood in a nonreligious way, along with their obvious religious import. But whether I am right about that or not, the Pledge represents Congress's attempt to state formally who we are as a nation. Therefore the language cannot be ducked and must be measured against the requirements of the Establishment Clause.

And what does the "under God" language mean? Judge Goodwin's opinion for the Ninth Circuit described what it means to be a nation "under God," treating the language straightforwardly as an endorsement of a form of biblical monotheism:

> In the context of the Pledge, the statement that the United States is a nation "under God" is a profession of a religious belief, namely, a belief in monotheism. The recitation that ours is a nation "under God" is not a mere acknowledgment that many Americans believe in a deity. Nor is it merely descriptive of the undeniable historical significance of religion in the founding of the Republic. Rather, the phrase "one nation under God" in the context of the Pledge is normative. To recite the Pledge is not to describe the United States; instead, it is to swear allegiance to the values for which the flag stands: unity, indivisibility, liberty, justice, and—since 1954—monotheism. A profession that we are a nation "under God" is identical, for Establishment Clause purposes, to a profession that we are a nation "under Jesus," a nation "under Vishnu," a nation "under Zeus," or a nation "under no god," because none of these professions can be neutral with respect to religion.[21]

When the case came before the Supreme Court, Justice Stevens held for the majority that the plaintiff, the non-custodial father of a school child subject to a school district's policy of requiring daily teacher-led recitation of the Pledge, lacked prudential standing to challenge the school district's policy. The major ground of this holding was that the custodial parent had filed a motion to intervene or dismiss on the ground that as a matter of state law, only she was legally entitled to represent her child's best interests.[22] Chief Justice Rehnquist, joined by Justice O'Connor and joined largely on this point by Justice Thomas, called this standing holding "novel," which it may well have been.[23]

Even if one considered this standing holding to be persuasive, it is obvious that if the justices wanted to hear a challenge to the daily recitation of the Pledge of Allegiance in public schools, a case raising the issue certainly could have been found since 2004. That fact, even more than the strained standing conclusion, suggests that the Court was ducking, and continues to duck, the Pledge of Allegiance issue. Apparently a majority of the justices do not wish either to uphold or strike down the words "under God" in the Pledge of Allegiance.

Because they would have upheld standing, three justices had occasion to indicate their views on the merits of including these words. Justice Thomas concluded that while he does not believe that the Pledge of Allegiance violates the Establishment Clause, the opinion below holding that it does was "based on a persuasive reading of our precedent."[24] Justice Thomas quoted *County of Allegheny v. Greater Pittsburgh ACLU* to the effect that "the Establishment Clause 'prohibits government from appearing to take a position on questions of religious belief.'"[25] Since the "under God" language in the Pledge affirms that God exists, the Pledge violates that precept of government neutrality. Justice Thomas, who disputes the thrust of precedent in the church/state area, stated that he would begin "the process of rethinking the Establishment Clause."[26] Justice Thomas made good on that promise, concluding that even if the Establishment Clause were held to be incorporated against the states, a violation would have to involve an "element of legal coercion" by the government.[27] No such coercion is present in the wording of the Pledge.

Chief Justice Rehnquist and Justice O'Connor would both have upheld the "under God" language in the Pledge of Allegiance. They presented visions of the Establishment Clause broadly congruent with the mix of religious and secular practices present in current American public life, and they claimed that this mix is generally consistent with existing precedent. Presumably, then, they would not have agreed that there is a crisis in Establishment Clause interpretation. But their views have an ad hoc quality that fails to explain what the role of religion is to be in American public life.

Chief Justice Rehnquist relied primarily on the presence in American history "of patriotic invocations of God and official acknowledgments of religion's role in our Nation's history. . . ."[28] From numerous examples, such as the national motto "In God We Trust" and the opening of Supreme Court sessions with the language "God save the United States and this honorable court," Chief Justice Rehnquist concluded that "our national culture allows public recognition of our Nation's religious history and character."[29]

Chief Justice Rehnquist's examples, however, prove much more than mere recognition of the nation's religious history and character. These references to God were presumably expressions of genuine faith. Justice Thomas is right that the language in the Pledge reflects the belief that God actually exists, not that people used to believe that God exists. By calling this language patriotic rather than religious, Chief Justice Rehnquist seems to be asserting that this language means very little. Through this approach, he did not have to confront the gap between genuine neutrality and the "under God" language in the Pledge. His conclusion, however, is belied by the determination of many religious believers to retain the words "under God" in the Pledge and the equal determination of many nonbelievers to remove it.

Justice O'Connor, in addition to joining the Chief Justice, would have upheld the "under God" language under the rubric of "ceremonial deism." Such references to God and other religious symbols "serve, in the only ways reasonably possible in our culture, the legitimate secular purposes of solemnizing public occasions, expressing confidence in the future, and encouraging the recognition of what is worthy of appreciation in society."[30] This minimal reference to God "cannot be seen as a serious invocation of God or as an expression of individual submission to divine authority."[31] While the reference to God does seem to contradict nontheistic religious belief, and thus might violate the core Establishment Clause prohibition against preferring one religion to another, "one would be hard pressed to imagine a brief solemnizing reference to religion that would adequately encompass every religious belief by any citizen of this Nation."[32]

Justice O'Connor did not seem enthusiastic about upholding the words "under God." She called the language a "tolerable attempt" to use religious language to acknowledge religion and to solemnize public occasions.[33] Fundamentally, she believes that this language is not really religious and indeed that it must not be genuinely religious. If public references to God were actually intended to induce a "penitent state of mind" or were "intended to create a spiritual communion or invoke divine aid" they would violate the Establishment Clause.[34] To be acceptable, public religious language must therefore either remind us that we were once religious or must have no more than a formal, rather than a substantive, character.

Again, however, as is the case with Chief Justice Rehnquist's view, Justice O'Connor is denying meanings that both sides in the struggle attribute to the words "under God" in the Pledge. Her hypothetical observer does not intuit genuine religious meaning in these words. But many believers and nonbelievers do intuit such meaning. She can uphold the "under God" language only by denying its authoritativeness. She denies its authoritativeness in order to make the claim that she is upholding neutrality.

The next set of Supreme Court cases raising the issue of religious neutrality in light of American religious practices were the Ten Commandments display cases in 2005—*McCreary County* and *Van Orden*—and *Pleasant Grove City, Utah v. Summum* in 2009.[35]

As noted in chapter 1, Justice Souter's majority opinion in *McCreary County* relied on the neutrality principle to strike down the posting of the Ten Commandments in two Kentucky County courthouses:

> The point is simply that the original text viewed in its entirety is an unmistakably religious statement dealing with religious obligations and with morality subject to religious sanction. When the government initiates an effort to place this statement alone in public view, a religious object is unmistakable.[36]

In dissent, Justice Scalia, joined by Justices Kennedy and Thomas, and by Chief Justice Rehnquist, took dead aim at the neutrality principle, both from the perspective of history and current American practices:

> Presidents continue to conclude the Presidential oath with the words "so help me God." Our legislatures, state and national, continue to open their sessions with prayer led by official chaplains. The sessions of this Court continue to open with the prayer "God save the United States and this Honorable Court." Invocation of the Almighty by our public figures, at all levels of government, remains commonplace. Our coinage bears the motto, "IN GOD WE TRUST." And our Pledge of Allegiance contains the acknowledgment that we are a Nation "under God."
>
> With all of this reality (and much more) staring it in the face, how can the Court *possibly* assert that the "First Amendment mandates governmental neutrality between . . . religion and nonreligion," and that "[m]anifesting a purpose to favor . . . adherence to religion generally," is unconstitutional? Who says so? Surely not the words of the Constitution. Surely not the history and traditions that reflect our society's constant understanding of those words. Surely not even the current sense of our society, recently reflected in an Act of Congress adopted *unanimously* by the Senate and with only five nays in the House of Representatives, criticizing a Court of Appeals opinion that had held "under God" in the Pledge of Allegiance unconstitutional. Nothing stands behind the

Court's assertion that governmental affirmation of the society's belief in God is unconstitutional except the Court's own say-so, citing as support only the unsubstantiated say-so of earlier Courts going back no further than the mid-twentieth century.[37]

In *Van Orden,* which upheld the Ten Commandments display, there was no majority opinion. Chief Justice Rehnquist's plurality opinion, like his concurrence in *Elk Grove,* did not directly challenge the neutrality principle:

> This case, like all Establishment Clause challenges, presents us with the difficulty of respecting both faces. Our institutions presuppose a Supreme Being, yet these institutions must not press religious observances upon their citizens. One face looks to the past in acknowledgment of our Nation's heritage, while the other looks to the present in demanding a separation between church and state. Reconciling these two faces requires that we neither abdicate our responsibility to maintain a division between church and state nor evince a hostility to religion by disabling the government from in some ways recognizing our religious heritage.[38]

Although Chief Justice Rehnquist's opinion did point to similar displays, for example, in the nation's capital, these practices were not actually relevant, since the Ten Commandments display was being upheld as a matter of religious "heritage" rather than as an acceptable form of the promotion of religious belief. Neutrality was not attacked in the plurality opinion. This failure led Justice Scalia to complain in a concurrence that, although he joined the plurality opinion, he "would prefer to reach the same result by adopting an Establishment Clause jurisprudence that is in accord with our Nation's past and present practices, and that can be consistently applied—the central relevant feature of which is that there is nothing unconstitutional in a state's favoring religion generally, honoring God through public prayer and acknowledgment, or, in a non-proselytizing manner, venerating the Ten Commandments."[39]

One might think that the law about Ten Commandments displays remains unsettled given the close division on the Court in 2005. That no longer seems to be true given the most recent treatment of a Ten Commandments display in *Pleasant Grove.* In that case, the City of Pleasant Grove maintained a public park with a number of privately donated displays, including a Ten Commandments display. Summum, a religious organization, requested that the City erect a monument containing the "Seven Aphorisms of Summum," which amounted to an alternative account—a "Gnostic" Christian one—of the Sinai story.[40] The city denied this request and Summum sued.

Summum claimed that by accepting the privately donated Ten Commandments display while rejecting its offer, the city was violating its free speech rights. Thus Summum was arguing that the existing Ten Commandments display was a form of private speech and that the city was in effect preferring one entity's private speech over that of another in what should be treated as a public forum. A panel of the Tenth Circuit agreed with this argument and ordered the city to accept the proffered monument,[41] but the Supreme Court reversed—unanimously on this point—viewing the Ten Commandments display (and indeed, by implication, all the monuments in the public park) as forms of government speech, however they came into possession by the city.

In the manner the case came to the Supreme Court, the decision was an easy one on the surface. After all, if monuments in public parks were treated as private speech in a public forum, governments might have to accept any such monuments, which would be impossible and would inevitably lead to exclusion of all such monuments.

But underneath the surface, the case was being litigated "in the shadow . . . of the *Establishment* Clause," as Justice Scalia put it in his concurrence.[42] If the existing Ten Commandments display represented private speech, it was immune from Establishment Clause challenge. On the other hand, if the Ten Commandments display were the government's own message, then the next challenge by Summum would amount to a replay of the Establishment Clause Ten Commandments challenges previously litigated to split decisions in *McCreary County* and *Van Orden.*

Summum sharpened this tension by asking the city to "adopt a resolution publicly embracing 'the message' that the monument conveys."[43] Such a resolution might easily have run afoul of the Establishment Clause in any later litigation. If the city had admitted, for example, that the message it meant to convey by accepting the Ten Commandments display was acknowledgment of the God of monotheism, as Justice Scalia had argued is permissible in his dissent in *McCreary County*,[44] there might later have been five justices on the Supreme Court who would find an Establishment Clause violation.[45]

Justice Alito's majority opinion, avoiding this controversy, stated that monuments do not have "simple" messages, but "may be intended to be interpreted, and may in fact be interpreted by different observers, in a variety of ways."[46] Justice Alito illustrated this theme by reference to the "Imagine" display "donated to New York City's Central Park in memory of John Lennon."[47] Justice Alito even quoted the lyrics of the Lennon song, "Imagine." Thus government may speak a mixed and rich message.

This was pretty fancy footwork by Justice Alito. It is noteworthy that in a case about a Ten Commandments display, he quoted a pop song rather than the Ten Commandments themselves. If he had quoted those verses, he would have had to begin with something like, "I AM THE LORD THY GOD."[48] Justice Alito did not wish to acknowledge this possibility, so he was content to leave the record silent as to the content of Pleasant Grove's government speech.

Certainly, on the surface, upholding a new Ten Commandments display does not seem consistent with any form of religious neutrality. What has happened to the Court's confident neutrality rhetoric that began in *Everson* and continued in later cases? Why hasn't the Court purged our public life of religious expression, or at least prohibited new public religious expressions? The answer is politics, in two different senses. First, the abolition of prayer in the schools, in combination with other controversial rulings, led to a conservative backlash against the Supreme Court in the 1970s and thereafter. The emergence of a politically powerful Christian right in the 1980s put additional pressure on the Court. And I think this backlash undermined even those justices who felt strongly that government should be neutral toward religion.

The other political aspect of the religion cases lies in the makeup of the Court. The substitution of Chief Justice John Roberts for Chief Justice Rehnquist in 2005 probably did not change much in terms of the Establishment Clause. But the substitution of Justice Samuel Alito in 2006 for Justice O'Connor might change a great deal. Justice O'Connor, as we have seen, was the author of the endorsement test and though she often voted to uphold government religious expression and government financial support to religion, she did not always do so, and she always maintained in theory a commitment to the notion that government could not endorse religion over irreligion. Justice Alito is not likely to share her commitment, or at least not to the same extent. Chief Justice Roberts, along with Justices Alito, Kennedy, Scalia, Thomas, and even perhaps Breyer, constitute if not a pro-religion bloc, at least a non-neutrality bloc. And this bloc remains dominant as Justice Stevens leaves the Court, no matter how pro-neutrality his replacement turns out to be.

The foregoing cases demonstrate acceptance by majorities of the justices of seemingly non-neutral government practices. If the neutral state conception has, therefore, failed to achieve complete jurisprudential victory, what, if anything, has?

The answer is that no one conception of the Establishment Clause is unambiguously accepted today. Certainly it is common ground among the justices that the government may not prefer one religion over another. But it is not universally agreed whether government may or may not prefer religion to irreligion. It is also clear that government may not coerce citizens into religious participation, but it is not clear what coercion means in this context. Finally, under the Free Exercise Clause and principles of free speech, there is a commitment among the justices to prohibit government from discriminating against private religious speech. In a culture as religiously infused as this one, that last point ensures a fairly religious public square.

But all of these points are only partial delineations of the reach of the Establishment Clause. Has any approach emerged as a possible next overall vision of the Establishment Clause, one that can serve as a substitute for the principle of government neutrality between religion and irreligion? Given the changes in Court personnel, the principle of neutrality probably lacks majority support today. But what will emerge in its place? That is not yet known.

We thus are in the following situation today: the American people as a whole seem to have rejected important aspects of the Court's fundamental vision of the proper relationship of government and religion—government neutrality; the justices seem unwilling or unable to defend and insist on their vision; and no alternative understanding of the Establishment Clause has emerged to take the place of government neutrality. Using a variety of stopgaps and exceptions, the Court has upheld a variety of government religious symbols and images, including Ten Commandments displays[49] and legislative prayers,[50] in the face of its promise of neutrality. Thus the law of the Establishment Clause is, in the words of John Bickers, in "current chaos."[51]

Should the American people be concerned about what I have called a crisis in interpretation of the Establishment Clause? Of course, the outcomes of cases in the field of church and state are significant for many people for many reasons. But should we be particularly concerned about the role of the Supreme Court when the Court says one thing—the Constitution requires government neutrality—and we do something different, and the justices allow this to go on without adjusting what they say?

Perhaps this gap in constitutional understanding is not important. There have been worse controversies involving judicial review. For example, in the area of abortion, the Court's decision in *Roe v. Wade*[52] sparked great controversy that forced the justices to narrow their original interpretation of the right of privacy. It is indisputable that the right of abortion was not as broad in *Planned Parenthood of Southeastern Pennsylvania v. Casey*[53] in 1992 as it had been in *Roe* in 1973.

But the crisis in the Establishment Clause is different. Even in *Casey,* in that judicial retreat, the Court held to *Roe*'s essential holding—a law actually outlawing abortion would still have been struck down. That is not the case in regard to the establishment of religion. The "under God" language in the Pledge of Allegiance would seem to be an endorsement of religion. Yet the Court allows it to stand.

As another example of controversy over a judicial decision, in enforcing the anti-segregation decision, *Brown v. Board of Education,*[54] the justices were aware of the depth of opposition to their decision. So they delayed enforcement of *Brown,* holding the next year that *Brown*'s mandate of ending segregation should proceed "with all deliberate speed,"[55] a purposely ambiguous construction. Thus justice was delayed.

Yet the Court's action in the religion cases, specifically in permitting the Pledge of Allegiance to be said in public school and permitting Ten Commandments displays to remain on public property, is far worse. In retaining the rhetoric of neutrality while refusing, rather than delaying, neutrality's enforcement, the Court denigrates its role in our system of government.

It might be argued that there is no crisis, that the Court is simply divided about the meaning of the Establishment Clause. After all, the majority in *McCreary County* did reassert the neutrality principle and acted on it. The contrary plurality in *Van Orden* might have been willing to overturn neutrality if Justice Breyer had been willing to go along. On this view, the Establishment Clause problem is just that Justice Breyer is unable to make up his mind.

But the Court's unwillingness to tackle the Pledge of Allegiance and the Court's silence on the Establishment Clause issue in *Pleasant Grove*, thus in effect upholding both without the willingness to explain how they satisfy neutrality or why neutrality is no longer required, along with the Court's upholding obviously religious practices like legislative prayer as either historical aberrations or religiously meaningless, all suggest a loss of judicial nerve accompanied by a lack of integrity. The Court should not be saying one thing and doing another.

There is no dishonor in caving in to public pressure. Indeed I will argue in the next chapter that judicial attentiveness to public opinion is necessary and healthy in a democratic system. When, in 2008, the Court finally concluded that the Second Amendment entails a personal right of some kind to possession of firearms,[56] the Court was changing course under public pressure. Perhaps the Court will do something similar eventually in the area of religion. I hope so. But right now all we have is a gap between what the Court says and what the Court is willing to enforce.

This crisis cannot be attributed solely to Justice Breyer's indecision. Certainly he is not the reason the Court is ducking a Pledge of Allegiance case, for example. Justice Breyer would also deny that he prevented the Court from reaching a principled result in the Ten Commandments cases. In casting the deciding vote in *Van Orden*,[57] upholding a Ten Commandments display on the grounds of the Texas state capital, Justice Breyer introduced a kind of situational judging in Establishment Clause cases. He did this in the name of avoiding social division.

Justice Breyer insisted in *Van Orden* that "no single mechanical formula" can draw the constitutional line of separation of church and state in every case.[58] "[G]overnment must avoid excessive interference with, or promotion of, religion," but this does not imply that government must "purge from the public sphere all that in any way partakes of the religious" for that would "tend to promote the kind of social conflict the Establishment Clause seeks to avoid."[59] That is an Establishment Clause principle of a sort.

In a way, when Justice Breyer wrote these words, he was simply acknowledging the crisis in Establishment Clause jurisprudence that is the subject of this book. No test proposing separation or neutrality can really explain why the Court has upheld so much in the way of public religious practices. In a borderline case, which Justice Breyer thought *Van Orden* represented, one should consider the context.

Despite the opinion's emphasis on the inapplicability of any test or rule, two themes predominate for Justice Breyer. First, the message of the Ten Commandments display in the case is "predominantly secular." The Ten Commandments themselves combine religious meaning with "a secular moral message" and their display can convey a historical connection of the moral and the legal. There was nothing in the history of this display or of its physical setting to suggest that anything sacred was intended by the government or that the display represented any religious message.

The second theme is that the absence of any previous challenge to the Ten Commandments display during its forty-year history shows that the display is not "divisive." This absence of strife distinguished *Van Orden* from the *McCreary County* case decided the same day, in which Justice Breyer joined the four *Van Orden* dissenters to strike down two courthouse Ten Commandments displays. In *McCreary County,* "the short (and stormy) history of the courthouse Commandments' displays demonstrates the substantially religious objectives of those who mounted them, and the effect of this readily apparent objective upon those who view them."[60] To hold that a Ten Commandments display must be removed simply because of its religious content, "might well encourage disputes concerning the removal of longstanding depictions of the Ten Commandments from public buildings across the Nation" thus creating the "very kind of religiously based divisiveness that the Establishment Clause seeks to avoid."[61]

It should not be hard to see that the result of this situational judging might be precisely the opposite of what is intended by Justice Breyer.

One rational response to his opinion would be to stimulate strife. A dedicated separationist would want to show there is a lot of opposition to the Texas monument. One way to do that would be to organize demonstrations on the capitol grounds. To put it another way, you don't obtain peace by ruling in favor of one party to a dispute on the basis of the absence of strife. Doing that teaches that the wages of strife are a better chance of winning your lawsuit.

Undoubtedly, non-divisiveness is a goal of the entire constitutional system. But it is not case-by-case judging that brings peace. The principle of separate-but-equal, for example, invited litigation about particulars of segregated institutions in a way that the principle of no segregation at all did not. To put the matter more generally, clear principles acceptable to a consensus of the American people are the constitutional path to peace.

The political consequences of the crisis of the Establishment Clause are severe. On the one hand, supporters of the neutral state cling to supportive judicial rhetoric and criticize the Supreme Court for its perceived duplicity. They look at *Everson* and the cases since then and conclude that government religious neutrality is plainly what the framers intended. The unwillingness of some conservative religious believers to accept neutrality is then viewed as bad faith.

On the other hand, the failure of the Court to promote any constitutional interpretation other than neutrality, while at the same time permitting public religious expression, invites extreme formulations of the Christian state that probably no justice would support. This is what happens when the Court is unable to present a clear vision of what the Constitution means. As we shall see in the next chapter, any such vision by the Court must be accepted by the American people. On the question of the establishment of religion, however, the justices have not taken even the first step toward a popular constitutional consensus by offering to the people a new general principle that the majority of justices endorse.

An illustration of the political consequences of the Court's failure to resolve the Establishment Clause crisis occurred on July 9, 2009, when the House of Representatives passed Resolution 131, by a vote of 410 to 8, with twelve abstentions, directing the Architect of the Capitol to engrave the Pledge of Allegiance and the national motto "In God We Trust" in the Capitol Visitor Center. The next day, the Senate passed the same resolution by unanimous consent.

This episode shows how the word "God" has become a wedge issue in the political culture wars. Many secularists, and even many religious liberals, oppose the addition of God-language in the public square on principle. Letters to the editor all over the country fumed over this congressional action. Lawsuits against it have been filed, which will almost certainly fail. Yet only ten representatives voted against the resolution in the House, and in the Senate not one senator wished to go on record opposing it. In terms of political advantage, Republicans have good reasons to press the word "God" into every public space they can. By doing so, they discomfort Democrats who might oppose these kinds of government-sanctioned forms of public religious expression, but are afraid to vote that way.

What makes all this unhealthy identity politics is that the underlying goals of the two sides are not clear. Proponents of the resolution spoke of our nation's "heritage," as if no one currently believes in God and as if this kind of action has no current political fallout. Opponents of the resolution are unable to specify what kinds of references to God in the public square might be constitutional. The answer might be none, but I have never heard that answer stated candidly by any politician. In fact, I have rarely heard that from anyone, no matter how secular.

What is clear is that when the words "under God" go up in the public square, there are perceived to be winners and losers. This kind of damaging struggle over public religious symbols appears likely to continue and even intensify.

What is needed to bring peace to the realm of church and state is an *answer* to the crisis of the Establishment Clause. The Court's obligation is to present the American people with a vision of the proper relationship of religion to public life that the people can understand and accept. The neutral state has proved not to be such a principle. Separation and neutrality have led us down a path of culture war and constant litigation.

Perhaps there is no principle of church and state that will reconcile most Americans. America has a long history of public religious practices along with a growing secular commitment. We have been overwhelm-

ingly Protestant and now we are fragmenting into a country predominantly Christian but with many religions and much secularism. In this
context, conflict may be inevitable.

But the justices should at least keep clarifying their conflicting visions so the people will have choices put before them.[62] And legal academics have a similar role to play. This book constitutes one such attempt. It is to be hoped that common ground among believers, minority
believers, and secularists can eventually be reached.

Where does such a constitutional interpretation come from? The
main source in the field of church and state has been history. The next
chapter suggests that the answer to the Establishment Clause crisis does
not lie in history.

THREE

Why Only the People and Not History Can Resolve the Establishment Clause Crisis

The Establishment Clause crisis consists of the gap between what we say in constitutional law about government neutrality toward religion, on the one hand, and the obvious endorsement of religion by government in practice. In effect, the crisis reflects an inability to choose between the alternatives that Ronald Dworkin starkly sets forth: a secular society tolerant of religion or a religious society tolerant of nonbelief. In part 2 of this book, I will propose the higher law reinterpretation of much of American public religiosity in order to resolve the crisis without overturning the neutrality principle. Before doing so, however, I must examine the historical claims that each side brings forth in order to support neutrality or oppose it and consider whether history provides the kind of support that can resolve the crisis. Then, in the next chapter, I will set forth several alternative proposals that have been made to resolve the crisis.

American arguments about church and state, both on the Supreme Court and in society generally, almost always end up as arguments about American history. One side quotes George Washington while the other quotes Thomas Jefferson. This approach has not resolved our religion issue; nor could it. Not only is American history indeterminate about religion in the public square, but constitutional issues in general can rarely be decided this way.

I was once interviewed by the liberal radio personality Thom Hartmann on the subject of church and state. The segment did not last long on the air—about ten minutes—and at least eight minutes, it seemed, were taken up with his reading a series of quotations from Thomas Jefferson and James Madison about the evils of mixing church and state and about how government and religion were to have nothing to do with each other. Perplexed, I finally replied, "How can someone who supports *Roe v. Wade*[1] rely on history this way? You sound like Justice Scalia."

Liberals normally interpret the Constitution as what is called a *living* document. For example, despite the lack of historical justification, the Due Process Clause is interpreted to protect the right to an abortion; the Equal Protection Clause is interpreted to require recognition of gay marriage; Free Speech is interpreted to protect pornography. History, in the sense of the original meaning of these provisions when they were introduced and ratified, would not support outcomes like these. That does not usually matter to liberals, who often argue that the Constitution must be interpreted flexibly to keep its protections fresh and up to date. Interpretation must not be constrained by slavish adherence to history. Thus the Constitution lives in a new time.

But when it comes to the Establishment Clause this liberal attitude toward history alters. In the context of church and state, the commitment of Thomas Jefferson to the wall of separation between church and state and the notion of government unconcerned about the salvation of individual citizens is elevated to an eternal norm.

As my response on the radio suggested, we usually associate conservative constitutional jurisprudence, such as that of Justice Scalia, with an emphasis on the claims of history. I will return below to the historical approach to the Establishment Clause held by Justice Scalia and other conservative justices. First, we will examine the reliance on history by those who favor government religious neutrality and the strict separation of church and state.

Hartmann was quoting Jefferson and Madison to establish the legitimacy and necessity of the secular state. His point was that government and religion are separate realms and, therefore, government has no legitimate reason to concern itself with religion in any way. Here is Jefferson as the secularists like to portray him:

> The legitimate powers of government extend to such acts only as are injurious to others. But it does me no injury for my neighbor to say there are twenty gods or no god. It neither picks my pocket nor breaks my leg.[2]

and

> The clergy ... believe that any portion of power confided to me [as President]
> will be exerted in opposition to their schemes. And they believe rightly: for I
> have sworn upon the altar of God, eternal hostility against every form of tyranny
> over the mind of man.

and, most famously,

> Believing with you that religion is a matter which lies solely between Man & his
> God, that he owes account to none other for his faith or his worship, that the
> legitimate powers of government reach actions only, & not opinions, I contem-
> plate with sovereign reverence that act of the whole American people which
> declared that their legislature should "make no law respecting an establishment
> of religion, or prohibiting the free exercise thereof," thus building a wall of sepa-
> ration between Church & State.[3]

There is also the example that Jefferson as president refused to issue
a Thanksgiving proclamation, as George Washington and John Adams
had done, on the ground that doing so would be a "religious exercise,"
which the Constitution had left in the hands of the citizenry and not
the government.[4] One could certainly add here quotations from James
Madison's 1785 *Memorial and Remonstrance Against Religious Assessments,* which was so influential to the Court in *Everson.* And there is, in
addition, the argument that the Constitution omitted mentioning God
at all and thus founded a secular state.[5]

But what is the point of this kind of authority? For argument's sake,
let us assume that Jefferson and Madison are the right historical sources
to understand the American history of church and state correctly. (There
actually would be a great deal of controversy about that.) We can also assume, for the moment, that these quotations and practices and actions—
and other such evidence as could certainly be gathered—really do reflect
a general consensus from the founding period about the desirability of a
strict separation of church and state. (As we will see, some justices have
specifically argued otherwise.)

The problem with using history this way is that there is no necessarily normative weight to this kind of historical evidence. In other words,
merely announcing what these figures from American history thought
is not necessarily a reason to change our society's current practices. We
need to be told why we should listen to them and why we should be influenced by what they thought.

Secularists like Hartmann already believe that religion is properly a private matter. They don't believe that because, as they say, Jefferson believed it. They believe it for other reasons. Those are the reasons that the listener needs to hear.

Similarly these secularists don't want a neutral state because the Constitution creates one. They want a neutral state because, for example, they think that religion is a divisive and negative influence on society. Again, the listener needs to know why they think that.

These reasons—the real reasons—are what must be debated. They form the potential normative basis for the strict separation of church and state. These reasons, and not history, are the underlying explanation for the movement toward a secular state.

Granted, there may be people who so admire Jefferson and Madison that the fact that these men are portrayed as supporting a neutral state might of itself be a reason to support the same goal. But even people like that cannot really support the neutral state just because Jefferson did. For his situation is not our situation. For example, part of the reason Jefferson felt the way he did about religion and government was theological. In *Everson,* Justice Black quoted the Preamble to the "Virginia Bill for Religious Liberty," originally written by Thomas Jefferson, as follows:

> Almighty God hath created the mind free; that all attempts to influence it by temporal punishments, or burthens, or by civil incapacitations, tend only to beget habits of hypocrisy and meanness, and are a departure from the plan of the Holy author of our religion who being Lord both of body and mind, yet chose not to propagate it by coercions on either.[6]

Jefferson's argument here is that God, in whom Jefferson clearly believed, chose not to use coercion to force faith. Therefore government action to promote religion, by its nature always coercive in some sense, violates the divine plan. But, obviously, if I don't believe in God, this argument for separation of church and state would not persuade me.

This reference to Jefferson is a small example of a larger problem. History as such, even when it seems clear, simply cannot resolve questions like what the relationship of church and state ought to be. Our situation is different from the situation people were in two hundred years before. Even if we seem to be asking similar questions, we usually are not. As C. S. Lewis, the author and Christian thinker, once said, "There is no more tiresome error in the history of thought than to try to sort our ancestors on to this or that side of a distinction which was not in their minds at all."[7]

But there might be an exception to the claim that history cannot decide constitutional claims. Conservative constitutional theory argues that history is precisely the way that a provision like the Establishment Clause should be interpreted *in the courts.* Justice Scalia is known for a position called textualism, which usually means that a constitutional provision should be interpreted to mean what it was understood to have meant when it was adopted. It is closely related to what is known as interpretation according to original intent. In limiting interpretation this way, it is said, a judge keeps her own value system from improperly influencing case outcomes.

In my radio interview, Hartmann was not making this kind of technical, legal, claim. But Chief Justice Rehnquist, Justice Scalia, and others have been making just that claim about the Establishment Clause. Is their opposition to neutrality on historical grounds any more persuasive than that of Hartmann and other secularists?

The resort to history for general interpretive principles concerning the Establishment Clause began, on the Court, in *Everson* itself, by reference to Jefferson's metaphor of the wall of separation between church and state and Justice Black's account of colonial and early American history culminating in its "dramatic climax in Virginia in 1785–86" when "Madison wrote his great Memorial and Remonstrance."[8] Justice Black famously concluded that "[n]either [a state nor the federal government] can pass laws which aid one religion, aid all religions, or prefer one religion over another."[9]

The full conservative counterattack against this version of history was made years later, in then-Justice Rehnquist's dissent in *Wallace v. Jaffree,* the public school silent prayer case.[10] Justice Rehnquist explained that he was expressly challenging a "mistaken understanding of constitutional history."[11] He concluded that Madison in particular, in introducing the precursor language to the Establishment Clause, "did not see it as requiring neutrality on the part of government between religion and irreligion."[12]

As we saw in chapter 1, the *Jaffree* decision was the highpoint of strict separation between church and state in which the bare intention by the

Alabama legislature to promote prayer led the Court to strike down a moment-of-silence law for public schools. Justice Rehnquist's dissent in that case took dead aim at Jefferson's "wall of separation" metaphor as the proper description of the relationship between religion and public life. The dissent began with the different versions of the Establishment and Free Exercise Clauses that Congress debated. That history, Justice Rehnquist claimed, demonstrates that James Madison saw the Establishment Clause as prohibiting congressional endorsement of a national religion and preventing discrimination among religions, not as "requiring neutrality on the part of government between religion and irreligion."[13]

Justice Rehnquist then traced the history of government support of religion in America. The same First Congress that passed the Bill of Rights called for "religion" in the schools of the Northwest Territory and passed a resolution asking President Washington to issue a Thanksgiving Day Proclamation, which he did.

In the 1800s Congress appropriated moneys for sectarian Indian education. Scholarly legal authorities of the period held that public religious worship did not violate the Constitution. Rehnquist concluded, "As its history abundantly shows . . . nothing in the Establishment Clause requires government to be strictly neutral between religion and irreligion."[14]

This historical counterattack has continued ever since *Jaffree*, most recently with Justice Scalia's reference in his dissent in *McCreary County* to "the demonstrably false principle that the government cannot favor religion over irreligion."[15] What made the principle *demonstrably* false was historical fact and current practices that the Court has been unwilling to strike down.

The cases referred to above tried to draw general principles or at least themes from history, taken as a whole. There is also in the case law an alternative use of history, much more restricted, limited to the long term presence of some practice in American history. This parallel historical approach to deciding Establishment Clause cases based simply on the pedigree of the challenged practice at issue was most fully utilized in *Marsh v. Chambers*.[16] In that case, in 1983, the Court upheld the practice of a state legislature beginning its session with a prayer by a chaplain paid with public funds. Chief Justice Burger found it dispositive for upholding this practice that the same Congress that approved the Bill of Rights in 1789, had, three days before, provided public funds for a chaplain and has always since then opened sessions of Congress with prayer. The Court has also, on various occasions, suggested that our national motto "In God We Trust" and other historical references to God and prayer, such as national declarations of Thanksgiving, are constitutional for the same reason of historical longevity.

Deciding cases by reference to historical practices was succinctly defended by Justice Kennedy in the Allegheny County crèche case, in which a divided Court struck down the prominent singular display of a crèche at Christmastime, but upheld a Chanukah menorah as part of a combined holiday display.[17] In his opinion concurring in the judgment in part and dissenting in part, Justice Kennedy explained the significance of the Court's upholding legislative prayers in *Marsh,* given the long American tradition of such prayers:

> *Marsh* stands for the proposition, not that specific practices common in 1791 are an exception to the otherwise broad sweep of the Establishment Clause, but rather that the meaning of the Clause is to be determined by reference to historical practices and understandings. Whatever test we choose to apply must permit not only legitimate practices two centuries old but also any other practices with no greater potential for an establishment of religion. The First Amendment is a rule, not a digest or compendium. A test for implementing the protections of the Establishment Clause that, if applied with consistency, would invalidate longstanding traditions cannot be a proper reading of the Clause.[18]

It is important to note what is and is not being claimed here by Justice Kennedy. The existence of historical practices does not excuse the interpreter from a coherent understanding of the meaning of the Establishment Clause. Nor does such a history insulate a specific practice, or an analogous practice, from constitutional challenge. Admittedly Justice Kennedy's last sentence introduces some ambiguity about that latter claim. But Justice Scalia some years later, in his dissent in *McCreary County*[19] made the point plainly. Also referring to *Marsh,* Justice Scalia scorned the tendency of Court majorities to ignore the principle of government neutrality in some cases but not others:

> The only "good reason" for ignoring the neutrality principle set forth in any of these cases was the antiquity of the practice at issue. That would be a good

reason for finding the neutrality principle a mistaken interpretation of the Constitution, but it is hardly a good reason for letting an unconstitutional practice continue.[20]

Thus all that the existence of historical practices can properly do is to suggest the general outline of a coherent approach to interpretation of a constitutional provision. For Justice Rehnquist, for example, that coherent approach was nonpreferentialism, the view that the government may legitimately prefer and promote religion over irreligion. We will deal with that perspective in the next chapter. The point here is that historical practices alone generally do not resolve any constitutional disputes, including our current crisis in understanding the Establishment Clause.

There are a number of examples in constitutional law in which a general principle deduced from a constitutional provision was later applied to overturn a practice well established at the time the provision was adopted. Most famously, the Congress that drafted the Equal Protection Clause in the Fourteenth Amendment in 1866 had, in the same year, appropriated funds to support segregated public schools in Washington D.C., thus suggesting that Congress conceived of segregation as compatible with equal protection. Yet, of course, in *Brown v. Board of Education*[21] and later cases, the Supreme Court would hold otherwise.

A similar example, but one not as much remarked upon, concerns legal discriminations against women. Clearly when the Fourteenth Amendment was adopted in 1868, these discriminations, which were widespread—including restrictions on ownership of property, prohibitions on participation in certain professions and, of course, exclusion from the right to vote—were assumed to be consistent with "equal protection of the laws." Much later the Supreme Court and state courts would dismantle this regime of gender discrimination in the name of equal protection at the same time that they were also being removed by legislation.

So history, whether a general view of the time a provision was adopted or by reference to particular practices that came down from that time, does not by itself decide the meaning of a constitutional provision. That alone would seem to discredit attempts to define the reach of the Establishment Clause purely by reference to history.

But there are, in addition, several particular reasons that the use of history by both sides in the religion cases has not been decisive. First, history in this area is contentious. Despite Justice Rehnquist's confident rhetoric in *Jaffree,* the actual difficulty of extracting a clear verdict from history on religious matters can be seen from his treatment of James Madison. Madison's views had been emphasized by the Court in *Everson* on the way to holding that the Establishment Clause requires the kind of government neutrality toward religion that Justice Rehnquist was opposing in his dissent. Yet, in coming to a different conclusion about the meaning of the Establishment Clause, Justice Rehnquist did not deny Madison's central role in the adoption of the Bill of Rights, including, of course, the Establishment Clause.

Justice Rehnquist surmounted this difficulty by attributing to Madison a different goal in Congress's adoption of the Bill of Rights than he had had before. There were, in effect, two Madisons: the earlier one, whose views on separation of church and state dominated in *Everson,* versus the one who framed the First Amendment, who "was James Madison speaking as an advocate of sensible legislative compromise, not as an advocate of incorporating the Virginia Statute of Religious Liberty into the United States Constitution."[22]

The question is: how can such a schizophrenic historical portrait tell us anything about interpreting the Constitution? This is not an interpretation of history. It is a debater's move.

The second problem with the use of history to define the Establishment Clause is that the concept of irreligion is not an eighteenth-century concept. The invention of the secular in the sense intended in this context is a nineteenth-century conceptual change.[23] Trying to interpret the failure of the framers to have anticipated the secular and to have made it clear how large-scale cultural irreligion relates to non-establishment, makes as much sense as trying to figure out their views on whether heat-imaging devices represent searches.[24] It simply cannot be true, therefore, that the claim of government neutrality is "demonstrably false," as Justice Scalia has put it.

While the struggle over history never went away in the Court's Establishment Clause cases after *Jaffree,* an important renewal of that debate took place in the 2005 Ten Commandments cases—*McCreary* and

Van Orden—which split on the constitutionality of displays of the Ten Commandments. Although history was referred to in a number of the opinions in those cases, the principal debate took place between Justice Scalia's dissent in *McCreary County* on the one hand, and Justice Souter's majority opinion in that case and Justice Stevens's dissent in *Van Orden,* on the other.

The reason these cases are so important is twofold. For one thing these cases are recent and, therefore, as will be discussed in the next chapter, these cases, plus personnel changes on the Court, may usher in a new era in the law of church and state.

In addition, in the Ten Commandments cases, history had to play a somewhat different role than it had in *Jaffree.* Justice Rehnquist could discuss, in *Jaffree,* government neutrality between religion and irreligion in almost a pure form. The question in the case was silent prayer in public school. It is fair to say, and Justice Rehnquist assumed, that all religious believers pray. Thus Justice Rehnquist did not face a question about divisions among religious believers. Perhaps more importantly, even nonbelievers can at least do something like pray. They can meditate, for example. Silent prayer is certainly the least excluding religious practice one can imagine.

In contrast, the Ten Commandments cases concerned public displays of a particular religious object with quite specific content. This meant both that all nonbelievers would, in effect, be excluded, and also that some religious believers might also be excluded. In his dissent in *McCreary County,* Justice Scalia was willing to go that far, but no further. He was willing to uphold public religious expression that would be broad enough to include all monotheists, and only monotheists, but could not be used to uphold sectarian Christian religious expression. Justice Scalia used history in an attempt to walk a pretty narrow line.

Like Justice Rehnquist earlier, Justice Scalia took aim directly at the notion that the First Amendment mandates neutrality between religion and nonreligion and that the government may not favor adherence to religion generally. Justice Scalia responded to these claims with typical flair, calling them "false" and asking "Who says so?"[25]

Of course, this question was rhetorical, since as Justice Scalia knew, the Court itself had said so, on many occasions. It was precisely this precedent upholding a wall of separation between church and state that Justice Scalia was attempting to overturn.

Justice Scalia began his dissent by referencing the attacks on 9/11. President George W. Bush could end his presidential address after the attacks "with the prayer 'God bless America.'" In contrast, a foreign judge told Justice Scalia, "sadly," that it would be absolutely forbidden for a Head of State in his country to conclude an address that way. That kind of separation of church and state, stated Justice Scalia, is the French model, "spread across Europe by the armies of Napoleon, and reflected in the Constitution of France, which begins, 'France is [a] . . . secular . . . Republic.'" Under the French Constitution, "[r]eligion is to be strictly excluded from the public forum. This is not, and never was, the model adopted by America."[26]

By calling "God bless America" a "prayer," Justice Scalia was already telegraphing that, unlike Justice Black in *Engel,* he would not treat traditional public religious references and practices as ceremonial and essentially nonreligious, but as manifestations of genuine and constitutionally proper religious worship in American life.

Justice Scalia then went on to note many other references to God in American history. His first example was that George Washington added to the end of the presidential oath prescribed in Art. II, Section 8, of the Constitution[27] the words "so help me God"—a custom by presidents that has continued to this day.

This reference to the oath of office was a double-edged sword for Justice Scalia. On the one hand, it served to counter the claim that we have a "Godless Constitution"[28] that does not mention God, and therefore that we are supposed to have a neutral state. But, on the other hand, having to add the words "so help me God" to what is, of course, the actual legal document—the constitutional text—suggests that these separation critics are right about the "Godless Constitution." If the question is whether the Constitution is neutral about religion, the answer would have to come, as surely Justice Scalia would agree, from the document itself and not from its informal amendment by even as canonical a figure as George Washington.

Justice Scalia also, later in the opinion, noted that the First Amendment, in the Free Exercise Clause, "accords religion (and no other manner of belief) special constitutional protection."[29] There is a certain bitter irony in this reference since it came from the author of the opinion in *Employment Division v. Smith*[30] that did so much to eviscerate the protections of the Free Exercise Clause.

Justice Scalia's references to American religious practices were familiar from prior cases. The Supreme Court opens with the words "God save the United States and this honorable court"—also called a "prayer" by Justice Scalia. Congress begins its sessions with prayer. President Washington issued the first Thanksgiving proclamation, "thus beginning a tradition of offering gratitude to God that continues today." This characterization—"gratitude to God"—was plainly intended, like the references to prayer, to mark these practices as genuinely and seriously religious and not as rote or pro forma.

All of these early religious practices represented, claimed Justice Scalia, the beliefs of "[t]hose who wrote the Constitution . . . that morality was essential to the well-being of society and that encouragement of religion was the best way to foster morality."[31]

According to Justice Scalia, the framers were believers in God and in the rights of man rooted in God. Not only did George Washington and John Adams believe that, but Thomas Jefferson and James Madison as well. And in a general sense the American people continue to believe all of the above. There is a direct line between that day and our day.

In the face of this history, asked Justice Scalia, how can it be asserted that the First Amendment mandates neutrality between religion and nonreligion?

To this point, Justice Scalia's historical evidence was similar to that of Justice Rehnquist earlier. But Justice Scalia had to answer a challenge that Justice Rehnquist did not face in *Jaffree*—the claim that posting the Ten Commandments favored one religion over another. Unlike silent prayer, the Ten Commandments are the doctrinal expression of, first Judaism, and then later, Christianity. They are in no sense the common commitment of all religious believers. At the very least, polytheists and believers in gods unresponsive to human beings are not included in the practice of posting the Ten Commandments. How would historical analysis deal with that?

Justice Scalia did not deny that the posting of the Ten Commandments did exclude some religious believers. His justification of this was that the Establishment Clause, interpreted in light of these historic practices demonstrating the permissibility of prayers to God, "permits this disregard of polytheists and believers in unconcerned deities, just as it permits the disregard of devout atheists."[32]

All of these historic religious practices are monotheistic and therefore "the acknowledgement of a single Creator"[33] simply cannot be viewed as establishment of a religion.

Of course, the Ten Commandments are not a simple acknowledgment of a single creator God, but a rather detailed, divinely inspired code of conduct. But, argued Justice Scalia, since almost all believers in the United States are members of the three monotheistic faiths that "believe that the Ten Commandments were given by God to Moses, and are divine prescriptions for a virtuous life . . . [p]ublicly honoring the Ten Commandments is thus indistinguishable, insofar as discriminating against other religions is concerned, from publicly honoring God."[34]

At this point in his dissent, Justice Scalia responded to criticisms of his position presented by Justice David Souter's majority opinion that struck down the Ten Commandments displays at issue in *McCreary County,* as well as criticisms offered by Justice Stevens's dissent in the other Ten Commandments case, *Van Orden,* which upheld the Ten Commandments display on the Texas State capitol grounds.

Justice Souter's response on behalf of the majority to Justice Scalia's historical evidence was that Justice Scalia had failed "to consider the full range of evidence showing what the framers believed."[35] While it is true that some of the framers would not have agreed that government must be neutral between religion and irreligion, there is also evidence to the contrary, including the broad language of the Establishment Clause itself. Justice Souter then presented some of this counter evidence, especially statements and actions by Jefferson and Madison, supporting government neutrality toward religion and concluded "that there was no common understanding about the limits of the establishment prohibition. . . ."[36]

Justice Souter also denied that history supported Justice Scalia's particular claim that monotheism could be endorsed by government without violating the Establishment Clause. If history were taken to show that any one religion could be favored, it would not be some generic monotheism, but Christianity alone. Justice Souter then added in a footnote that George Washington himself might not have been a monotheist, but a deist and thus, by implication, one of those very believers whose God is unresponsive to human beings. Justice Souter did not press this point.[37]

Justice Stevens in his dissent in *Van Orden* did not spend as much time on American historical practices as did Justice Scalia, who, it should be remembered, had the burden of arguing against settled precedent supporting the neutrality principle. Justice Stevens recognized the ubiquity of official acknowledgments of religion in American life, both in the past and in the present. But Justice Stevens seemed to deny the specifically religious significance of these practices. Either these expressions were merely acknowledgments of the religious beliefs of the American people or they were associated with important, secular, historic events.

In contrast, argued Justice Stevens, the Ten Commandments display in *Van Orden* was neither mere history nor mere acknowledgment. For one thing, this display contained the full text of the Ten Commandments, with "especially large letters that identify its author: 'I am the Lord thy God'" and thus was much more of a religious, doctrinal claim than have been most expressions of religion in American history.[38]

Justice Stevens also responded to Chief Justice Rehnquist's plurality opinion in *Van Orden,* which, in common with Justice Scalia, had also cited "[r]ecognition of the role of God in our nation's heritage."[39] But, Justice Stevens responded, the speeches and rhetoric of the founding era, including many references to God, are inapposite in this case because a Ten Commandments display is much more dogmatic than these generic expressions, and because public speeches by government officials are not just government expressions but include "personal views of the speaker. . . ."[40] In that sense these religious practices, including Thanksgiving proclamations and presidential inaugural speeches are not "the sort of governmental endorsement of religion at which the separation of church and state is aimed."[41]

Justice Stevens agreed with Justice Souter that there is not "a unified historical narrative" in the American history of religion and public life. Both Chief Justice Rehnquist and Justice Scalia failed to account for the views of other influential leaders and of the debates over the proper role of religion that took place throughout American history.

Justice Stevens echoed Justice Souter's argument that history used the way Justice Scalia was using it would allow governmental endorsement of Christianity itself. Justice Stevens gave even more emphasis than had Justice Souter to the history of the Establishment Clause as prohibiting only discriminations among Christian denominations. Endorsement of Christianity, these authorities would have said, does not violate the Establishment Clause. Justice Joseph Story's *Commentaries on the Constitution* was one such source. Story specifically excluded Judaism, Islam, and all other non-Christian religions from the concern of the Establishment Clause. The Supreme Court itself, in *Church of Holy Trinity v. United States* in 1892 had proclaimed this country "a Christian nation."[42] This support for Christianity, Justice Stevens claimed, is as historically grounded as the claim by Justice Scalia that endorsement of monotheism is permitted. Therefore history alone—what the text meant to observers at the time of the adoption of the Bill of Rights—cannot serve as the final word for the interpretation of the Establishment Clause.

Of course, Justice Scalia responded to Justice Stevens by pointing out that his own references were more official than those of Justice Stevens. Also Jefferson's refusal to issue a Thanksgiving proclamation was only *inaction*—Justice Scalia even put the word in italics. Most of the neutrality references were against "enforced contribution to religion rather than public acknowledgment of God. . . ." Jefferson was "notoriously self-contradicting" and himself believed in God. Justice Scalia, perhaps stung, called Justice Stevens's criticism that he was marginalizing non-monotheists a "gross exaggeration." There are *competing* interests among believers, which, Justice Scalia assumed, could not all be accommodated.[43]

By this point, the reader has a sense that these debates among the justices have been inconclusive. Justice Stevens is clearly right that Justice Scalia's reading of history is somewhat arbitrary. The national practices that Justice Scalia happens to call normative are said to be the ones that define the Establishment Clause. But why these particular practices? One could make the same kind of argument about the endorsement of Christianity—that history tells us that preferring Christianity is not an establishment of religion. Just as one example of that history, it was the Continental Congress that issued the first Thanksgiving Day proclamation, in 1777, addressing it to "GOD through the Merits of JESUS CHRIST."[44]

Justice Scalia absolutely rejects the proposition that Christianity could be the endorsed religion of America. He made it clear in his *Mc-Creary County* dissent that he would not, for example, permit the government to add "One Nation under Christ" to the Pledge of Allegiance.[45] But this distinction is just his preference. It is not a simple reading of history.

In the end Justice Scalia may have had more historical evidence on his side. But, given Justice Scalia's assumptions about constitutional interpretation, it was not enough for him to have the marginally better of the historical argument. As he was well aware, the historical record was quite varied. Some authoritative figures wanted neutrality and the separation of church and state, while others wanted that only in part (by including God as part of public life). Furthermore some wanted no true separation at all between government and religion, while others wanted Christianity broadly conceived to be intertwined with public life. These wide variances in historical record would leave the Court without clear guidance as to how to interpret the Establishment Clause. For Justice Scalia, history has to "show *what it* [the Establishment Clause] *meant.*"[46] Thus the historical record has to be clear. That is why Justice Scalia had to overstate the degree of clarity in the historical record, by insisting that the government neutrality views of some of the framers "were plainly rejected" and that the invocation of the Christian views of other authoritative figures was "as clearly rejected."[47] That is why he proclaimed with such overweening confidence to all polytheists and other non-monotheists: "Our national tradition has resolved that conflict in favor of the majority."[48]

Justice Scalia's invocation of history to reject neutrality fails for lack of determinatively clear evidence. History just does not tell a clear story about church and state.

Nor does Justice Scalia obey his own prescription concerning what use an interpreter may make of history. In the case of the public acknowledgment of God that Justice Scalia believes excludes "polytheists and believers in unconcerned deities," the applicable principle is one that everyone agrees is at the heart of the Establishment Clause—"that the government cannot favor one religion over another."[49] When Justice Scalia says that this principle does not apply because of our historical practices, he is guilty of misusing history to immunize particular practices that he does not wish to submit to principled constitutional inquiry. That is, in part, what caused Andrew Koppelman to label this kind of appeal to history as "phony originalism."[50]

In contrast to Justice Scalia's conclusion that monotheism is permissibly favored, it would be more plausible to suppose that the invocation of God on public occasions in the past had not been thought to violate the principle of non-discrimination among religions because there was at that time no substantial non-monotheistic believing community in America to offend. Looked at in that light these invocations of God should be regarded as seriously suspect today because there are now in America substantial communities of Hindu and Buddhist believers.

Nor should we stop there. Historical determination of the reach of the Establishment Clause is even more conflicted than the treatment of these excluded non-monotheistic believers would suggest. For the atheist may today plausibly construct the following principled syllogism in arguing for the protection of the Establishment Clause. When the religious divisions among Americans concerned differing interpretations of Protestantism, the Establishment Clause was understood as prohibiting the endorsement of any one of these Protestant interpretations. When Catholic immigration grew, the Establishment Clause came to be understood as prohibiting the preference among any interpretations of Christianity. When Jews became full members of the political community, the Establishment Clause came to be understood as not allowing the endorsement of Christianity in preference to Judaism. When Muslims entered the national consciousness, the Establishment Clause came to be understood as permitting only the endorsement of monotheism. As the numbers of Hindu and Buddhist believers grow, the Establishment Clause must change to allow only the preference of religion itself rather than the endorsement of monotheism. And, finally, as society becomes more secular, so that a substantial community of genuine nonbelievers exists for the first time, the Establishment Clause must come to be understood as prohibiting the endorsement even of religion itself and as requiring instead government neutrality between religion and irreligion. This would be a plausible interpretation of the Establishment Clause, and it is one that is consistent with our history.

This kind of reasoning is a significant challenge to the reliance on history in upholding practices like the public posting of the Ten Commandments. History is not to be thought of as a dictatorial ipse dixit—because he said so. Instead history functions properly as the foundation from which principled interpretation grows. A judge must always be able to explain decisions in a consistent rather than an ad hoc way. That is how Justice Scalia understands the use of history, but it is not the method that he practiced in his *McCreary County* dissent.

When Justice Scalia tried to use history simply to declare a winner in the religion wars, and a winner from among religions that are all plainly protected by both the Establishment and the Free Exercise Clauses, he was really not interpreting the Constitution at all, but was simply declaring that we shall do in the future what we have always done in the past.

If history is not to be the source of interpretation of a provision like the Establishment Clause, then what is? The answer, ultimately, is the people. The Court may offer an interpretation of this or any other constitutional provision, and may use history or any other sources of interpretation, but that interpretation must stand the test of popular acceptance.

Professor Charles L. Black, Jr.—a giant in American jurisprudence —made this point in a classic book he wrote in 1960 defending judicial review. The book, entitled *The People and the Court*,[51] argued that judicial review—the power of the courts, and especially the United States Supreme Court, to pass on the constitutionality of government action—is a healthy aspect of American governance and should be encouraged rather than regarded as a usurpation by the courts.

Black did not address his book to judges, lawyers, or government officials. He understood that defining the proper role of the courts was a decision the American people would have to make, in some kind of organic fashion. Here is how he put that thought early in the book:

> The decision whether this is to happen lies in the power of the people. No institution can survive in this country unless the people want it to survive. The fate of the constitutional role of the courts will be decided in the making up of many minds, until at last we may speak of a national decision.[52]

This "national decision" was not to be a new law or even the result of some election. In fact, I doubt that Black had a clear idea as to how one would know that such a decision had been made. The courts would come to practice judicial review vigorously, or they would not. And the decision one way or the other would be a popular one.

The notion of "popular constitutionalism" has received a lot of attention in recent years. But what the proponents of this concept, such as Larry Kramer and Mark Tushnet, have usually meant is limiting the role of courts in deciding constitutional issues.[53] That is more or less the opposite of Black's intention. Black clearly thought that the courts would have an important role—a crucial role—to play through judicial review, but that this judicial role would take place within an overall sovereignty of a free people. In other words, the courts would propose what the Constitution means, but then the people would ultimately decide. If they rejected judicial review as an institution, it would wither.

To see this kind of popular constitutionalism in action, consider the role of free speech in our society. Until World War I free speech was not considered to be the foundational value that it is today. In 1918, the Sedition Act punished disloyal or profane language and Postmaster General Albert Burleson cancelled the mailing privileges of magazines deemed unpatriotic. When the famed socialist Eugene Debs was convicted of obstruction of the draft for an anti-war speech, Justice Oliver Wendell Holmes wrote a short affirmance for a unanimous Supreme Court on basically criminal law and evidence grounds.[54]

But then popular opposition arose. As Anthony Lewis has written, "Debs was a national figure, respected by many as he was disliked by others. He was sixty-three years old, and a ten-year prison sentence aroused considerable sympathy."[55] The Holmes opinion sparked an influential critique by University of Chicago law professor Ernst Freund in the *New Republic*. A campaign began for a presidential pardon. Debs became a candidate for president from prison, winning almost a million votes. Ultimately Warren G. Harding commuted Debs's sentence and then invited him to the White House. When a majority on the Court finally held that intense opposition to wartime policies could not be punished, it was following popular opinion.

This sense of popular constitutionalism has been manifest as well in the field of church and state. While the Supreme Court has rendered important decisions requiring government neutrality toward religion, these decisions have not actually decided the matter. They have only been an important part of the popular judgment that continues to take place—a national decision we are in the process of making. The role of religion in American public life is not the kind of thing that courts alone can ultimately decide. The Establishment Clause crisis is just another name for this national decision-making process.

If we now return to the situation the Supreme Court faced in 1947, after *Everson* was decided, we can see why the Establishment Clause crisis happened. In 1947, President Roosevelt's D-Day radio address was still a living memory for most Americans. Religious displays in public life were common. Prayer and Bible reading were widely practiced in the public schools. American public officials routinely invoked God. America was a religious society whose government practices reflected that reality.

Against this background, the declaration in *Everson* that the First Amendment had erected a wall, "high and impregnable," between church and state was wildly incompatible with then-existing American practices. I am not referring to the holding of the case—that tax money could be given to parents to pay for transportation to private religious schools—but to the standard of government neutrality toward religion that the case declared. The fact that, in effect, all nine justices agreed with this neutrality standard is all the more remarkable given the distance between the ideal announced by the Court and the everyday reality of American life. This was a Court out-of-step with the commitments of the American people on a very important subject.

Undoubtedly, during the entire postwar period, America was becoming a more secular society. One can see this, for example, in the long-term decline of Sunday Closing Laws, which were generally repealed by legislative action rather than judicially overturned, and which the United States Supreme Court never held to be a violation of the Establishment Clause.

Also, during this time, America was becoming more religiously pluralistic, with greater social acceptance of Catholics and Jews. By the time the Supreme Court again challenged established religious cultural practices in the early 1960s—striking down school prayer and Bible reading—America was much more ready to accept a limited separation between religion and public life.

In the years following *Engel* and *Schempp*, the Court held some government aid to private school programs unconstitutional. But these decisions have been mostly overturned. School-sponsored prayer has been banished from public schools, but student organizations and student private speech are more religious than ever. Just go to the average high school graduation and listen to the students thanking Jesus. And, now that a large-scale school voucher program has been upheld, the private school aid issue would appear to be resolved.

In other words, even though the Court has not yet rescinded its language of government religious neutrality, our society, including its public manifestations in motto, creed, and display, remains quite religious. Political candidates invoke God probably more often than in the 1940s. The walls of our public buildings still contain Ten Commandments displays. We still say the Pledge of Allegiance. The judicial effort to declare a religiously neutral state has failed and is probably over, at least for the foreseeable future. Everyone knows that the words "under God" will not be taken out of the Pledge of Allegiance.

What happened? Why did such a determined beginning in *Everson* yield so little change? Part of the reason is that society *did* change to an extent. The Court was part of a movement that eliminated almost all vestiges of coercion in matters of religion in American life. Undoubtedly religious minorities and nonbelievers are freer today from majority pressure than they have ever been. And America is less officially Christian than ever, as well. The Court has had a hand in all that.

In addition, the fundamental commitment in *Everson*—that public money not be used to aid religious proselytizing—has become an accepted principle. It was a core aspect of President George W. Bush's faith-based initiative that public money could not be used to persuade people to accept a religious message. No doubt this principle was sometimes violated in practice, but it was accepted in principle by the religious charities that took public money.

The American people seem to have reached a balance in the relationship of church and state. It is a balance to which the Court contributed.

But it is clearly not government neutrality toward religion, and it is not the wall of separation.

This gap was inevitable, given the failure of the Supreme Court to convince the American people that religious neutrality was an appropriate national commitment. The Supreme Court could not insulate public life from the religious commitments of the American people. The Supreme Court is not the kind of institution that can, by itself, change the fundamental nature of national life. Those fundamentals are determined by "the power of the people" as Charles Black put it. Again that power is not a narrow "political" matter but a broader, cultural one. All the Court can do is announce constitutional principles; all it has in the end, is the power of persuasion.

There is another instance in American history in which the Court tried to alter a fundamental social arrangement in American life. But in that instance—the opposition of the Supreme Court to the emergence of the social welfare state—the Court was actually attempting to prevent a change rather than usher one in. In any event, the effort collapsed in 1937 and is now universally viewed as having been a serious mistake.

This is a well-known story. In the late nineteenth century, Supreme Court opinions upholding state regulation of economic activity began to suggest that there might be limits on the power of the state to regulate. This tendency culminated in *Allgeyer v. Louisiana,*[56] in which Justice Rufus Peckham, writing for a unanimous Court, struck down a state statute regulating insurance contracts. The decision was the first time the Court struck down a state economic regulation on the grounds that the regulation violated the substantive protections of the Fourteenth Amendment's Due Process Clause.[57] This was the beginning of the so-called liberty or freedom-of-contract cases.

Allgeyer led to a significant line of cases. Between 1897 and the end of this judicial effort in 1937, the Court invalidated state economic regulations on Due Process or similar grounds around 175 times.[58] This period is sometimes referred to as the Lochner Era in reference to a case—*Lochner v. New York*—decided in 1905.[59] In *Lochner,* the Court invalidated a New York statute that limited bakers to a sixty-hour work week and a maximum workday of ten hours.

The Lochner Era cases were premised on the notion that people, or at least "grown and intelligent men," should be able to decide for themselves how many hours they wish to work and at what wages and, to a certain extent, under what conditions. An interference with the free market was deemed by the Court to be unconstitutional unless there was some special reason why the persons subject to the law might need special protection.

The Lochner-Era cases concerned primarily regulation of the economy by the states. With exceptions, such as regulations in the District of Columbia, federal law did not regulate ordinary contractual relationships during this period.

That division shifted radically, however, with the onset of the Depression and resulting New Deal legislation. The Supreme Court, in addition to limiting the power of the states to pass economic regulation under the Due Process and Equal Protection Clauses, also struck down efforts by Congress to regulate trade practices, wages, hours, and collective bargaining in industry on the ground that to do so went beyond congressional power under the Commerce Clause.

All of this judicial effort to fend off government regulation of the economy ended in 1937—although the Court had begun to allow more state regulation a few years before that. In the course of just a few weeks, the Court upheld a state minimum-wage law using language that seemed to signal a retreat from laissez faire philosophy,[60] and upheld wideranging congressional authority to regulate all aspects of the national economy.[61]

What does this failed episode tell us about the proper role of the Supreme Court? In *Lochner*, Justice Holmes wrote a famous dissent that raised the question of the Court's proper role in resolving fundamental national issues. Holmes introduced his thought as follows:

> This case is decided upon an economic theory which a large part of the country does not entertain. If it were a question whether I agreed with that theory, I should desire to study it further and long before making up my mind. But I do not conceive that to be my duty, because I strongly believe that my agreement or disagreement has nothing to do with the right of a majority to embody their opinions in law. . . . [A] Constitution is not intended to embody a particular economic theory, whether of paternalism and the organic relation of the citizen to the state or of *laissez faire*. It is made for people of fundamentally differing views.[62]

Did Holmes mean that legislative majorities can do whatever they want? Did Holmes oppose judicial review itself and thus "reject . . . the premises of limited government," as one observer has suggested?[63] Apparently not, since Holmes would come to be known as a great defender of free speech on the Court.

Holmes was not an anti-court majoritarian. The problem in *Lochner* and the Lochner-Era cases was the attempt by the Court to foist on the country the justices' own vision of a proper economic starting point. According to Holmes, the Court should not try to decide what kind of economic system America should adopt. Something that basic must be decided by the people.

Holmes here really did mean the people. When Holmes referred to "a large part of the country" he was saying that the Court must defer to the coming "national decision," as Charles Black put it, between laissez faire and the welfare state.

Holmes's approach does not mean the end of judicial review. For example, let us examine a really unpopular decision—*Texas v. Johnson* in 1989,[64] holding that there is a First Amendment right of free speech to burn the American flag. This was a widely unpopular decision. Congress immediately tried to reverse the decision by statute—an attempt the Court also struck down.[65]

But as unpopular as the decision was, no one could say that it was "decided upon [a] . . . theory which a large part of the country does not entertain." The case was decided upon a theory or principle that almost everyone accepts—that generally under the First Amendment, people are free to express even opinions that we hate. The unpopularity of the decision, which could yet be overturned one day by constitutional amendment, in no way damaged the prestige of the Court. In *Johnson,* the Court stood up for a principle embedded in the Constitution, which is what the people expect from the Court even when they disagree with the Court's application of the principle. And this is why the Court would probably decide the case the same way today despite the decision's unpopularity.

If we assume that *Johnson* is the Court doing its job and that *Lochner* is the Court not doing its job, we can see both what Holmes was getting at in his dissent, and also the outline of the proper role of the Court in constitutional interpretation. The job of the Court is not to resolve the fundamental social arrangements of American life, but to announce principles that the American people either already accept or will come to accept once the justices point them out, and then to apply these principles to particular legal issues. Or, to put it bluntly, it is the Court's job to state what can, and does, become the obvious.

Notice that I am not adverting to the method by which individual justices come to state the obvious. Some justices rely on history or text—or claim they do—while others argue from prior case law or from morality or from other sources. Law professors and judges love to debate which interpretative methods are legitimate.

But the Supreme Court is a part of the government. It is not a debating society. Its legitimacy lies in popular acceptance of its decisions and nothing else. So the method by which a justice comes to a principle that the people can accept is not particularly important. Nor is it important whether a particular legal right is enumerated in the text of the Constitution or not. The important point is whether the principle announced by the Court becomes accepted by the people. The method of its derivation may play a part in that popular acceptance, but I think usually it does not.

The problem in *Lochner* was not its outcome. The problem was that the country was still deciding whether the government should determine the rules by which the economy would run, or whether that should remain a basically private decision. If a national decision to return to laissez faire had ultimately been made, then a case like *Lochner* would have ended up being seen as legitimate. Since that did not happen, *Lochner* is today regarded as a fundamental error.

The way I am representing judicial review makes it seem like a very political practice. And so it is, in a deep sense. Some legal thinkers imagine that constitutional decision is just ordinary law. In fact, in an abortion case, Justice Scalia once suggested that when the Court really does its job, which he assumed was not to render value judgments, the people leave the Court alone:

> As long as this Court thought (and the people thought) that we Justices were doing essentially lawyers' work up here—reading text and discerning our society's traditional understanding of that text—the public pretty much left us alone. Texts and traditions are facts to study, not convictions to demonstrate about. But if in reality our process of constitutional adjudication consists primarily of making value judgments . . . then a free and intelligent people's attitude towards us can be expected to be (ought to be) quite different. The people know that their value judgments are quite as good as those taught in any law school— maybe better.[66]

Justice Scalia is right that in the context in which this observation was made—abortion cases—the Court had not done its job well. The justices have not identified a principle in the abortion cases that has come to be generally accepted.

But Justice Scalia is wrong to think that just because the American people can render value judgments, they do not want a government institution to do so as well. Justice Scalia imagines a wall of separation of his own—between the Court and the people. He thinks that when the Court does "real" law, the people have nothing to say because the work is technical in some sense. The real situation, though, is, and has always been, that the Court makes value judgments and then offers its value judgments to the people for their ratification or reversal.

Everson is a good example of why Justice Scalia is wrong in his assumption that the problem with controversial decisions is that they rely on value judgments. Undoubtedly, in *Everson* Justice Black believed that he was reading texts and discerning what they meant in their original context. He certainly would have denied that he was imposing his own value judgment.

Justice Scalia would respond that the Court in *Everson* plainly erred in how the Establishment Clause was traditionally understood. But making a lawyer's mistake, that is, misreading a text, is still not making a value judgment. Yet the people have not, of course, left the matter of church and state alone. This shows that it is not enough for a Court to try to go about things in the right way. The Court must ultimately get the matter right, and that is essentially a political judgment. *Everson* failed because the people never accepted the Court's proffered neutrality principle, not because of a failure in method.

In light of the Establishment Clause crisis, the obligation of the Court is to present to the American people a principle of church and state that they can accept. Thus far, no such proposal has attained popular legitimacy. But attempts to do so have been made. We turn to these attempts in the next chapter.

FOUR

Proposals That Have Failed to Resolve the Establishment Clause Crisis

I wrote in the last chapter that the Supreme Court's job is to state the obvious. In the context of church and state, this means giving a principled account of the meaning of the Establishment Clause. The Court's job is to determine what the Establishment Clause means so the people may ultimately render their own judgment. This is the only way the crisis over the meaning of the Establishment Clause can be resolved.

"Principled" here does not necessarily exclude a pragmatic account, such as that of Justice Breyer. We saw in chapter 2 Justice Breyer's attempt to make non-divisiveness the touchstone of Establishment Clause analysis in his concurrence in *Van Orden*. Non-divisiveness is certainly an admirable goal. However, the trouble with Justice Breyer's kind of pragmatism is that it does not work. An interpretation stating, in effect, that government may utilize religious symbols if there are no protests will obviously lead to more protests.

What are the possible interpretations of the Establishment Clause? The most obvious possibility for resolving the crisis in Establishment Clause interpretation is for the justices to reaffirm the neutrality principle and to enforce it consistently. This course would return the Court to the original impetus of *Everson, Engel,* and *Schempp* and would continue to move us in the direction of a secular society. In theory that would mean the words "under God" would be removed from the Pledge of Allegiance, at least in its official versions, and new religious public monuments would be barred at some point. This course would close the gap between what we say and what we do.

Admittedly, a reinvigoration of government neutrality does not seem very likely today given the balance of political pressures in the country and the trends on the Court. The Democratic Party has attempted to make itself more faith-friendly since the 2006 elections. President Obama reinforced that trend while running for president in 2008. In addition, his first appointment to the Supreme Court, Justice Sonia Sotomayor, had not shown any sign of a strong neutrality position prior to her appointment. Of course, that does not necessarily mean much once a nominee actually joins the Court. But one can at least say that Justice Sotomayor was not picked because of her reputation for a strict separation position.

Nor do decisions from the Court show any signs of moving toward enforcing neutrality. The Court's most recent decisions—upholding public school vouchers, ducking a challenge to the Pledge of Allegiance, first splitting on the issue of public Ten Commandments displays and then later upholding one—certainly do not augur a renaissance of neutrality.

In terms of personnel on the Court, there is also no reason to anticipate a renewed commitment to government neutrality. Justice Souter, whose seat Justice Sotomayor now assumes, was probably the second most pro-neutrality justice on the Court. Justice Stevens, who is retiring, has been the most pro-neutrality justice. Thus even if Justice Sotomayor turns out to be as pro-neutrality as had been Justice Souter, which is by no means certain, with Justice Stevens's retirement, the Court would be more likely to shift away from neutrality, rather than toward it.

Of course, predictions like these are never certain. Neutrality could stage a comeback. Although Chief Justice John Roberts and Justice Samuel Alito are regarded among many law professors as pro-religion in the Establishment Clause context,[1] that does not necessarily mean they are. Justice Alito did write the *Pleasant Grove City* opinion allowing a Ten Commandments display, which Chief Justice Roberts joined, but that case is not directly on point, since it was technically a free speech case. In addition, Justice Sotomayor might turn out to be strongly pro-neutrality, as perhaps was indicated by her decision to join Justice Stevens's dissent in *Salazar v. Buono,* the cross-in-the-desert case that will be discussed in chapter 6.

Future nominees by President Obama might also be pro-neutrality. The reason the current pro-religion case law is not really settled is that there has been no accepted substitute for neutrality as an overall interpretation of the Establishment Clause. Thus the case law is actually just at equipoise and could easily move in one direction or another. President Obama's first nominee for a Court of Appeals position was District Judge David Hamilton, who had once strongly suggested in an opinion that Justice Brennan had been right in his *Marsh* dissent that legislative prayer is unconstitutional.[2] It is possible that this is President Obama's position as well, that he is a closet separationist whose future judicial nominees will reopen the debate over the religiously neutral state.

What would a renewed neutrality regime actually look like? It is hard to imagine the Court removing the words "under God" from the Pledge of Allegiance or taking down Ten Commandments displays. That does not mean an end to the neutrality principle, however. Another possibility is that a majority of the justices would retain a commitment to government neutrality—a formal commitment—but would refuse to enforce neutrality with full consistency.

In a way, that is the situation now. For example, no justice on the Court would allow tax money to be used by government to build churches or pay clergy in a program to promote religion in order to improve social behavior. To that extent, government already may not endorse or promote religion and must remain neutral. On the other hand, many government-sponsored religious practices remain vibrant in the public square.

There are two ways in which the Court could retain the neutrality principle but not decide fights over the words "under God" in the Pledge of Allegiance or public displays of religious imagery. The Court either, first, could engage in a kind of strategic abstention from deciding religion cases or, alternatively, could reinterpret what neutrality requires to lessen the conflict between what we say and what we do.

The first course—simply ignoring politically sensitive cases—may be the Court's current preference. For example, the Court is now ducking any Pledge of Allegiance challenge. The Court might also reject future Ten Commandments cases, having more or less approved such displays as long as the government is silent as to its purpose.

Is such judicial passivity possible? Are certain government uses of religious symbols so insignificant that they could be allowed, or at least overlooked, despite the requirement of government neutrality? If we consider legal theorists who generally support the concept of government neutrality, this kind of grudging acceptance is what they seem to practice. While most of them expressly oppose public religious expressions and symbols, such as the words "under God" in the Pledge of Allegiance, they do not seem in any hurry to press this unpopular stance.

There are exceptions. Proponents of a strict separation of church and state, such as Steven Gey,[3] Isaac Kramnick, R. Laurence Moore,[4] Suzanna Sherry,[5] and Kathleen Sullivan,[6] strongly oppose openly religious imagery and practices in the public square. They might be willing to take the political heat for removing the words "under God" from the Pledge. Steven Gey writes that there is a great deal at stake in the Pledge controversy and theorists have no business surrendering to illegitimate and even unconstitutional political pressure. He asks in reference to "the growing conflict over the most basic principle of Establishment Clause jurisprudence: Does the Constitution continue to mandate a secular government, or has the subtle sectarian dominance of government become an accepted constitutional fact?"[7] Gey wants the Court to enforce neutrality, indeed separation, consistently. Yet we still do not see prominent academics representing litigants who, for example, want to ban prayer from public occasions, such as presidential inaugurations.

Less stringent opposition to the public use of symbolic religious imagery is also present in the ideas of neutrality theorists like Douglas Laycock[8] and Arnold Loewy[9] and in the various strands of equality theory—equal liberty by Christopher Eisgruber and Lawrence Sager,[10] equal protection by Susan Gellman and Susan Looper-Friedman,[11] and equal liberty of conscience as religious equality by Martha Nussbaum.[12] So it is not only the strongest opponents of mixing church and state who oppose putting "under God" in the Pledge of Allegiance and who oppose putting up Ten Commandment displays. Most legal thinkers who support the thrust of *Everson* oppose, in theory, any government use of religion in the public square.

Yet, while most of these law professors agree with Gey on some level, they seem wary of taking on anything like the Pledge of Allegiance. Loewy sounds this kind of note of resignation about public references to God: "[S]adly, the majority likes the endorsement so much, that there would be hell to pay if we were to remove it."[13] Steven Shiffrin writes that "we would have a better Constitution if we did not have what amounts to a monotheistic established religion" but it is "inconceivable" that we will.[14] Kramnick and Moore refer to separationists living "more or less easily with the accumulated chinks in the wall of separation"[15] Sullivan is not ready to take up arms either, although she is not certain.[16] Nussbaum suggests that "given public feeling on the issue" the Court "should avoid the issue as long as possible"[17] That seems to be precisely what the Court is currently doing.

That judicial avoidance is harmful and dishonest. The tone above suggests that these manifestations of religion are not worth fighting about because they are insignificant, whereas they cannot be taken on because they are so politically potent. Both cannot be true. If they are that potent, they are not insignificant. Gey is right about that.

The crisis in the interpretation of the Establishment Clause will not be resolved by pointing to the political obstacles preventing enforcement of the constitutional norm of neutrality. The reality of such political obstacles is just another way of stating that there is a crisis. Attempting to ignore violations of neutrality is not an answer. Either the neutrality norm is wrong, in which case neutrality should be modified or abandoned, or the neutrality norm as currently understood is right, and these public religious practices should be vigorously opposed.

If the public instinct in favor of government religious imagery is legitimate, then, to resolve the crisis, we must turn to interpretations of the Establishment Clause that suggest this public support is not a threat to constitutional values. That would be a second way in which the Court could retain the neutrality principle but permit some or most public religious imagery in the public square. The justices could reinterpret what neutrality requires.

One such proposed reinterpretation comes from Noah Feldman in his book *Divided by God*.[18] Feldman proposes essentially reversing the current trend in Supreme Court case law, which he characterizes as acceptance of public money going to religious institutions—such as educational vouchers—but careful review of public religious expression, especially in the public schools. Feldman wants to reverse these tendencies by permitting more government religious expression through the elimination of the requirement that government action have a secular purpose and not endorse religion; but, at the same time, Feldman wants to limit public subsidies to religious institutions. Feldman defends this reversal on historical grounds of the core concerns of the religion clauses and because, while he is Jewish and thus an outsider himself, he does not feel excluded by broad Christian references in American public life.

As someone who also grew up as a Jew and was educated in an Orthodox environment, I agree with Feldman that a person ought not to feel uncomfortable at manifestations of a country's majority religion. However, I think that Feldman's Jewish experience actually blinds him to the American context he is describing. Orthodox Jewish education constantly reminds a Jewish person that he or she is in exile. Thus a Jew educated in that tradition perhaps expects to be treated at a certain level as an outsider. This might even be true of non-Jewish immigrants who come to the United States knowing that it is a predominantly Christian country.

But this is not necessarily the case with a person who is born in the United States and grows up either a nonbeliever or a believer in a minority religious tradition. That person may absolutely feel what Feldman and I do not—exclusion in a deep political sense by certain public majoritarian religious displays. It is ironic that Justice Scalia in his dissent in *McCreary County* is careful not to distinguish among Jews, Christians, and Muslims but endorses instead a kind of supra-biblical monotheism.[19] Justice Scalia is apparently not as sanguine as is Feldman at the prospect of non-Christians accepting majoritarian religious expression.

In any event, Feldman's proposal for a new approach to neutrality has not been influential. The current trend on the Court is actually the worst of both worlds for Feldman. There has been no movement away from the Court's support for educational vouchers or other forms of tangible aid to religion, but at the same time, the Court has lessened its careful review of public religious expression. The careful compromise Feldman was hoping for may no longer be possible.

A quite different form of reinterpretation of what neutrality requires has been the assertion by some of the justices—that public references to God are not necessarily religious and thus are not a threat to government neutrality toward religion. We saw in chapter 2 that Justice O'Connor would uphold the words "under God" in the Pledge of Allegiance under the rubric of "ceremonial deism." This concept originally emerged in the case law in *Lynch v. Donnelly* in 1984.[20]

In *Lynch,* Justice O'Connor joined in Chief Justice Burger's opinion upholding a nativity scene in a municipality's Christmas display. That display could be justified on the grounds of a secular purpose to recognize the national holiday. Justice O'Connor, however, went beyond the context of the crèche to explain why these other government acknowledgments of religion, such as the national motto "In God We Trust," are constitutional. The crèche was no more an endorsement of religion than other public expressions of religion the Court had already allowed such as prayer to open legislative sessions or other practices using religious language that had not even been challenged (for instance, the announcement "God save the United States and this honorable court" to open Supreme Court sessions).

The problem for Justice O'Connor was to explain why these other expressions did not endorse religion. They seemed to, after all. But these expressions are permissible, she argued, because they serve, and are understood to serve, nonreligious purposes:

> Those government acknowledgments of religion serve, in the only ways reasonably possible in our culture, the legitimate secular purposes of solemnizing public occasions, expressing confidence in the future, and encouraging the recognition of what is worthy of appreciation in society. For that reason, and because of their history and ubiquity, those practices are not understood as conveying government approval of particular religious beliefs.[21]

Justice Brennan wrote the principal dissent in *Lynch* for three other justices. He discussed these same kinds of public religious expressions. Justice Brennan first dismissed any religious content in them, referring to them as ceremonial deism, a phrase he borrowed from Dean Rostow.[22] He essentially agreed with Justice O'Connor's concurrence as to why these other government practices might be constitutional:

> I would suggest that such practices as the designation of "In God We Trust" as our national motto, or the references to God contained in the Pledge of

Allegiance can best be understood . . . as a form a [*sic*] "ceremonial deism," protected from Establishment Clause scrutiny chiefly because they have lost through rote repetition any significant religious content. Moreover, these references are uniquely suited to serve such wholly secular purposes as solemnizing public occasions, or inspiring commitment to meet some national challenge in a manner that simply could not be fully served in our culture if government were limited to purely non-religious phrases. The practices by which the government has long acknowledged religion are therefore probably necessary to serve certain secular functions, and that necessity, coupled with their long history, gives those practices an essentially secular meaning.[23]

So, according to these justices, these governmental practices either are not religious anymore or are not understood to be religious anymore.

These observations do not serve, as Justices O'Connor and Brennan thought they did, to justify religious language under the neutrality doctrine. As Justice Kennedy would later suggest,[24] the fact that religious language is necessary to certain public purposes still does not turn religious language into something secular. You could say, as I will suggest in the next part of this book, that there may be something universal about this language that includes even the secularist. But this is an argument that must be explained. One cannot simply decree that obviously religious language is indeed secular. What Justices O'Connor's and Brennan's language actually suggests is the opposite of their stated conclusion that apparently religious imagery has lost its religious content. Instead they end up positing that religious language can express a notion of transcendence that need not be understood as purely religious in nature.

However, it is wrong to simply assert that government use of religious imagery is not really religious. If these practices were not understood by the opposing sides to be religious, we would not be struggling so much over the words "under God" in the Pledge of Allegiance. Atheists would not be arguing strenuously for the exclusion of this language and believers would not be pressing hard for its retention. And if the words "under God" are removed from the Pledge of Allegiance, the next round of litigation will be aimed at the national motto or the invocation of God in opening courts or legislative prayers and so forth.

In other words, as Ronald Dworkin sees it, this fight over the use of the word "God," and other religious acknowledgments, is actually a fight about the kind of country we are. Are we a secular society or a religious one? The neutrality principle is an answer to that question. As currently understood, the concept of neutrality implies we are a secular society tolerating religion. Ceremonial deism attempts to retain that basic definition disingenuously. Despite asserting neutrality, it permits religious symbols in the public square that identify us as a religious society. This is why parties on both sides reject ceremonial deism as a kind of cop-out.

In the next part of this book, I set forth a different understanding of neutrality and religious expression. These expressions can be thought of as genuinely religious for the believer while containing secular meaning as well. But for now, let us look at other proposals to end the Establishment Clause crisis. Another approach would be to reject the neutrality principle as the basic understanding of the Establishment Clause in favor of something else—some approach that does not clash with the practice of allowing public religious imagery. Justice Thomas has been clear on the need to do this. He referred specifically to the need for "rethinking the Establishment Clause," and he offered two such suggestions as to how to do this, in his concurrence in *Elk Grove.*

The first justification that Justice Thomas offered for his conclusion that the school policy of daily recitation of the Pledge of Allegiance does not violate the Establishment Clause was that the Establishment Clause is best understood historically as a "federalism provision" that prevents Congress from interfering with the states.[25] The Clause does not in any way limit the discretion of state and local governments in regard to the expression of, or even the payment for, religion. Nor does the Clause create any right enforceable by an individual, even against a congressional religious policy. It followed, therefore, that the Elk Grove School District could not violate the Establishment Clause no matter what its policy.

There is a great deal of historical support for the proposition that, whatever else the Establishment Clause was intended to do, it certainly was intended to prevent Congress from interfering with state religious establishments that already existed—Massachusetts, for example, was the last state to abandon such an establishment, in 1833.

This federalism argument by Justice Thomas is not, however, likely to resolve the issue of the relationship of religion and American public life. Even in the unlikely event that the Establishment Clause is ever interpreted by a majority of the justices to leave the states free to pursue any religious course they wish, state courts would still have to resolve the issue of the constitutionality of government religious policy under state constitutions. Many states have provisions in their constitutions similar to that contained in the Constitution of Pennsylvania: "[N]o preference shall ever be given by law to any religious establishments or modes of worship."[26] So the issue of church and state would still need to be resolved.

In addition, even under a federalism approach, individuals would still have a good chance of being permitted to challenge federal religious practices under the Establishment Clause. The historical argument that the Establishment Clause creates no private rights in individuals is not nearly as strong as the evidence that states were intended to be protected from congressional interference. Given the fact that the Bill of Rights has been interpreted overwhelmingly to protect individual rights as well as to protect the states, including most recently the Second Amendment right to bear arms,[27] it is much more likely that both individuals and states are protected by the Establishment Clause. So an individual would still be able to bring an Establishment Clause case against the federal government, and, again, the issue of church and state would still have to be resolved.

Justice Thomas's second suggestion in *Elk Grove* for an overall interpretation of the Establishment Clause was that, even if state and local governments are bound by the Establishment Clause, and even if individuals are deemed protected by it so that they may sue for its infringement, the Clause would only prohibit government from practicing "actual legal coercion" on behalf of religion, such as penalties for non-participation in religious events or taxation on behalf of religions in particular or even religion in general. He stated, "The traditional 'establishments of religion' to which the Establishment Clause is addressed necessarily involve actual legal coercion."[28] Because the mere recitation of the Pledge of Allegiance in the *Elk Grove* case involved none of these things—the school district permitted students who objected to saying the Pledge to abstain from the recitation—there was no violation of the Establishment Clause.

Although the degree of Justice Thomas's concentration on coercion is an interpretation unique to him among the justices, coercion itself has been a consistent theme in Establishment Clause cases. One example has been the religion-in-the-public-schools cases. Coercion there has been a particular concern to the Court because of the pressure to conform inherent in mandatory school laws.[29] But even in the school cases, coercion has not been considered to have exhausted Establishment Clause factors.[30]

Coercion has also sometimes functioned as an alternative ground for decision in Establishment Clause cases. For example, in *Santa Fe Independent School Dist. v. Doe*,[31] a case holding that student-led prayer before a high school football game violates the Establishment Clause, Justice Stevens's majority opinion held that the policy at issue was not genuinely student speech, but constituted speech encouraged by the school. In so holding, the opinion stated that "[s]chool sponsorship of a religious message is impermissible because it sends the ancillary message to members of the audience who are nonadherents 'that they are outsiders, not full members of the political community, and an accompanying message to adherents that they are insiders, favored members of the political community.'"[32] Clearly this by itself would have been sufficient to strike down the policy. The Court had held as early as *Engel v. Vitale* that government may not sponsor a religious exercise.[33] Nevertheless, Justice Stevens then went on to dispute the school district's argument that there was in the school program "no impermissible government coercion."[34]

Undoubtedly the absence or presence of coercion will always be considered a factor in determining whether an Establishment Clause violation has taken place. But the presence of coercion is unlikely to be adopted as a threshold requirement for such a violation. For one thing, the concept of coercion has proven to be elusive. The justices have not always been able to agree as to whether coercion is present in a particular context. This was particularly true, for example, in the high school graduation prayer case, *Lee v. Weisman*.[35]

In addition, Justice Thomas's coercion proposal does not even "bar . . . governmental preferences for *particular* religious faiths," which, Justice Thomas admitted, is a view of the Establishment Clause with "much to commend" it.[36] Under the coercion test, Congress would be free to rewrite the Pledge of Allegiance to declare the United States to be one nation "under Christ" or simply to be a "Christian nation." Justice Thomas was aware of such possibilities and tried to forestall them. He suggested that legal compulsion would generally be part of any preference for one religion over another, or perhaps alternatively that such a policy might be unconstitutional under the Free Exercise Clause. But these suggestions are stopgaps to paper over the inherent implausibility of the coercion test.

Similar to the spirit of the actual coercion principle, Justice Kennedy's partially concurring opinion in *Allegheny County* suggested that the government may recognize and accommodate "the central role religion plays in our society" as long as the government does not make an effort "to proselytize on behalf of a particular religion." According to Justice Kennedy, the government was recognizing and accommodating, but not proselytizing, when it displayed the crèche on the courthouse staircase. Justice Kennedy added that the government would be proselytizing, and thus violating the Establishment Clause, if, for example, it permanently erected "a large Latin cross on the roof of city hall."[37]

This distinction between recognizing or accommodating, on the one hand, and proselytizing, on the other, is important both because it could aid Establishment Clause jurisprudence and because Justice Kennedy is today a swing vote on church–state matters on the Supreme Court. Justice Kennedy's opinion about these matters may thus decide what the law is.

Justice Kennedy would probably acknowledge that the distinction between accommodating religion or recognizing religion, on the one hand, and proselytizing for religion, on the other, is unclear. We could give specificity to the proselytizing test by assuming that what Justice Kennedy was getting at is that the crèche in the courthouse was just a part of the celebration of Christmas and not an attempt by the government to convince people to convert to Christianity. Justice Kennedy no doubt assumed that everybody understood the government was not trying to convert people. If this is what he meant, then it is true that the government was not proselytizing on behalf of Christianity in the *Allegheny County* case.

But Justice Kennedy failed to consider that his Establishment Clause test in effect permits the erection of a hierarchy of religions in America. Under his test, Christianity becomes the religion that government practices even though no one is forced to convert. Preventing just that outcome is the major reason for not permitting government to establish a religion. The government should not be free to treat Christian symbols differently from the way it treats the symbols of every other religion. By making proselytizing the test, Justice Kennedy was suggesting that we are in fact a Christian nation, with officially recognized Christian symbols, although we all are free to worship as we please or not to worship at all.

But we are *not* a Christian country. The government has no legitimate purpose in giving a preferred place to Christian symbols. Justice Kennedy is simply wrong here.

I do not mean to suggest that the official recognition of Christian symbols is always unconstitutional. Making Christmas a national holiday, for example, is constitutional even though doing so treats a Christian holiday differently from the treatment accorded the holidays of other religions. The reason the government is permitted to do this is because only by creating a national holiday can the majority of citizens, who do wish to celebrate the holiday, actually celebrate it. If Christmas were not a holiday, inevitably some people who want to celebrate it would have to work. Declaring Christmas a national holiday is thus a legitimate government accommodation of the needs of a religion that the majority of citizens belong to. Indeed it is almost a necessity if the majority of citizens are to be able to celebrate the holiday as they wish to do.

But a public display of a crèche is not necessary in that way. Because the government in the *Allegheny County* case did not display the religious symbols of any other religion with such centrality and solemnity, the display of a crèche was in fact a manifestation of government preference for Christianity. As such the Supreme Court properly found it to be unconstitutional.

Another proposal to resolve the Establishment Clause crisis by dropping religious neutrality and permitting endorsement of religion, at least in certain contexts, is support for the promotion of civil religion. Borrowing largely from Robert Bellah, Frederick Gedicks and Roger Hendrix define "civil religion" as

> a set of nondenominational values, symbols, rituals, and assumptions by means of which a country interprets its secular history. Civil religion aims to bind citizens to their nation and government with widely shared religious beliefs, thereby supplying a spiritual interpretation of national history that suffuses it with transcendent meaning and purpose.[38]

Although they oppose current efforts to impose civil religion status on Judeo-Christian symbols such as displays of the Ten Commandments, Gedicks and Hendrix acknowledge that in the past shared Protestantism, shared Christianity, and shared Judeo-Christian heritage have formed the basis of a kind of civil religion in the United States.

As I have pointed out elsewhere,[39] a debate exists in American politics and jurisprudence over just how religious American "civil religion" is or has been. For some observers, civil religion retains some of the trappings of religion—references to God at presidential inaugurations, for example—but substitutes entirely secular meanings for religious ones. Conversely, in Bellah's original use of the term, there is a surprising amount of actual piety.[40] As we shall see in chapter 6, Bellah is using the term civil religion in part to describe the higher law tradition that I believe can contribute to a resolution of the Establishment Clause crisis.

Gedicks and Hendrix object to the use of Judeo-Christian symbols in civil religion on the grounds that such symbols have been taken over, rather recently, by "Christian conservatives"[41] and thus can no longer partake of whatever universal appeal they used to have. Therefore public displays of the Ten Commandments should not be defended as constitutional on the ground of a widely shared civil religion.

Steven Smith objects to Gedicks and Hendrix's conclusion, arguing that the interpretation of the meaning of a symbol by some particular group cannot be thought to exhaust the totality of the meaning of that symbol.[42] A religious symbol is not hijacked in this way unless a majority of people begin to interpret the symbol in the same terms as does the sectarian group. This is a matter of "perceived social meaning," and Smith claims that, at least until now, a transference of meaning of religious imagery along the lines described by Gedicks and Hendrix has not taken place.[43]

Smith is right that Judeo-Christian symbols have not become an inappropriate carrier of civil religion because of some conservative plot. But civil religion has lost some or most of its universality all the same. The problems for civil religion in the United States today can be illustrated by what occurred with regard to predictions made by Ira Lupu in 2001.

Lupu was trying to describe the overall trends of Establishment Clause jurisprudence.[44] He concluded that during the 1990s the Court had come to distinguish government message cases from government money cases, regarding government religious messages of "dubious constitutionality" while allowing government "substantial room to provide resources to religious entities engaged in projects of secular value."[45] Lupu's description of the prevailing case law here paralleled those of Noah Feldman, though of course Feldman wanted to reverse the trend. Like Feldman, Lupu noted how unhistorical the Court's emphases had become. Lupu noted in particular that reviewing government religious messages skeptically, "rather dramatically undo[es] . . . the general understanding of the late-eighteenth century that religious speech on behalf of the branches of government . . . constituted a universally accepted part of the political culture. . . ."[46]

At the end of the article, Lupu considered the future of Establishment Clause jurisprudence in the twenty-first century. He thought government would be kept "from taking positions on matters of religious faith, celebration, and observance."[47] But Lupu concluded this would lead to "preservation, not condemnation of significant aspects of the 'civil religion' by which government and its officials acknowledge a religious force in the society."[48] Lupu thought such civil religion would include the "In God We Trust" motto, the National Day of Prayer, and so forth, but believed our civil religion would "become more abstract, more generically theist, and not necessarily more monotheist. . . ." In particular, he predicted that displays of the Ten Commandments would be "perceived as Judeo-Christian, and therefore sectarian, and therefore constitutionally inappropriate."[49]

Lupu's prediction about Ten Commandments displays has proven dramatically false and his more general prediction that Judeo-Christian tradition would appear sectarian has certainly not yet occurred, at least in Supreme Court majorities. The fact that these reasonable predictions did not prove true says a great deal about the inability of civil religion to resolve the crisis in Establishment Clause jurisprudence.

Lupu's predictions were reasonable because of demographic changes occurring in American religious life. In March 2009, the American Religious Identification Survey published results that emphasized two trends, both of which supported Lupu's assumptions: America was becoming more secular and less Christian.[50]

Since the point of civil religion is the use of "widely shared" symbols and language, these trends away from religion, and specifically away from Christian identification, could well have been expected to weaken judicial acceptance of biblical images like the Ten Commandments and monotheistic appeals in general, just as Lupu had predicted. Instead, since Lupu's article appeared, the Court has upheld public displays of the Ten Commandments[51] and has reversed a challenge to the "under God" language in the Pledge of Allegiance. In addition to those actions, Justice Scalia, joined on this point by Chief Justice Rehnquist and Justice Thomas, practically endorsed monotheism as our national religion in his dissent in *McCreary County*,[52] contrary to Lupu's expectations.

To accomplish its goal of widespread consensus, civil religion must be unexceptional rather than controversial. Clearly there could be some dissent from ritualized invocations of watered-down religious imagery, but it would have to be genuinely marginalized dissent for civil religion to accomplish its inclusive goal. But objections to biblical symbols and even objections to God-language can no longer be reasonably described as marginal. The invocation of the term "civil religion" to embrace language where there is no consensus is not an escape from the crisis of the Establishment Clause but another manifestation of it.

An example of the attempted use of a genuinely new form of civil religion, according to Wade Clark Roof, was President Barack Obama's express recognition of "non-believers" in his inaugural address:

> [T]his past January we saw a president in his Inaugural Address openly and honestly wrestling with the nation's diversity—a "patchwork," as he described it, "of Christians and Muslims, Jews and Hindus, and non-believers." Nonbelievers? Their inclusion in the same breath with religious communities, especially on civil religion's holiest of days, unsettled some, inspired others. Clearly, Obama would like to defuse this tension. More than just carefully chosen words, his was a performative act aimed at uniting believers and nonbelievers in a common citizenship.[53]

Considering our traditional invocations in light of our increasing diversity, Roof asks, "[I]s this God symbolism expandable?" That is, is there a kind of symbolism that can be the equivalent of the invocation of God for a society in which substantial numbers of people do not believe in God? Or, as another possibility, can the word "God" be reinterpreted for such a context? These are the questions for a renewed civil religion. But they are not questions the justices are asking yet in the Establishment Clause context.

The most likely short-term resolution of the Establishment Clause crisis is the adoption by the Court of the position of nonpreferentialism. This position argues that government is permitted under the Establishment Clause to aid and endorse religion as against irreligion but is not permitted to discriminate among religions.[54] It is a position with serious support in the legal academy,[55] albeit with more critics.[56] Yet even critics of nonpreferentialism seem resigned that the Court will be moving toward nonpreferentialism in the future.[57]

Nonpreferentialism is usually associated with then-Justice Rehnquist's dissent in *Wallace v. Jaffree* in 1985, which was meant to challenge the foundation of the Court's Establishment Clause neutrality jurisprudence since *Everson* by rejecting the implications of Thomas Jefferson's "wall of separation between church and state metaphor."[58] From a reexamination of the history of the adoption of the Establishment Clause, Rehnquist concluded that the amendment was "designed to prohibit the establishment of a national religion, and perhaps to prevent discrimination among sects . . . [not as] requiring neutrality on the part of government between religion and irreligion."[59]

Is nonpreferentialism a healthy and persuasive alternative to neutrality? It would seem that nonpreferentialism might resolve the crisis in Establishment Clause jurisprudence. After all, the very existence of the Free Exercise Clause suggests that the Constitution in some sense protects religion as a special case.[60] So it might be reasonable to suppose the Establishment Clause prohibits only discrimination among religions and the Free Exercise Clause protects the practices of all religions. A case such as *Jaffree*, in which Justice Rehnquist's dissent expressly proposed the nonpreferentialist position,[61] seems like the perfect situation for allowing government to endorse religion. In that case, the government was endorsing "prayer"—a vague and broad concept that all religions share at least in some form.

But nonpreferentialism turns out to have a fatal flaw. Rather than representing a potential trend, *Jaffree* was actually an anomalous case that masked an inherent contradiction within nonpreferentialism. As critics have noted,[62] in practice nonpreferentialism cannot resolve the tension between endorsing religion over nonreligion and not discriminating among religions. Preference for religion over nonreligion usually leads to discrimination among religions.

The tendency toward discrimination among religions can be seen in Justice Scalia's dissent in *McCreary County*. Based on the fairly one-sided reading of American history we saw in the last chapter, Justice Scalia argued in favor of nonpreferentialism in much the same way that Justice Rehnquist had done in *Jaffree*. As a kind of summary, Justice Scalia described the "principle that the government cannot favor religion over irreligion" as "demonstrably false."[63]

But immediately after that assertion, Justice Scalia was forced to confront the criticism that upholding a government-owned Ten Commandments display "violates the principle that the government may not favor one religion over another."[64] Obviously this was a more significant challenge in the context of a biblical symbol like the Ten Commandments than of the silent prayer at issue in *Jaffree*. There are obviously religions that do not revere the Ten Commandments, whereas that might not be the case with something like prayer.

In responding to the religious discrimination challenge, Justice Scalia stated that the non-discrimination principle is binding in some contexts but it "necessarily applies in a more limited sense to public acknowledgment of the Creator."[65] Even though some religions do not acknowledge such a divine Creator, "it is entirely clear from our Nation's historical practices that the Establishment Clause permits this disregard of polytheists and believers in unconcerned deities, just as it permits the disregard of devout atheists."[66]

Lest the reader imagine that Justice Scalia could not have meant what he seemed to be saying and that he surely meant to reinterpret God-language more broadly, along the lines suggested by Wade Clark Roof,[67] Justice Scalia emphasized that he did indeed mean to privilege essentially the God of the Bible and, to be fair, maybe the God of the Qur'an as well. Justice Scalia responded to the criticism in the majority opinion that his understanding of God was too small by observing:

[t]his reaction would be more comprehensible if the Court could suggest what other God (in the singular, and with a capital G) there *is*, other than "the God of monotheism." This is not *necessarily* the Christian God (though if it were, one would expect Christ regularly to be invoked, which He is not); but it is *inescapably* the God of monotheism.[68]

In his *McCreary County* dissent, Justice Scalia put a stake through the heart of nonpreferentialism. According to Justice Scalia's approach, the words "under God" in the Pledge of Allegiance would not be understood as including all believers, let alone nonbelievers. Seven million American believers in non-monotheistic religions would be expressly excluded from our "One nation." Whatever this position is, it is certainly not nonpreferentialism. Justice Scalia is proposing quite a different resolution of the Establishment Clause crisis, and his proposed resolution demonstrates the failure of nonpreferentialism.

Instead of nonpreferentialism, Justice Scalia proposes that the American people, assisted by their government, be allowed to "honor ... God through public prayer."[69] This is a serious proposal for a reinterpretation of the Establishment Clause, and it has a great deal of merit in its own way. Although I think he has gone horribly wrong, Justice Scalia is the only justice on the Court today who seems to grasp the depth and significance of communal expressions of reverence. There is a kind of deep politics at work here that most of the justices, as well as most of legal academia, have overlooked.

Justice Scalia presented his analysis of communal religious expression better in his dissent in *Lee* than in his dissent in *McCreary*, with its dismissive tone toward atheists and polytheists. In *Lee*, Justice Kennedy's majority opinion struck down nonsectarian prayer at a high school graduation. The majority opinion sounded the usual notes of concern about coercion and requiring government neutrality. Justice Scalia's dissent, on the other hand, looked at the context of the case in a different way:

The reader has been told much in this case about the personal interest of Mr. Weisman and his daughter, and very little about the personal interests on the other side. They are not inconsequential. Church and state would not be such a difficult subject if religion were, as the Court apparently thinks it to be, some purely personal avocation that can be indulged entirely in secret, like pornography, in the privacy of one's room. For most believers it is *not* that, and has never been. Religious men and women of almost all denominations have felt it necessary to acknowledge and beseech the blessing of God as a people, and not just as individuals, because they believe in the "protection of divine Providence," as the Declaration of Independence put it, not just for individuals but for societies; because they believe God to be, as Washington's first Thanksgiving Proclamation put it, the "Great Lord and Ruler of Nations." One can believe in the effectiveness of such public worship, or one can deprecate and deride it. But the longstanding American tradition of prayer at official ceremonies displays with unmistakable clarity that the Establishment Clause does not forbid the government to accommodate it.[70]

In Justice Scalia's way of looking at religious culture, any prohibition against government religious expression becomes, in effect, a ban against biblical religion. And there is a sense in which he is right about this. The Bible tells the story of the fate of a people, not the fate of individuals. In the Old Testament, that people is Israel. In the New Testament, that people is the "new" Israel of the Church. Public, that is communal, expression of worship and thanks is a necessary practice according to the Bible. If the Establishment Clause prohibits this, there is nothing "neutral" about it. The Constitution would then be read as banning religion of this type.[71]

For Justice Scalia, alone among the justices, the clash of interests between the believing majority on the one hand, and nonbelievers and minority believers on the other, cannot be avoided. It is a tragedy of constitutional dimensions. He returned to this clash in his *McCreary County* dissent:

> Justice Stevens fails to recognize that in the context of public acknowledgments of God there are legitimate *competing* interests: On the one hand, the interest of that minority in not feeling "excluded"; but on the other, the interest of the overwhelming majority of religious believers in being able to give God thanks and supplication *as a people,* and with respect to our national endeavors. Our national tradition has resolved that conflict in favor of the majority. It is not for this Court to change a disposition that accounts, many Americans think, for the phenomenon remarked upon in a quotation attributed to various authors, including Bismarck, but which I prefer to associate with Charles de Gaulle: "God watches over little children, drunkards, and the United States of America."[72]

Justice Scalia suggests in *Lee* that, while the blessings of God may be irrelevant, the government may allow these expressions at communal events because many people believe in them. This is the meaning of the word "accommodate" in his *Lee* dissent. But in *McCreary County,* there is a shift in Justice Scalia's thinking in which it now appears that the Court would act to bar communal supplication of God at its peril because disaster might follow as surely as the plagues in Egypt followed from disobedience of God's will. Clearly these are high stakes.

Other justices have acknowledged the communal desire in America for public expressions of reverence, but they have not taken account of its depth. In *Lynch v. Donnelly*,[73] which upheld a city's nativity scene as part of a Christmas display, Justice O'Connor's concurrence referred to various government "acknowledgments of religion," such as the motto "In God We Trust," as serving secular purposes.[74] As we saw above, Justice O'Connor would have upheld the words "under God" in the Pledge of Allegiance by means of a similar "occasion solemnizing" rationale. But, as Justice O'Connor expressly stated, these religious-sounding words are not a "serious invocation of God."[75] Justice Brennan, dissenting in *Lynch,* described the same phenomena of the public use of religious language as "ceremonial deism,"[76] a term Justice O'Connor also has used. Justice Brennan agreed with Justice O'Connor that rote repetition of these phrases had deprived them of "any significant religious content."[77]

Presumably, if Justice Scalia had not recused himself from the *Elk Grove* case, his justification of the words "under God" in the Pledge of Allegiance would have been almost diametrically the opposite—that these words represent a genuine attempt by the majority to express gratitude for, and acknowledgment of, God's blessings. Justice Scalia would thus presumably not be surprised that although Justices O'Connor and Brennan find this religious language to be devoid of genuine meaning, they both acknowledge that the language cannot be discarded because it has no substitute. Justice Kennedy objected in the courthouse crèche case[78] that he failed to see "why prayer is the only way to convey these messages. . . ."[79] If the messages are so devoid of meaning, why is their religious form so crucial?

Justice Kennedy seems to have some feel for the importance of the communal expression of reverence that is akin to that of Justice Scalia. In *Lee,* although he wrote the majority opinion striking down communal prayer at high school graduations, Justice Kennedy sounded as if he had almost decided the case the other way:

> We are asked to recognize the existence of a practice of nonsectarian prayer, prayer within the embrace of what is known as the Judeo-Christian tradition,

prayer which is more acceptable than one which, for example, makes explicit references to the God of Israel, or to Jesus Christ, or to a patron saint. . . . If common ground can be defined which permits once conflicting faiths to express the shared conviction that there is an ethic and a morality which transcend human invention, the sense of community and purpose sought by all decent societies might be advanced. But though the First Amendment does not allow the government to stifle prayers which aspire to these ends, neither does it permit the government to undertake that task for itself.[80]

It also sounds as if Justice Kennedy would like to find a mechanism for communal expression of reverence that would not involve state action.

Even Justice Stevens, who is certainly committed to the neutrality principle, has had to admit the importance that these shared expressions have for people: "We recognize the important role that public worship plays in many communities, as well as the sincere desire to include public prayer as a part of various occasions so as to mark those occasions' significance. But such religious activity in public schools, as elsewhere, must comport with the First Amendment."[81]

Despite the power of Justice Scalia's analysis, however, I doubt that his proposed resolution to the Establishment Clause crisis will ever be accepted by a majority of the Supreme Court. It is significant that Justice Kennedy did not join these portions of the Scalia dissent in *McCreary County.*

I think the reason that Justice Scalia's proposal will not achieve majority status is that Justice Scalia is much less inclusive than are the American people. Whereas Justice Scalia is ready to "disregard" Buddhists and Hindus from prayerful occasions, as he wrote in *McCreary County,* there is no reason to think that most Americans agree with him about this. I am certain that most Americans would welcome the addition of representatives from polytheistic religions on occasions like high school graduations.

There is an underlying premise behind this gap between Justice Scalia's views and what I assume to be the views of most Americans. Justice Scalia is too narrow in his understanding of what public expressions of reverence are about. For Justice Scalia, God is exclusively the "benevolent, omnipotent Creator and Ruler of the world."[82] That God is what Justice Scalia is referring to in his *McCreary County* dissent as the God of monotheism. But this image of God is too specific to the Bible and indeed is too specific to a particular kind of reading of the Bible.

It neglects all sorts of theological expansions of the meaning of God, even within the Judeo-Christian tradition. And it certainly also neglects formulations like the God of pantheism. Americans probably are looser in what they mean by the invocation of the divine than is Justice Scalia. This is why I say that Justice Scalia's defense of the words "under God" in the Pledge of Allegiance will probably never redefine the meaning of the Establishment Clause.

Before leaving Justice Scalia's proposal, however, I must add that something along the lines of what he is asserting is necessary if the American experiment in self-government is to be genuinely continued. The Declaration of Independence, after all, grounded universal human rights in their bestowal by the Creator. Unless that reference to God is reinterpreted to be consistent with the requirements of the Establishment Clause, the Declaration of Independence runs the risk of becoming historically antiquated. Indeed Justice Black dared to refer to the Declaration of Independence in just such a dismissive tone in *Engel v. Vitale*.[83] But the understanding that rights are inherent and are not the gifts of government is not merely "historical." It is a view of government that must be hard won anew in every generation. If the word "Creator" cannot be legitimately confined to one literal understanding of the God of the Bible, it must nevertheless mean something significant or we have lost our connection to our founding. The establishment of that kind of broad and inclusive understanding is the goal of the next part of this book.

Justice Scalia's proposal brings us to the limits of the current case law. Thus far, we have seen neutrality as unsupported by the American people and the justices as undecided about what direction to take in its interpretation. In addition, the other directions currently proposed are all highly problematic in different ways. Justice Thomas is right that the Establishment Clause must be rethought. But it must be rethought in a way that recognizes the validity of the neutrality principle as well as the legitimacy of public religious practices. Part 2 of this book introduces a possible way out of the crisis of the Establishment Clause through utilization of the doctrine of government speech and the higher law tradition.

PART TWO

Using Government Speech and Higher Law to Resolve the Establishment Clause Crisis

FIVE

The Establishment of Higher Law

The last chapter ended at the limits of Establishment Clause jurisprudence. The current law of the Establishment Clause allows wide-ranging use of God-language in government displays, creeds, and events, at least outside of special contexts, like schools, in which coercion is a particular concern. Thus the national motto "In God We Trust" is constitutional, the Pledge of Allegiance is constitutional, legislative prayers are constitutional, and prayers at public ceremonies are constitutional. Biblical images are also generally constitutional. Ten Commandments displays and oaths of office sworn on the Bible will be upheld, especially if the government is silent as to why the Bible or a biblical reference is being used.

While a majority on the Supreme Court has not adopted any one explanation as to why this array of public religious imagery is constitutional, the outcomes of these types of cases seem unlikely to change in any important way. The majority that supports the presence of this religious imagery in the public square is composed of Chief Justice Roberts and Justices Alito, Breyer, Kennedy, Scalia, and Thomas, although their commitments differ in degree. On the other side, Justice Ginsburg seems opposed to most of this. No one can be sure of Justice Sotomayor's overall approach to religious imagery in the public square, but, judging by her decision to join Justice Stevens's dissent in *Buono*, she is probably no more open to it than was Justice Souter, whom she replaced. Justice

Stevens's replacement may oppose all government use of religious imagery, but is unlikely to do so as determinedly as did Justice Stevens.

As the reader can see, an alteration in personnel on the Supreme Court of one justice, or even two, is probably not going to change this lineup very much in the near future. So this is our constitutional law, at least for now.

In chapter 2, we looked at the destructive political consequences of the Supreme Court's drift without explanation in Establishment Clause jurisprudence. What is needed to bring peace to the field of church and state is an answer to the Establishment Clause crisis that the American people can accept. It is especially divisive to proclaim neutrality while at the same time practicing government religious expression. We need a clear judicial statement of the legitimate role of religion in government policy that pays homage to our history, our current beliefs and practices, and our diversity.

In this chapter and the next, I try to formulate such an answer to the Establishment Clause crisis. This chapter begins that process with a more or less nonreligious question: can the government establish higher law in the public square? Once that question is answered affirmatively, I turn in the next chapter to the more controversial question of whether government may use religious imagery to do so.

We start by returning to the Robert Cochran story in the introduction. As a law student, he was brought by his professor of jurisprudence to the front of Clark Hall at the University of Virginia. The inscription at the entrance to the building called on those who study law to "promote justice" in their legal careers. Inside the building, in a very noticeable placement, were two murals, one of Moses and the Ten Commandments and the other of Greek philosophical debate. For Cochran, these images "seemed to represent the higher aspiration of the law," and in particular, these images represented the aspiration of law to serve justice.

Now imagine that the image of Moses and the Ten Commandments was not present. Imagine that the university, perhaps out of sensitivity to the feelings of its nonreligious and non-monotheistic students, had carved the same message about justice on the front of the building, but had put up only one mural, that of Greek philosophical debate. Would it be constitutional for the university to do that?

The University of Virginia is a public university. Thus, in my example, the government would be disseminating an inspirational message of a nonreligious type, or at least of a not obviously religious type. No one doubts that Cochran read the message in the way it was intended to be read—that lawyers should serve justice. The question is whether the government may send messages communicating ideas of this kind. The answer to this question is yes, the government may do this. In this chapter I will present the constitutional-law context that supports this kind of speech by the government.

Given that Cochran was a student at a university, the reader may find the very question an odd one. How could a university, or indeed any educational entity, not communicate with its students on a whole range of subjects? Communication of ideas, after all, is at the heart of education.

It turns out, however, that the constitutional authority of government to communicate ideas is not directly connected with the government's particular role as educator in any literal sense. The government's right to communicate goes beyond that context. The government has a general power to speak, largely similar, though with important exceptions, to the right of individuals to speak. This constitutional doctrine is aptly called the government speech doctrine.

In its essence, the government speech doctrine is simple: "when the State is the speaker, it may make content-based choices."[1] Thus the government of the United States is free to praise democracy and the free market. The government may condemn the deprivation of human rights around the globe. Public officials can criticize premarital sex and the taking of illegal drugs. The government can choose to subsidize art and scientific research. Government teachers, subject to school-board guidelines, may offer particular views in the classroom. All of this is government communication of ideas.

In all these contexts, the government is communicating ideas that citizens have a right to controvert—ideas that the government could not support through its coercive powers. Government may attempt to persuade, but that is all it may do. The government speech doctrine is a right to speak, not a right to regulate.

The discretion in the government to discriminate in the messages it chooses to disseminate distinguishes government speech contexts from

the usual free speech content restrictions that apply when the government is, for example, regulating the speech of private parties or oversee-
ing a public forum.[2] In the context of its coercive powers, government
almost always must be neutral as to content of speech by citizens.

There is some dispute about the origin and pedigree of the government speech doctrine. Although Justice Stevens called the government
speech doctrine "newly minted" in his concurrence in *Pleasant Grove*,[3]
he was referring to a particular set of controversies that have emerged
since 1991, involving government authority to enforce limits on content
when it is subsidizing speech by private parties. In contrast to that narrow aspect of the doctrine, Justice Alito's majority opinion in *Pleasant
Grove* traced the government speech doctrine back to a concurrence by
Justice Stewart in 1973.[4] And, if Justice Scalia is correct that "[i]t is the
very business of government to favor and disfavor points of view," as
also quoted in Justice Alito's majority opinion in *Pleasant Grove*,[5] the
substance of the doctrine goes back much further than that.

When the government is speaking on its own, it enjoys something
like the discretion that any private speaker would have in what to communicate. Its choices are not judged by viewpoint discrimination standards. In contrast, in what Mary Jean Dolan calls "'speech selection'
judgments by government entities,"[6] government choices must be reasonable and, at least sometimes, viewpoint neutral. Speech selection
cases concern government selection of private speech. In a pair of such
cases decided in 1998, *Arkansas Educational Television Commission v.
Forbes*[7] and *National Endowment for the Arts v. Finley*,[8] the Court held,
respectively, that public broadcasters enjoy substantial editorial discretion in programming decisions and that the same is true of the government decision to fund particular art exhibits. In *Forbes*, the government
standard for participating in a televised debate on a state-owned public
television station—the degree of public support for a candidate—was
upheld as "a reasonable, viewpoint-neutral exercise of journalistic discretion consistent with the First Amendment."[9] In *Finley*, the Court held
that a legislatively imposed funding restriction requiring "consideration
[of] general standards of decency and respect for the diverse beliefs and
values of the American public" was not unconstitutional on its face. This

aspect of government speech recognizes some, but not total, discretion in the government to choose speech that it prefers.

The government speech issue that Justice Stevens called new in *Pleasant Grove* emerged in 1991, in *Rust v. Sullivan*,[10] concerning the free speech rights, if any, of private recipients of government funding while participating in a government program. In *Rust*, a statutory provision limiting federal funding for family-planning services to those that did not offer advice concerning abortions was challenged as violating "the free speech rights of private health care organizations that receive Title X funds, of their staff, and of their patients. . . ."[11] The limiting provision was upheld. Although Chief Justice Rehnquist's majority opinion appeared to rely on government spending discretion, later cases have viewed *Rust* as squarely within the government speech doctrine, despite the use by the government of private speakers to convey the government's message.[12] Thus when the government uses private speakers to convey its own message, its discretion is the same as if the message had been presented solely through government channels.

One continuing issue that comes up in the field of government speech is whether, in a variety of contexts, speech should be characterized as government speech or as something else. In *Legal Services Corp. v. Velazquez*,[13] the Court held that speech by government-funded attorneys is not government speech, but is private speech by a lawyer on behalf of a client. In *Rosenberger v. University of Virginia*,[14] the Court held that university subsidies for printing costs of student organizations likewise did not constitute government speech, but instead an encouragement by the government of the expression of a wide variety of private views. In contrast, in *Johanns v. Livestock Marketing Association*,[15] a case involving a mandatory assessment supporting a beef advertising campaign, the Court upheld the program as government speech against a facial challenge. In dissent, Justice Souter, joined by Justices Stevens and Kennedy, would have required the government to label the speech it claims to be government speech as its own, at least in targeted tax cases.[16] Justice Souter was arguing that the government should make it clear when it is doing the speaking, especially when identifiable private parties who are required to pay for the speech may not agree with its content. Justice Scalia's majority opinion in *Johanns* held that private parties could be compelled through taxation to support a government message with which they disagree, but that doing this to fund a non-government message might raise serious First Amendment issues, at least if the unwilling taxpayer were identified with the message.

The issue of characterizing speech in a government religious speech context as either government speech or private speech also arose in *Pleasant Grove*.[17] In that case, a religious group, Summum, claimed that by accepting for public exhibition the privately donated Ten Commandments display while rejecting its offer of its own monument on the same general subject, the city was violating its free speech rights. The city argued that the Ten Commandments display was the city's own speech and not the private speech of the original donor. Summum argued, against the city, that these monuments in a public park constituted private speech in a public forum, where government is prohibited from making content distinctions among private speakers. The Supreme Court held that all the monuments on public property represent the government's own message and are thus government speech, which is not subject to content restrictions.

While the *Pleasant Grove* case vindicated government speech, it also illustrated an important limit on the government speech doctrine. Although free speech content restrictions do not apply to government speech, other constitutional restrictions do apply, most notably "the Establishment and Equal Protection Clauses."[18] Thus, once the city adopted the Ten Commandments display as its own, it substituted a potential Establishment Clause challenge for the free speech challenge that it survived. Summum could not insist that its private message be promoted by the government, but it might be able to insist that the government not establish religion through government use of a religious image, such as the Ten Commandments. We will return to this issue in the next chapter.

Several justices have suggested, in addition to Establishment Clause and Equal Protection restrictions, that there are other substantive limits on government speech—that government speech may not, for example, "promote candidates nominated by the Republican Party"[19] or "communicate . . . partisan messages."[20] However, if the content limits of free speech do not apply to government speech, it is not clear why this should be so. Years ago, Robert Kamenshine argued there might be a kind of Political Establishment Clause implied by our Constitution, which prevents the government from interfering with the democratic process.[21] Kent Greenawalt has suggested that partisan government speech might violate a principle "of our Constitution taken more broadly in its assurance of free voting."[22]

These constitutional intuitions have not yet been worked out. The following quote from Justice Scalia shows that there must be a limit on government speech that some justices sense but cannot articulate:

> I suppose it would be unconstitutional for the government to give money to an organization devoted to the promotion of candidates nominated by the Republican Party—but it would be just as unconstitutional for the government itself to promote candidates nominated by the Republican Party, and I do not think that that unconstitutionality has anything to do with the First Amendment.[23]

Justice Scalia's reference to the First Amendment presumably means that government subsidy of one political party would not violate any individual's right to free speech. But, despite that, Justice Scalia still thinks it would be unconstitutional for the government to do so, though he cannot say why it is unconstitutional.

Whatever this limit on partisan government speech turns out to be, it will have something to do with the structure of democracy. We all assume that President George W. Bush was not permitted to use government resources to promote the presidential candidacy of Senator John McCain in 2008, even though President Bush might have sincerely felt that the election of Barack Obama would harm the United States. Undoubtedly this constitutional instinct is correct, and the only reason we have no constitutional law on the subject is that it is obvious that partisan government speech would not be permissible.

The point for our purposes—the establishment of higher law—is that this political limit, whatever its contours turn out to be, is not a restriction against government promotion of controversial ideas. It is a protection of democracy, not a ban against having substantive content in government speech.

Let us then turn back to the promotion of an idea by the University of Virginia in its mural. The university was promoting the idea that pur-

suing justice is the essence of lawyering. The university was also suggesting that justice is in some sense objective. I will call this position the
higher law tradition.

It is not my purpose in this book to attempt to fully define the higher
law tradition. A general introduction is all that is necessary. I just want
the reader to have a sense of what the University of Virginia might have
been suggesting about the concept of justice in its law school building
display and what the opposition to that claim might be asserting.

Generally speaking, there are disputes and differing approaches to
what the higher law doctrine actually encompasses. These disputes, however, do not greatly affect the point I am making here. Edward Corwin,
who introduced, or reintroduced, the term "higher law" to American
jurisprudence, was referring to the way in which certain principles of
common law became superior in the sense of judicial enforceability.[24]
I am not referring to that claim by my reference to higher law. Nor am I
referring to, in any strict sense, the Thomist synthesis of natural law.[25]
I am not even referring to the roots of the constitutional doctrine of
substantive due process.[26]

Closer to what I am asserting here by the use of the term "higher law"
is what Oliver Wendell Holmes once called a "naïve state of mind"—
that there is something binding on all human beings everywhere.[27] The
higher law position disputes Holmes's criticism.

C. S. Lewis described this something-that-is-binding, contrary to
Holmes, in the lecture that became the book, *The Abolition of Man*.[28]
Lewis began by examining a classic instance of debunking that is readily familiar to a modern reader. Lewis told of two authors of a book—he
doesn't name them or the book—who themselves quote a well-known
story about the poet Samuel Taylor Coleridge, who was present at an
impressive waterfall along with two tourists. One tourist called the waterfall "sublime" and the other called it "pretty." In the story, Coleridge
endorsed the former judgment and rejected the latter.

Lewis is interested in what the authors make of this story. He quotes
them as follows: "When the man said *That is sublime,* he appeared to be
making a remark about the waterfall. . . . Actually . . . he was not making
a remark about the waterfall, but about his own feelings."[29] Lewis has
much to say about this comment, but he concluded very much to our
purpose here:

Until quite modern times all teachers and even all men believed the universe to
be such that certain emotional reactions on our part could be either congruous
or incongruous to it—believed, in fact, that objects did not merely receive, but
could *merit*, our approval or disapproval, our reverence, or our contempt.[30]

This understanding that our feelings could respond to something
real in the universe, in contrast to asserting that everything is a matter
of opinion, and thus subjective and relative, is the theory of objective
value—that certain things really are pleasant and unpleasant and, more
importantly, just and unjust. Lewis knew well that this was not the modern temper in 1950. Certainly it is not a universal perspective today. In
context, the theory of objective value asserts that the waterfall in the
story was either sublime or it was not and that an observer could in a
meaningful way make a judgment about that.

People who you might suppose would reject the theory of objective value sometimes express acceptance for it. For example, I would
have guessed that Sam Harris, the atheist writer, would think that values
are chosen by people and are only real in that sense. But in a *Newsweek*
debate with Rick Warren in 2007, Harris stated, "I'm not at all a moral
relativist. . . . I think there is an absolute right and wrong."[31] So, in arguing for the theory of objective value, and in suggesting that many people
reject this theory, I run the risk of presenting a straw-man argument.
Nevertheless, it does seem to me that Lewis's view of values is controversial today—indeed, those who share his view often are on the defensive,
at least in academic circles.

The rejection of the theory of objective value has been particularly
significant in American law. Charles Black described that rejection in
terms similar to those of Lewis. He referred to

the widespread modern view that only delusion beckons when we conceive of
"justice" as having anything remotely like the objective reality which invests the
positive institutions of law. We have no warrant, say the followers of this view,
for supposing that there exists any "justice" which can be "discovered"; "justice"
is merely a name for our own reactions.[32]

The University of Virginia might not have been promoting the
theory of objective value. The university might have meant to suggest
only that a lawyer should follow his or her conscience in the practice
of law—that the lawyer's "own reactions" should govern conduct. And,
undoubtedly, the school officials who put up the inscription did believe

that a lawyer should follow conscience. But the university evidently did not wish to emphasize that obligation in this instance, or it would have inscribed the words, "To Thine Own Self Be True."

When the university enjoined on lawyers the obligation to "promote justice," it was emphasizing that there is such a thing as justice and suggesting that with proper study—the very activity a law student would be pursuing in that law school building—the student might come to know what justice requires. Indeed, justice might be discovered in just the way that Black describes, which he claims modern thinking rejects.

Granted, under the theory of objective value, no necessary division exists between judgments of conscience and judgments about values. Subjective judgments by people will only be arbitrary if there are no norms inherent in reality to which we should conform. If justice is absolute, the healthy human conscience will tend to recognize it. Only if justice is not absolute, is there likely to be a disconnection between a person's moral reactions and the actual state of things in the world.

In his lecture, Lewis traced the theory of objective value in a number of classic traditions, including the *Tao*, which he called "the Way in which the universe goes on." Lewis then suggested that, apart from its manifestation in individual traditions, there is an underlying universal tradition:

> This conception in all its forms, Platonic, Aristotelian, Stoic, Christian, and Oriental alike, I shall henceforth refer to for brevity simply as 'the Tao.' ... It is the doctrine of objective value, the belief that certain attitudes are really true, and others really false, to the kind of thing the universe is and the kind of things we are.[33]

As this manuscript was being finalized, scientific evidence was emerging that infants have an innate, though flawed, sense of right and wrong—infants reward altruism and punish selfishness, for example, though they greatly favor their own kind.[34] This evidence would come as no surprise to Lewis, who would have said it just proves his theory that the kind of things we are and the kind of thing the universe is are objectively related to the demands of justice.

This field of research holds the promise of refuting the claims of subjectivism, relativism, and nihilism. Years ago, Arthur Leff, the noted Yale law professor, wrote an agonized poem in which the assertion that various historical evils including the Holocaust were indeed objectively evil was met by the skeptic's question, "Sez who?"[35] Perhaps one day we will answer simply, "the babies, that's who."

Lewis did not limit this tradition of objective value to the religions of the world. Certain philosophical traditions, including the classic ones, also endorse the theory of objective value, according to Lewis. Indeed, philosophy might have been thought once to have as its goal the study of objective value. Alfred North Whitehead once wrote of philosophy giving "a sense of the worth of life."[36]

It is this overall tradition of objective value that is reflected in a political/legal context in the Declaration of Independence, when that document affirms that certain truths are self-evident and that human rights are not the gift of men to other men: "We hold these truths to be self-evident, that all men are created equal, that they are endowed by their Creator with certain unalienable Rights. . . ."

In terms of my argument, the Declaration of Independence raises two questions. Clearly it raises the question of establishing religion because of its reference to the Creator. We will return to that question in the next chapter. But, more significantly for the purpose of the theory of objective value, it raises the question of whether human rights actually are absolute. If you do not live in a culture of objective value, you run the risk of treating the reading of the Declaration of Independence the way Justice Black did for the majority in *Engel*—as if you were going to a museum "to express love for our country by reciting historical documents."[37] It did not occur to Justice Black that school children might need to be taught that the Declaration's view of reality is true. The theory of objective value presupposes that all human beings in all historical periods actually are imbued with inalienable rights—rights that are objectively real. Today the assumption that human rights are intrinsic, and objective, is often denied.

As the reader can see, I am using the terms "theory of objective value" and "higher law" interchangeably. When Oliver Wendell Holmes famously criticized the whole notion of objective justice by writing "I hate justice," Cochran, the professor who entered law school under an entrance praising justice, describes him as arguing that "there is no higher law."[38] C. S. Lewis and Charles Black would describe Holmes as rejecting the theory of objective value. We may say that acceptance of objectively real values constitutes the higher law position.

There is nothing unique in Lewis's description of the higher law tradition. Nor did Lewis claim otherwise. That is why he emphasized that the notion of objective value was very widely held until relatively recent times. And, of course, that position is still held by many. I recently read an article by Howard Lesnick that quoted the anthropologist Clifford Geertz to the same effect as Lewis, but in the context of religion:

> Clifford Geertz describes "the heart of . . . the religious perspective" as "the conviction that the values one holds are grounded in the inherent structure of reality, that between the way one ought to live and the way things really are there is an unbreakable inner connection."[39]

I presume that Geertz, like Lewis, would not limit this "unbreakable connection" between values and reality to religion but would agree that nonreligious traditions make the same claim.

Here is another, recent example of the theory of objective value. Pope Benedict wrote the following in his 2009 encyclical letter *Caritas in Veritate* (Charity in Truth):[40] "Without truth, it is easy to fall into an empiricist and skeptical view of life, incapable of rising to the level of praxis because of a lack of interest in grasping the values—sometimes even the meanings—with which to judge and direct it."

Pope Benedict's use of the word "truth" here is important because it shows the trans-religious nature of the theory of objective value. As Lewis put it, the tradition assumes only that one can speak intelligibly about the kind of thing the universe is and the kind of thing we are. For Pope Benedict, our ability to act in the world is founded on our capability to recognize this truth of life.

The higher law tradition has certain implications for positive law, that is, law created in accordance with specified social norms, such as legislation. The higher law tradition inevitably asks about the relation of morality to positive law. This issue is usually described in American law as the tension between the positivist and natural law positions. Indeed, the issue of the relationship of law to morality is often what interests American jurisprudence about higher law. Connie Rosati describes that concern in the symposium about higher law that Cochran introduced:

[S]ometimes when people ask whether there is a higher law, they do not appear
to be interested in the question of whether there are moral truths, at least not
directly. Rather, they seem to be interested in the question of the relationship
between such moral truths as may exist and our law; in asking whether there is
a higher law, they mean to ask about the limits, authority, and binding force of
positive law. This suggests a second question about the existence of higher law:
Is positive law in some way normatively dependent upon or partially constituted
or conditioned by morality?[41]

The traditional assertion of the natural law position is "that it is a
necessary condition on the legal validity of rules that they comport with
morality."[42] Of course, as Rosati points out, people who reject the theory
of objective value might agree that unjust laws have no legitimate claim
on our obedience. They would just have to explain what they mean by the
use of a word like "unjust." And the reverse is also true—a person might
believe in the theory of objective value, but assert that even unjust laws
should be obeyed, at least most of the time, for reasons of prudence. All
of these matters, and many more, were the subject of the famous Hart-
Fuller debate in the *Harvard Law Review* in 1958. H. L. A. Hart took
the positivist view in arguing that morality and law were separate. Lon
Fuller's reply argued for morality as the source of law's binding power.[43]

According to Steven Smith, all lawyers are actually higher law lawyers, whether we think of ourselves that way or not.[44] We act and talk
as if higher law is a norm against which we judge the justice or injustice
of positive law, even if many lawyers do not actually believe in objective justice. We use higher law to establish the authority of law and to
evaluate the justice of law and even the meaning of law. As Smith put it
in this same symposium, "When we human beings make and interpret
and apply law, we are in a sense joining in a sort of cooperative venture
with an intrinsically normative cosmos."[45] All of this is implicitly being
asserted by the University of Virginia in its display. Now the question is:
is that assertion by the government constitutional?

On one level, the answer is obviously yes. The point of the doctrine
of government speech is that the government may assert substantive
ideas. The government does this all the time. Many government monuments glorify themes and events to which some people might object. The
mural at the University of Virginia is just one example of a very common
public practice.

But this simple answer is not sufficient. Although I criticize in this book the concept of ceremonial deism because it defends religious speech by robbing it of its meaning, nevertheless there is some truth in the idea that some speech is merely pro forma. Some speech is not even really noticed. And that could be true of the display at the University of Virginia. Absent the religious element that might attract attention, the message of the mural depicting Greek debate is too much of a background element to elicit any kind of constitutional challenge. So the supposed constitutionality of the hardly noticeable display—no one would think to challenge an image of Greek debate by itself—does not necessarily answer the question.

In order to judge the constitutionality of government higher law speech fairly, we would have to imagine more robustly public examples of such speech. What if the government recast the Pledge of Allegiance so as to provide, instead of "one Nation under God," the phrase "a Nation dedicated to Truth"? Putting the matter this way reminds us that the Pledge of Allegiance already asserts the reality of justice "for all." But the addition of the category of Truth would greatly sharpen the claim of higher law and objective value in the Pledge.

There would be at least four objections to this new national creed of "a Nation dedicated to Truth." First, this formulation, with its capital "T" for Truth, would be challenged as nothing more than a religious formulation with a slightly different phrasing. Thus the same Establishment Clause challenge would be brought to this creed as to the phrase "under God." Second, there would be the charge that the assertion about Truth is nebulous and incoherent and is not within the proper role of government. Third, there would be passionate objection from people who do not share the metaphysical comportment of the doctrine of objective value. They would feel just as disenfranchised by this version of our national creed as atheists and non-monotheists do by the phrase "under God." Finally, there would be the objection that a national creed of this kind is coercive, indeed totalitarian. This final objection would be deepened if, as I will hypothesize below, the government sought seriously to teach the theory of objective value in its public schools.

The first objection—that Truth is a religious category—has an excellent pedigree. The point of this claim is not that a national creed about

Truth and justice is necessarily unconstitutional, but that such a creed should be judged by the same constitutional standard that would be applied to formally religious terms. In other words, this new Pledge of Allegiance is religion by another name and should be treated the same as our current Pledge.

Christianity has always asserted a strong and close connection between Truth and the Gospel. Jesus' statement, "I am the Way, the Truth, and the Life,"[46] must be contrasted, and was no doubt meant to be contrasted, with the weary question of Pontius Pilate, "What is truth?"[47] Pope Benedict, writing before he became Pope, formulated this Christian claim simply and succinctly: "The three questions, concerning truth and good and God, are but one single question."[48]

At one point in his magnum opus, *A Secular Age*, Charles Taylor appears to assert that any account of objective truth must be founded on a strictly religious basis. Taylor says that a secular account of objective value—he does not use that actual term—does not fit "our favoured ontology":

> [W]e are starting from Hume's attempt to understand morality as a species of "natural" human sentiment among others, rather than as something that reason perceives as an intrinsically higher demand. The issue I raise here, without definitively answering, is whether such a "naturalist" account can make sense of the phenomenology of universalism.[49]

I have sympathy for the assertion that religion and metaphysics are closely related. The doctrine of objective value has deep religious roots, as Lewis stated. And in the next chapter, I will argue that traditional religious symbols can be used to represent claims such as the objectivity of values, because of those roots and that connection.

Nevertheless, whatever it is that the Establishment Clause prohibits the government from doing, that ban has always been applied to only traditional religious expressions. The Clause has never been invoked to prohibit the government from endorsing anything other than traditional religion. That narrow limitation has distinguished the Establishment Clause from the Free Exercise Clause.

The Free Exercise Clause has occasionally been expanded to protect nonreligious practices and beliefs that occupy the same role in the life of the person as that occupied by religion in the life of the believer.

This occurred in the Vietnam-era draft cases, for example. Although in these cases, the Court technically interpreted statutory draft-exemption language, the cases were decided against the background of a potential Free Exercise challenge.

In *United States v. Seeger*[50] and *Welsh v. United States,*[51] the Court was dealing with a statutory draft exemption for conscientious objection based on "religious training and belief," which was further defined in the statute as "an individual's belief in a relation to a Supreme Being." None of the four claimants in these cases believed in a traditional God, but they were granted exemption by the Court all the same.

In *Seeger,* Justice Tom Clark adopted a test for religious belief in relation to a Supreme Being that avoided the constitutional question whether Congress could have lawfully distinguished between theistic and nontheistic religious believers. The test, said the Court, was whether a claimant for draft exemption possessed

> [a] sincere and meaningful belief which occupies in the life of its possessor a place parallel to that filled by the God of those admittedly qualifying for the exemption comes within the statutory definition. [52]

Justice Black's plurality opinion in *Welsh* further refined the test to require that

> opposition to war stem from the registrant's moral, ethical, or religious beliefs about what is right and wrong and that these beliefs be held with the strength of traditional religious convictions.[53]

The draft cases illustrate that commitments that are within the doctrine of objective value might be regarded as protected by the Free Exercise Clause. For C. S. Lewis, an exemption claimant who believes as a matter of right and wrong that one may not kill in war is clearly religious in the sense of following the Tao, which is the understanding of objective value. Such a person is asserting that it is wrong for anyone at any time to kill. So Lewis might have said that the Court was right—not in the sense that there ought to be such a draft exemption, but that these young men were utilizing a religious justification for it.

But this expansive understanding of religion has not been applied in Establishment Clause challenges. The question of what is religious has been limited to Free Exercise claims. One reason for that difference must be that most of political life partakes of value commitments and what might be called quasi-religious orientations. If all such commitments could be considered violations of the Establishment Clause, political life would be emasculated.

This sense of deep political/religious values was discussed in a September 2008 oral exchange between Robert Bellah and Mark Juergensmeyer, which was reproduced on *The Immanent Frame* blog.[54] Juergensmeyer referred to a definition of religion that both parties seemed to share: "patterned activity or thought related to the deepest, most important things in a collective context." The reader can see that this definition also applies to political life. And so almost anything government says and does could be challenged as a violation of the Establishment Clause, if its breadth were treated similarly to that of Free Exercise.

If the search for deeper meaning were banned from the public square, on the ground that all such seeking is religious, the public square would be mostly empty. Expressions of reverence for nature in the context of environmental protection, for example, have never been treated as potential threats to Establishment Clause values. A government billboard asserting that "Nature is our home; protect it" simply cannot be thought to violate the Establishment Clause. Where would such a restriction end? It might end in a politics of pure, material self-interest. But even that is, after all, an assertion about Truth; perhaps it is the truth that there is no Truth. In any event, that renunciation of meaning is surely not required by the Establishment Clause.

Granted, there is something arbitrary about banning some words from government use while allowing others that carry similar weight to remain. In this instance, "a Nation dedicated to Truth" is not subject to Establishment Clause challenge, while "one Nation under God" is. But that arbitrariness is better viewed as a justification for restricting Establishment Clause prohibitions, rather than expanding them. The fact that we cannot practice our politics without words of deep meaning should teach us to open the public square to many more expressions of deep meaning, especially, as I argue in the next chapter, traditionally religious ones.

The second objection—that Truth is nebulous and incoherent and not within the proper role of government—is related to this last point.

Perhaps I have been hasty in assuming that political life must involve basic questions of meaning. Mark Lilla, author of *The Stillborn God*[55] and a supporter of the strict separation of church and state, has described our political life in very narrow terms compared to the political life of countries that mix politics and religion:

> We have made a choice . . . we have chosen to limit our politics to protecting individuals from the worst harms they can inflict on one another, to securing fundamental liberties and providing for their basic welfare, while leaving their spiritual destinies in their own hands. We have wagered that it is wiser to beware the forces unleashed by the Bible's messianic promise than to try exploiting them for the public good.[56]

So it may be that something like Truth is not a fit subject for politics.

Since in this part of the book I am dealing with the meaning of the Establishment Clause, I will have to return to this argument by Lilla later, in chapter 11, which deals with the politics of higher law assertions. Lilla would probably agree that his view of politics is not, and should not be, enforceable in court as a limit on legitimate conceptions of politics under the Establishment Clause. He is describing our politics, not creating a legal restriction. Lilla, and others who share his view, would not be one to challenge a new, Truth-oriented Pledge of Allegiance in court.

Steven Gey comes closer to making a legal challenge on this point. Gey writes of "our routine assumption that the government should not be deciding matters of metaphysics, theology, or ultimate truths on behalf of the government's own citizens."[57] Gey is writing in the context of the meaning of the Establishment Clause and he argues that any "[d]etermination of [u]ltimate [v]alue" by government threatens a strict separation of church and state.

Gey's candor, however, shows the weakness of this position as a supposed constitutional limit on politics. Government currently claims the power to coercively send young people to their deaths in war. If that is not a determination of ultimate value by the government, imposed on its own citizens, what would be? The government could just as easily write a creed stating, "These are matters worth dying for . . . ," which then listed Truth, Freedom, Democracy, and so forth. That is why, in *Wooley v. Maynard*,[58] for example, the plaintiffs were held to have a free speech right to place tape over the phrase "Live Free or Die" on their New Hampshire license plate, but could not have enjoined the license plate phrase itself as a violation of the Establishment Clause.

Certainly government may not decide matters of theology, strictly speaking. Religious neutrality is a shared starting point between Gey and me. But that limit, which will be discussed in the next chapter, is a narrow and formal one. The Establishment Clause applies to religion and not to anything else. Nor is there any parallel constitutional prohibition that applies to other kinds of government assertions of meaning.

Up to this point, I have left out the substantive dissenter from a national creed invoking Truth. This is the third objection—that persons who disagree with the theory of objective value are disenfranchised by a national creed that proclaims loyalty to Truth. The objection is that the relativist, the values skeptic, the nihilist, and so forth, are treated by this new creed as outsiders, much as the nonbeliever is said to be treated by the current use of the phrase "under God." As one critic of the establishment of higher law put it on her blog, "I believe that goodness and justice are concepts generated by our human brains after millions of years of evolution as social animals: more or less universal across humanity, but certainly not generated from a higher source.... Why should that make me a second class citizen?"[59]

This objection is fundamentally at odds with the government speech doctrine itself. If the government has the power to speak, that power cannot be limited to trivial matters. The government must be permitted to express fundamental ideas with which a particular citizen might disagree. Thus the objection cannot be accepted in regard to the commitment to Truth, for example, unless the government were prevented from substantively speaking at all.

It certainly is true that the government speech doctrine is potentially harsh toward any citizen's nonreligious beliefs that the majority does not share. As *National Endowment for the Arts v. Finley* suggests, the government may insist, using my and others' tax money, that a work of art is a genuine masterpiece, even though I know it to be a piece of junk. As *Rust* holds, I can, as a government employee or public grant recipient, be forced, at the risk of my livelihood, to tell people that this piece of art is a masterpiece. As *Johanns* makes clear, I can be compelled by the government through taxation to contribute to a public subsidy for an award to this false artist. All of this is justified in the name of government speech.

In terms of Justice O'Connor's endorsement test, one emblem of forbidden establishment of religion is that such endorsement "sends a message to nonadherents that they are outsiders,"[60] and the government speech doctrine reminds us of how often this kind of treatment occurs outside the context of public religious expression. The socialist must feel like an outsider, for example, when the government praises capitalism. Feeling that one is an outsider is not intrinsically a religious issue. It is a matter of encountering fundamental ideas and commitments that the citizen does not share expressed by her own government.

Of course Justice O'Connor did not mean "outsider" in any general sense. She added the qualifying phrase "not full members of the political community." But surely the socialist knows that to be true as well. And, assuming that such government speech would not run afoul of the political-speech exception mentioned above, a government advertising campaign, not aimed at any referendum, that touted marriage as a bond between a woman and a man, would certainly send a message to gay men and women that they are not full members of the political community, or at least not viewed as such by the majority. But such advertisements would not be thought to represent an establishment-of-religion issue, whatever other constitutional issues they might raise.

The government speech doctrine forces us to confront just how deep our disagreements can be with the messages of our own government. The values relativist would be right to feel excluded by a government endorsement of Truth. But that has never been considered a valid constitutional objection to the government speech doctrine. Indeed, the fact that the objection of the values relativist is to be discounted will be revisited in the next chapter as a ground for undermining Justice O'Connor's endorsement test in the context of traditionally religious expression in the public square.

The final objection that would be raised against a new national creed endorsing Truth is that it is coercive. It should be remembered that coercion is unconstitutional both in the context of religious endorsement by government and in the context of free speech itself. Here, then, is a potential objection to government speech that does not require us to characterize traditionally nonreligious speech by government as if it were religious.

In 1943, in *West Virginia State Bd. of Education v. Barnette,*[61] Justice Robert Jackson stated the rule against coercion in the context of upholding the right of public school students to refuse to salute the flag: "If there is any fixed star in our constitutional constellation, it is that no official, high or petty, can prescribe what shall be orthodox in politics, nationalism, religion, or other matters of opinion or force citizens to confess by word or act their faith therein."[62]

Although the children in *Barnette* were Jehovah's Witnesses, and thus raised both religious freedom and free speech issues, the case is regarded today as protecting the citizen from forced association with ideas to which the citizen objects, on any ground.

The anti-coercion principle, however, does not prevent attempted persuasion by the government. The result in *Barnette* was to invalidate "compelling" a flag salute. It did not prevent the state from holding flag-salute ceremonies in public schools. Thus the state continued at least to attempt to prescribe what was orthodox in politics and nationalism, but could only do so without coercion.

Would it violate *Barnette* if a teacher said to an elementary school class, "It is a good thing to honor our country by saluting the flag"? The answer to that question is difficult only because saying that to an impressionable student audience might amount to coercion. Yet, by performing the flag salute every day, the government is implying precisely that—honoring America in this way is a good thing. Some level of government endorsement of values is obviously permitted in public schools.

We can ask the same question about the government/teacher endorsement of the doctrine of objective value, that is, of Truth. Clearly the government may not coerce belief in that proposition. The student who states that the doctrine is false cannot be penalized in any way. To provide any kind of penalty would violate *Barnette*.

But can the teacher teach that the doctrine of objective value is true? In 2002 Martin H. Redish and Kevin Finnerty tried to develop what they called an "anti-indoctrination model" for public education in order to protect freedom of thought.[63] Earlier law review articles had raised similar concerns.[64] Thus there is at least some support in the legal literature for objection along these lines. These articles are not currently the law, but they could become the law at some point in the future.

Yet even if these scattered efforts were one day to constitute a new constitutional prohibition, it is hard to imagine a bar against teaching the objectivity of values. There is a sense in which that kind of teaching is too fundamental, too deeply embedded in all facets of education, to even evaluate in terms of its constitutionality. The teacher teaches the doctrine of objective value whenever reference is made in class to right and wrong or good and bad. The teacher is always going to teach students to respect the rights of other students, for example. The teacher is not going to say, "some people believe that you should wait to take your turn." Indeed, waiting to take your turn was for C. S. Lewis the best indicator of objective morality in the universe and it is a lesson every kindergarten teacher imparts. Terms such as indoctrination do not belong here. Or if it they do, then all education of any type is going to involve indoctrination.

Therefore, leaving aside for the moment the use of the word "Creator," I believe the state may post and proclaim the wisdom of the Declaration of Independence in every schoolroom. The government may teach that our rights are absolute and that they are beyond the reach of majorities and autocrats. Indeed, I wish the government would do so.

I have ignored one objection to government promotion of the doctrine of objective value. The doctrine may simply not be true. In a recent article, law professor Jeremy Waldron wrote, "we no longer say, as Lord Acton once said, 'Opinions alter, manners change, creeds rise and fall, but the moral law is written on the tablets of eternity.'"[65] Waldron is speaking here for many.

But he is not speaking, as he seems to suggest, for all of us. There are many citizens who retain the old worldview of objective right and wrong, however modified for a world of many cultures in contact with each other. I mention Waldron because his view perhaps serves as a good justification for why a government might want to self-consciously and expressly inculcate the doctrine of objective value, if the Constitution permits it to do so.

In any event, as the reader can see, the government speech doctrine has never asked whether government speech is true. The government may promote even a half-baked idea of higher law, even one that has been rejected by many thinkers on the subject. Government speech need not be logical or well grounded in order to be constitutionally permissible under the government speech doctrine.

I believe the doctrine of higher law is true. But I acknowledge that I have not defended it here. It may even be that no fully convincing defense can be given. Perhaps, like religion itself, a commitment to higher law may not ultimately be a matter of argument. In any event, it is enough for my proposal in this part of the book that the government may legitimately assert the higher law claim, whether or not that claim is indeed true or provable. In contrast, in part 3, I will attempt to present the higher law tradition as a substantively attractive alternative for a secularism prone to unthinking relativism.

Now we turn to the more difficult issue of government religious expression. The University of Virginia did seek to promote the doctrine of objective value. But it did so not only with secular images, but also with a religious one. Is it constitutional for the government to promote the doctrine of objective value through the use of religious expressions, such as "one Nation under God"?

SIX

Using Religious Symbols to Establish Higher Law

Government's use of religious symbols is a very different issue than government endorsement of higher law. The Pledge of Allegiance says "one Nation under God," not "one Nation under the Essential Unity of All Things." If the Pledge said the latter, not many people, and certainly no judges, would call it unconstitutional as a violation of the Establishment Clause. The question is, then, whether the use of specifically *religious* language, such as the word "God," is constitutional if used to endorse higher law? That question raises another: if government were permitted to use religious symbols for nonreligious purposes, what would be the standard by which one could determine whether religious language was being used in a nonreligious way?

Clearly, in some contexts, the use of religious imagery to endorse higher law principles is constitutional, no matter how one understands the Establishment Clause. For example, in chapter 1, we saw the two constitutional tests through which government neutrality toward religion has been enforced: the Lemon test and the endorsement test. Under the former, government action must have a secular legislative purpose; its principal or primary effect must be one that neither advances nor inhibits religion, and the action must not foster excessive government entanglement with religion. Under the latter, government must not endorse or disapprove of religion.

If we apply these two tests to the display of the Ten Commandments inside the building at the University of Virginia—the story with which we began in the introduction—we can conclude that the display is currently constitutional. Given the secular inscription on the front of the building, and given the nearby mural of the Greek philosophers, the Ten Commandments are pretty clearly being used to make a nonreligious point about justice. This point about justice satisfies the requirements of secular purpose and effect and thus conforms to the Lemon test. In addition, any reasonable observer of the inscription on the front of the building and the two displays inside would come to the conclusion that an essentially secular point was being made and that the government was not endorsing religion. Thus the building as a whole would satisfy the endorsement test.

I am not suggesting that these two tests define the reach of the Establishment Clause any longer. The crisis in Establishment Clause jurisprudence precludes any certainty about what test currently would be used by a majority of the justices to determine forbidden establishment of religion. But the Lemon and endorsement tests are as restrictive of government use of religious imagery as the Court is likely to get, at least any time soon. If the University of Virginia building satisfies these tests, it is certainly constitutional.[1]

What if the Ten Commandments display were present without the display of the Greek philosophers? Would it still be constitutional? In that instance, the inscription at the front of the building might still preserve the Ten Commandments display from constitutional invalidation, even without having to rely on the approval of a Ten Commandments display in a case like *Van Orden*. The reason for this is that the display could still be interpreted as illustrative of the motto, rather than as endorsement of any religious theme. This conclusion is buttressed by the approval of a divided Court in 1989, in the *Allegheny County* case, of a menorah and a Christmas tree in a public space with the title "Salute to Liberty." Beneath the title, the sign stated: "During this holiday season, the city of Pittsburgh salutes liberty. Let these festive lights remind us that we are the keepers of the flame of liberty and our legacy of freedom."

Just as this secular message supported the nonreligious symbolism of the menorah and Christmas tree, so the message of law and justice would presumably render the Ten Commandments display at the university secular rather than religious.

Finally, returning to the building at the University of Virginia, what if that Ten Commandments display appeared by itself at the law school? That question just restates the question of this chapter—can the government use religious imagery to establish higher law? In that hypothetical situation, the display might still represent a view of the law as embodying the thesis of objective value, but it might also be interpreted as promoting the view that American law reflects God's will. The express secular context in *Allegheny County* would not be present.

There are religious symbols that, even without special explanation, are understood to convey mixed religious and secular messages. One such religious symbol that arguably conveys a nonreligious message is a cross at a war memorial on public land used to symbolize the ultimate sacrifice. Such a cross was at issue in *Salazar v. Buono,* which was decided in April 2010.[2]

In *Buono,* the Court faced a complex legal and factual context. In 1934, the Veterans of Foreign Wars erected a Latin cross on federal land in the Mojave National Preserve to honor the dead of World War I. In 2002, Federal Judge Robert J. Timlin found that display of the cross on federal land violated the Establishment Clause and granted an injunction ordering the government to remove the cross. Meanwhile, Congress enacted a statute transferring the cross and the land on which it stands to the VFW in exchange for other land of equal value. Judge Timlin then found the land transfer statute unconstitutional and ordered that the 2002 injunction be enforced.

Justice Kennedy, joined by Chief Justice Roberts and Justice Alito in part, found that the judge should not have enjoined the land transfer without further study because the original decision applied only to a cross on federal land. The land transfer changed the circumstances. The case was remanded to the court below for further consideration because Justices Scalia and Thomas, who found that the plaintiff lacked standing, concurred in the Court's judgment, thus creating a five-justice majority.[3] On the other side, Justice Stevens dissented, joined by Justices Ginsburg and Sotomayor, arguing that the land transfer was a violation of the Establishment Clause. Justice Breyer also dissented, albeit on technical grounds of injunction law.

Buono was decided on narrow grounds concerning the private ownership of the land in question. It is clear from the opinions that land transfers in general will not usually decide Establishment Clause issues. That posture of the case kept the fundamental issue from being decided: can government use a cross to honor the dead in war?

That basic issue is clear enough. The cross became a traditional symbol of honoring the dead in America and the West because most of the soldiers were Christian and many of them wanted crosses above their graves. Honoring this wish was no more an endorsement of Christianity than was having military chaplains in the army. The government was accommodating the private religious wishes of its soldiers.

But because military cemeteries thus became the scene of row after row of crosses, the cross became a simple shorthand for honoring the military dead. Think, for example, of the opening lines of perhaps the most famous poem of World War I, *In Flanders Fields*:

> *In Flanders fields the poppies blow*
> *Between the crosses, row on row, . . .*[4]

As Justice Kennedy put it in *Buono*, "a Latin cross is not merely a reaffirmation of Christian beliefs. It is a symbol often used to honor and respect those whose heroic acts, noble contributions, and patient striving help secure an honored place in history for this Nation and its people. Here, one Latin cross in the desert evokes far more than religion. It evokes thousands of small crosses in foreign fields marking the graves of Americans who fell in battles, battles whose tragedies are compounded if the fallen are forgotten."[5]

Naturally, given changing demographics and changing religious commitments, the day will come, if it has not already, that the cross is not an appropriate universal symbol of military sacrifice. But it certainly has been such in the past, and it is significant that *Buono* involved a monument to the dead of World War I.

Buono actually was a much easier case than other government-religious-display cases because the nonreligious meaning of the cross in this context seems clear. In contrast, the justices have not yet been able to explain convincingly what the nonreligious meaning is in the motto

"In God We Trust." As we saw earlier, Justice Scalia, for example, would move in the opposite direction, giving such a phrase a candid, purely religious meaning of thanks and praise to God.

When there is dispute about the secular meaning of religious imagery in the public square, I suggest the standard by which public religious expression should be judged is whether it is plausible to view the government's use of religious language, imagery, or symbols as endorsing the principle of higher law or other related, nonreligious themes. If so, the government use is constitutional. If not, the use is unconstitutional. I believe the use of the Ten Commandments, for example, to endorse higher law satisfies this understanding of the Establishment Clause and thus would be constitutional.

I will explain below how plausibility works, why I suggest it, and how it differs both from the analysis of purpose in the Lemon test and from the observer perspective in the endorsement analysis. Before doing so, let me delineate some of my operating assumptions.

There are really only four courses open to the Supreme Court in the area of church and state. First, the Court can continue to muddle through, thus keeping the crisis of the Establishment Clause at a high pitch. Second, the Court can abandon the neutrality principle and allow the government to endorse religion openly, at least in certain contexts, as promoted by Justice Scalia. Third, the Court can retain neutrality and begin to enforce it consistently. Finally, as suggested in this chapter, the Court can keep government neutrality, while reinterpreting religious symbols along deeply meaningful secular lines that differ from, but do not conflict with, their original religious meaning. The first three paths promise, or are already leading to, great harm to law and political life. The latter path might be a path to peace.

The first path—muddling through—is the one that the Court will most likely follow. But this course is unsatisfying. The ceremonial deism approach associated with Justice Brennan, and to a lesser extent with Justice O'Connor, is too secular and too thin to apply successfully to public religious expression. Despite what Justice Brennan has suggested, public religious expression retains genuine religious meaning even when it can be interpreted plausibly along secular lines. And, despite what Justice O'Connor has suggested, that religious language communicates a variety of deep meanings, religious and secular, and not just vapid generalizations. The current approach is a compromise, and compromise in the field of church and state is something to be valued. But this is not a coherent compromise.

This incoherence has led to a crisis in Establishment Clause interpretation that is quite harmful for American law and political life. The Supreme Court should not continue to endorse government neutrality toward religion in theory while allowing numerous manifestations of plainly religious symbols in public life in practice. Despite the protestations of the justices, these religious images are obviously meaningful for religious believers and claiming they are not without convincing explanation encourages disrespect for the Court and for law in general.

The gap between announced doctrine and case result also encourages insincerity in political disputes. A good example is the recent fight, mentioned in chapter 2, over placing the Pledge of Allegiance and the national motto in the Capitol Visitor Center. Proponents of that successful effort said the placement had to do with acknowledgment of America's religious "heritage." But of course the fight had nothing to do with our heritage but with our present and future. Opponents of the motto and the Pledge regarded this effort as an attempt to publicly endorse religion in the present time. And they were right. I don't mean this as a criticism of those who supported the placement of the national motto and the Pledge of Allegiance in the visitor center. The fault here is with the Court. This fighting goes on in its current mode because the Supreme Court outlaws government endorsement of religion but then turns a blind eye when such endorsement happens. The justices were the ones who started allowing public display of religious symbols under the plainly false rubric of mere historical acknowledgment and mere ceremony. The justices are largely responsible for the toxic quality of the current political debate over religion. The absence of consistent enforcement of constitutional norms turns a deep and genuine disagreement about the proper place of religion in the public square into rivaling insincere claims.

Of the available courses, abandoning neutrality at least has the virtue of candor. The national motto "In God We Trust" does seem to endorse God, as does the Pledge of Allegiance. This is why Justice Thomas stated that the Ninth Circuit had properly interpreted past precedent in invalidating the Pledge of Allegiance. These uses of religious language seem to suggest that the government prefers the citizenry to believe in God. Calling the motto a manifestation of our religious heritage, or calling the Pledge ceremonial deism, does not change the impact of these religious words. Only Justice Scalia's proposal to allow public acknowledgment and thanksgiving to God seems an adequate description of what it means to retain the national motto and the Pledge of Allegiance.

But Justice Scalia does not seem to realize that his proposal would lead to political disaster in the future. Allowing the current majority in the country to use the government expressly and formally to praise and worship its God inevitably turns the worship of God into a political issue. Once Justice Scalia's approach was accepted, and it became clear that the courts were closed to challenges against public religious imagery—and indeed that the Court had actually allowed government endorsement of monotheism as akin to a national religion—opposition to such displays would turn to political action rather than legal action. At the moment, such political action would not mean much. America is overwhelmingly a monotheistic country. Many American believers, for whatever reason, prefer that generic references to God and, to a lesser extent, biblical imagery such as a public Ten Commandments display, remain in the public square. That is why not a single national political figure has proposed removing the words "under God" from the Pledge of Allegiance or altering the national motto. But it would still become a question of politics. Does God have more votes than not?

The harm this would do is that all elections in the future would turn to some extent into referenda on God. It is hard to imagine any political context more divisive and dangerous. In addition, secularism would be reinforced in its determination to oppose all aspects of religion, a subject we return to in part 3 of this book. And if eventually the rapidly increasing cohort of nonbelievers finally managed to put together a majority to purge God from the public square, religious believers would come to regard their fellow countrymen as spiritual enemies. There could hardly be a worse political future.

I would like to propose that the fiction we operate under now is healthier than the situation Justice Scalia's candor would lead us to. Because of the formal commitment to the neutrality doctrine, proponents of something like putting the national motto onto the wall of the Capitol Visitor Center now claim they are merely acknowledging our national religious heritage. That is a false claim, but it is better than fighting and voting about the truth, that is, about the existence of God. Yet the claim is still false, and we can do much better.

So why not just fully enforce the government neutrality position, which is the third option? The current political situation in America makes it easy to predict that the Court will not go in that direction. The most committed separationist on the Court, Justice Stevens, is retiring. President Obama has shown no inclination to press a strong neutrality position, even though neutrality may reflect his personal belief. The Democratic Party has clearly made a kind of cultural/political calculation that abortion and gay rights are, mostly, commitments worth fighting for, but gun control and separation of church and state are not. Thus, since the 2006 election, the Democratic Party has embraced God, ignored guns, and even tolerated some pro-life candidates.[6] Certainly there is nothing here to presage a revival of a strong church/state separation position on the Court.

In any event, it is not even clear what a consistent neutrality position entails. Supporters of government neutrality have never been forced to spell out their ultimate vision of the public square. Are all prayers on public occasions unconstitutional? Must the Pledge be found unconstitutional in general? Remember, even the Ninth Circuit ruled only on the Pledge in public schools. The national motto? The National Day of Prayer? How about religious references in speeches by public officials? Most separationists know that this list spells political impossibility.

What would be the political fallout if the Court really attempted to remove all references to God in the public square? For one thing, it would probably lead to a constitutional amendment that would enshrine at least monotheism, and maybe Christianity, as the national religion. Any effort by the justices to expunge God from the public square would likely fail in that sense.

But imagine what would happen if such a judicial effort succeeded. Millions of Americans would become convinced that constitutionalism and judicial review are evil. The American experiment itself would begin to fail. Eventually some Mussolini type might come along to give political expression to these resentments. The ground would be well prepared. Separationists do not see the danger their success in the courts might entail.

This leaves my proposal that the Court reinterpret religious imagery along the lines of higher law or some similar meaningful, but secular, context. What are the prospects of this proposal?

We can start with the proposition that the government is already permitted to endorse the higher law position—roughly speaking, that values are real. The government is permitted now to endorse that position.

The question then becomes, can government, consistently with the Establishment Clause, use a religious word like "God" to represent the higher law position? Can the words "under God" in the Pledge of Allegiance, for example, plausibly mean anything other than an endorsement of the God of the Bible?

American sociologist Robert Bellah provides a surprisingly strong affirmative answer to that question. Bellah, who popularized Rousseau's term, civil religion, in chapter 9 of his 1970 book, *Beyond Belief*,[7] argued that the use of the word "God" on public occasions was precisely an invocation of higher law thinking. Despite the American commitment to majority rule, the invocation of God in public discourse means, according to Bellah, that "the will of the people is not itself the criterion of right and wrong. There is a higher criterion in terms of which this will can be judged; it is possible that the people may be wrong."[8]

Bellah's understanding of the use of the word "God" is not much different from the use of the word "Creator" in the Declaration of Independence: "We hold these truths to be self-evident, that all men are created equal, that they are endowed by their Creator with certain unalienable Rights." Naturally some religious people look at that language as if it were an argument for the existence of God. But that is not a fair reading. The existence of God was not the issue at the time. Rather, the Declaration was making a political point about the nature of rights. Rights do not come from men, that is, not from the King or Parliament. And thus, as Bellah says of right and wrong, no positive political power has the authority to revoke rights with which all human beings are endowed. This was the major point of the Declaration of Independence.

This is also precisely the "common ground" that Justice Kennedy's majority opinion in *Lee v. Weisman* was seeking—"the shared conviction that there is an ethic and a morality which transcend human invention."[9] Since that conviction, which is the higher law position, is not uniquely "religious," why not allow government to express it with religious symbols that do embody it?

Bellah is making the point that the use of religious imagery actually does embody this claim about rights—that rights are absolute. It follows that these rights and values naturally impose ethical and moral demands on the society that utilizes such religious language, demands that are not themselves direct importations of revelation, and are secular in that sense, but that for religious believers overlap with their understanding of revelation. As Wilfred McClay wrote of Bellah's thought: "As Robert Bellah and others have observed, it is a good thing for our loyalties to the nation-state to be qualified by their being subject to a higher moral criterion: to being 'under judgment.'"[10]

The secularist has no reason to abandon the theory of objective value that is sometimes expressed through religious imagery. Certainly many, probably most, secularists agree both that the majority may be objectively wrong and that government, even though supported by the will of the majority, might violate our fundamental rights. Bellah was explaining that the use of the word "God" has been recognized in these contexts to serve as a kind of shorthand for these sentiments. It is particularly important to remember that Bellah was not writing about the Establishment Clause. He was not proposing some religious/political compromise but simply describing what he thought religious language meant in context.

But why use religious language, symbols, and images for an assertion that could be made directly and through purely secular appeals? This is indeed a crucial objection. The secularist would be wrong to argue that religious images lack deep secular meaning. But it certainly is correct to say that such images also contain religious and sectarian claims as well, even predominantly. So why use religious symbols to deliver any message if the government is supposed to be neutral toward religion?

The answer is there are unique attributes of traditional religious language that recommend its use to represent higher law. For many religious believers, overwhelmingly Christian in American history, the phrases "under God" or "by their Creator" serve a dual role. God is the foundation, the ontological basis, according to Charles Taylor, for the truth of the claims that right and wrong are inherent and human rights are not gifts of government. Like the believing and secular observers I described in the introduction, the believer and the nonbeliever both draw similar secular conclusions, along with disparate religious ones, from this type of religious language. The important point here is that the secular conclusions are just as sincerely held by the religious believer as they are by the nonbeliever. They both believe that justice and rights are real.

This is a very significant point and one that secularists tend to dismiss. Religious believers, at least believers in the biblical tradition, already associate God with the claim of objective value. That is why Pope Benedict asserted, as we saw in chapter 5, that truth, good, and God are one single question. So, in using the word "God" to illustrate higher law, the government already has strengthened the appeal to higher law for religious believers. Using the word "God" strengthens the case for higher law among a significant portion of the citizenry. That is one reason to use religious imagery.

Despite the believer's religious interpretation, the government is still making an appeal to higher law and is not making a uniquely religious assertion. In the same work, Pope Benedict describes "the natural law school of thought" in "constitutional democracy" without any reference to supernatural realities and in terms that Bellah would easily recognize:

> [P]rior to all systems of order, within man himself, on the basis of his nature, there are rights. . . . [T]he idea of human rights . . . stands against the absolutism of the state, against the arbitrary will of positive legislation. . . . [I]nherent in being itself there is an ethical and legal claim.[11]

So in using the word "God," as in "under God" or in a reference to the "Creator," the government attains double effectiveness. The believer hears the truth of objective value as religiously supported, while the nonbeliever also hears the claim of objective value but without religious support. It makes no sense for the separationist to assert that "one Nation under God" is unconstitutional while admitting that "one Nation under the Ethical and Legal Claims Inherent in Being Itself" is not unconstitutional. If one is genuinely committed to the higher law position, it makes no sense to surrender religious support for it.

This way of thinking about religious language not only bridges the gap between religious believers and nonbelievers, but it also does the same for religious believers who reject the biblical creator God. As C. S. Lewis assumed, just about every religion testifies that "inherent in being itself there is an ethical and legal claim." Thus this kind of reinterpretation of religious imagery promises genuine community, among disparate believers as well as between believers and nonbelievers, even when a particular religion rejects the biblical understanding of God.

There is nothing in these references to the writings of Pope Benedict that is unique to him. Listen to the words of Martin Luther King Jr. in 1967, for example, also blurring any border between religious and non-religious assertions about objective value in the universe:

> When our days become dreary with low hovering clouds of despair, and when our nights become darker than a thousand midnights, let us remember that there is a creative force in this universe, working to pull down the gigantic mountains of evil, a power that is able to make a way out of no way and transform dark yesterdays into bright tomorrows. Let us realize the arc of the moral universe is long but it bends toward justice.[12]

At this point I must remind the reader of two things. First, although the claim of higher law unites believers of all kinds and many nonbelievers, it does not reflect the views of everyone. As I stated in chapter 5, there are many, perhaps millions of Americans, who vociferously reject the notion that "inherent in being itself there is an ethical and legal claim." Such persons may even assert that the claim is nonsense and the words that make the claim have no meaning. But theirs is not an Establishment Clause objection. It is an objection to a form of secular government speech.

Second, for the religious believer, the assertion of higher law through the rhetoric of God and religious imagery absolutely *is* religious. It does not become secular just because it is asserted by the government. But that reception by the believer should not be considered a criticism of government use of religious language, a point I will return to below. Actually, the believer's view that religious language used by government is religious is another advantage of the use of religious language by the government. For the believer would then share with the nonbeliever, in the words of Teilhard de Chardin, "those aspirations, in essence religious, which make the men and women of today feel so strongly the immensity of the world, the greatness of the mind, and the sacred value of every new truth."[13] The use of religious imagery solidifies the social solidarity between believer and nonbeliever that other approaches to the Establishment Clause threaten to undermine.

But the word "God" does more than strongly reinforce higher law for the religious believer. Even for a nonbeliever, a word like "God" can serve as a stand-in for the concept of the Absolute. Because our culture in the West is Christian in its origin, our secularism also takes the shape of the Christian universe. In other words, even though some of us do not believe in God, we know approximately the kind of God we do not believe in. Thus our nonbelief has a Christian, or at least biblical, valence. When nonbelievers say a nation "under God" they know that this phrase can represent overweening pride—as in the false claim that we are a nation that faithfully obeys God—or can mean a nation subject to judgment for its wrongdoing. And that judgment can reflect the Absolute in history, which many nonbelievers instinctively accept.

It should not be forgotten that John Dewey, a foundational American secular figure, never gave up the use of the word "God," though in his mature thinking he did not believe in the traditional God of monotheism. In *A Common Faith* in 1934 Dewey refers to God as "a unification of ideal values that is essentially imaginative in origin." By "imaginative," Dewey does not mean unreal. He adds, so there is no mistake, "the reality of ideal ends as ideals is vouched for by their undeniable power in action."[14]

Justice O'Connor's reference to confidence in the future is an imitation of Dewey, though a pale imitation. Dewey meant much more than O'Connor did in his justification of religious imagery:

> Those government acknowledgments of religion serve, in the only ways reasonably possible in our culture, the legitimate secular purposes of solemnizing public occasions, expressing confidence in the future, and encouraging the recognition of what is worthy of appreciation in society. For that reason, and because of their history and ubiquity, those practices are not understood as conveying government approval of particular religious beliefs.[15]

Justice Brennan sounded the same thin theme:

> [T]hese references are uniquely suited to serve such wholly secular purposes as solemnizing public occasions, or inspiring commitment to meet some national challenge in a manner that simply could not be fully served in our culture if government were limited to purely nonreligious phrases. The practices by which the

government has long acknowledged religion are therefore probably necessary to serve certain secular functions, and that necessity, coupled with their long history, gives those practices an essentially secular meaning.[16]

There is a reason why religious language is so well suited in our society to the expression of depth. It is in its origin deep language. And it remains deep language for many nonbelievers as well as for the believer. Or, to put it simply, the word "God" always also reflects the assertion of higher law, and many nonbelievers feel this claim to be true even though they also believe that God does not exist.

This acknowledgment of the depth of religious language for both believer and at least some nonbelievers leads to the final reason for government to use religious language on public occasions and events to express higher law principles. The use of religious language provides needed symbolic continuity with our past. As long as this religious language can plausibly refer to an ideal such as the theory of objective value, the fact that some believers imbue the language with even more meaning, and in the past that most people may have regarded the language in the same way, does not matter. It is not a reason to give up such powerful rhetorical resources.

The claim about our religious heritage that comes up in political debate about issues such as the Capitol Visitor Center is cynical because on these political occasions, proponents of religious expression are actually trying to smuggle in current endorsement of biblical religion. And they are doing it for partisan advantage.

Nevertheless, there is in America a religious heritage. Continuity with that heritage and its language serves, as Abraham Lincoln said in his first inaugural, "[t]he mystic chords of memory." As long as it is possible to use religious language in something like its original framework, it should be done. That is the way a nation maintains its unity, both currently and with its past. Naturally, if the use of religious language is unconstitutional, this continuity must be broken. But if, instead, we can reinterpret religious language along secular lines in order to maintain and sustain our political traditions, it is of great benefit to do so.

I have been assuming up to this point that the government is proceeding in good faith when it uses religious imagery to endorse higher law. I have been assuming that although religious believers hear the words "under God" and believe they affirm the biblical God, this is a side benefit for them and was not the government's aim.

There is obviously no reason to assume such good faith by government officials. It might very well be that all references to religion in the public square are in fact motivated by the desire of government officials to endorse religion in general and even Christianity in particular. Without question, that is the motive of at least some government officials. Because I have here expressly abandoned the Lemon purpose test and the endorsement test, a party challenging religious expression in court under my proposal would not be permitted even to raise the question of the government motivation behind the religious words or argue about how the religious language being challenged is understood by reasonable observers. All the party could raise is the weak plausibility test. Am I therefore allowing a sham?

I recommend the plausibility standard, combined with the continued prohibition on the endorsement of religion, in order to force government officials to state officially and formally—that is, publicly—that particular instances of religious symbolism are being utilized for their secular meaning. I don't ask whether such assertions are true in the sense that this was in fact the motive of the government official involved, nor whether the assertions are true in the sense that the religious language is actually being received as an endorsement of secular values.

Why do I propose such a weak standard? When a government official claims plausibly that religious language is being used for a deep secular purpose, such a statement becomes self-authenticating. The religious symbolism, such as "under God," continues to have real religious content; in fact it is used, in part, because that religious content serves to make a secular point in a broader and more inclusive way than could secular language alone. So the language, image, or symbol remains genuinely religious. By forcing government officials to affirm a more universal, nonreligious justification for its use, the Court would be helping to create the broad community of believers and nonbelievers to which the justification refers. Though perhaps untrue immediately, the justification could become true over time. Eventually, traditional religious symbols could actually be understood in meaningful secular terms by both believers and nonbelievers.

A secular justification of a religious symbol keeps religious believers from formally asserting that the religious symbol endorses their beliefs uniquely. Instead the religious believer is forced to find common ground with the nonbeliever, at least in public pronouncements. In turn, the nonbeliever is forced to admit that her commitments are in large part shared by the believing community and that this traditional religious language emphasizes that shared belief. In other words, the government official claims that "under God" refers to universal moral standards, the believer acknowledges that morality can, in fact, be implied by the word "God," and the nonbeliever acknowledges that universal moral standards are being affirmed by both nonbelievers and believers. This is why I assert that this approach promises, or at least aims for, genuine community.

The Establishment Clause limit that remains on government—that the claim of secular meaning must be plausible—defines the outer boundary of government use of religious imagery. It is conceivable, for example, to use a crèche at Christmas-time as a symbol of recurring hope. But, in a context in which only the crèche is used for such purposes during the year, that is not a plausible claim. A judge would conclude that Christmas is being endorsed and that this use of religious imagery is unconstitutional.

My proposal is not all that different from the position taken by Justices O'Connor and Brennan that religious language is capable of expression that secular language, for reasons of history as well as theology, finds difficult to express. The difference between their position and mine is that they never wanted to acknowledge the transformational content that religious language was being used to express. The acknowledgment of the depth of meaning that religious language conveys, and the acceptance of the genuinely religious response to that language by believers, makes all the difference.

The goal at the end of the day is to find common ground where that is possible. Despite the growth of secularism, this is not yet a secular society. Any effort to force religious imagery out of the public square promises political and legal strife for years to come. Any contrary effort to use government to promote religion promises the same. But recognizing that traditional religious language is rich in its connotations and can be understood as promoting very broad claims about reality, including secular claims, might allow a new kind of consensus to emerge. We might come to agree as a nation that much religious expression can be accepted for its secular content, despite its continuing, genuine religious content.

Although there are clearly numerous objections that will be made to this proposal to resolve the crisis in the Establishment Clause, I want to mention in particular four such objections, two from the religious believer's side, one from the secular side, and one general objection.

1. THE HIGHER LAW JUSTIFICATION ROBS RELIGIOUS SYMBOLS OF THEIR RELIGIOUS CONTENT

Justice Scalia's interpretation of the Establishment Clause promises religious believers they may worship God through communal expression organized and sponsored by the government, and this is constitutional. Believers may feel that, although the higher law proposal in this book legitimates some of the same religious expressions that Justice Scalia endorses, it undermines their meaning by requiring an official commitment to secular interpretations of those forms of religious expression.

This criticism is certainly an accurate description of the proposal. The only way the Establishment Clause can allow what is essentially communal monotheistic worship is, as Justice Scalia candidly admits, by the "disregard of polytheists"[17] as well as, of course, the disregard of atheists and other nonbelievers. This callous disregard is not justified by Justice Scalia's appeals to "our Nation's historic practices."[18] America is demographically not what it used to be. It is not as Christian and not even as religious. Those changes must be recognized. By declaring monotheism to be the winner in the culture wars, Justice Scalia is ensuring that those wars of religion will continue forever. America currently has 15 percent of its population as nonbelievers with a small additional portion of polytheists. But those numbers may change. If the Constitution does not aid us in finding common ground among all these groups, we will end up voting for and against God in all future elections. This promises continuing political strife.

Believers should be satisfied that their preferred forms of life will be largely retained under my proposal. For example, if the words "under God" are kept in the Pledge of Allegiance, believers are free to experience devotion to God in reciting the Pledge. And they are free to do this not just as individuals but in group settings. They may not insist, however, that their understanding of God be adopted as the official meaning of such a text. According to my proposal, government need not deny that a religious meaning is present on an official occasion, as long as it may plausibly be asserted that a nonreligious meaning is present as well.

I expect that religious believers will come to the conclusion that secularists who share their commitment to higher law are participants in some sense in the religious traditions, as C. S. Lewis stated. These secular expressions of commitment to the higher law are akin to those described by Teilhard de Chardin, earlier in the chapter. By not insisting that communal expression endorse their religious commitments particularly, believers may come to see that in the long run, they may be bringing secularists back to religion. Whether that occurs or not, at least by ending debate about the use of the word "God," they would be removing a block that currently sets many secularists against God.

2. THE HIGHER LAW JUSTIFICATION ALLOWS GOVERNMENT TO HIJACK RELIGIOUS SYMBOLS

This criticism might be thought of as the mirror image of the former one. Some religious believers find the use of religious symbols, images, and language by government to be harmful to genuine religion and thus greatly offensive. Religious symbols used in this way become "Bleached Faith," as Steven Goldberg describes it in the title of his recent book.[19] Goldberg argues that religious symbols are only "real" when they can be affirmed in their fullness and not as some watered down version acceptable to secularists as well as believers.[20] Justice Brennan made a similar point in his dissent in the Pawtucket crèche case, *Lynch v. Donnelly:*

> the crèche is far from a mere representation of a "particular historic religious event." It is, instead, best understood as a mystical re-creation of an event that lies at the heart of Christian faith. To suggest, as the Court does, that such a symbol is merely "traditional" and therefore no different from Santa's house or reindeer is not only offensive to those for whom the crèche has profound significance, but insulting to those who insist for religious or personal reasons that the story of Christ is in no sense a part of "history" nor an unavoidable element of our national "heritage."[21]

As Steven Shiffrin puts it, "Religion is already damaged by using it for secular purposes."[22]

But this view underestimates the reach of religious symbolism. The Ten Commandments display that helped introduce Professor Cochran to the theory of higher law did not demean or trivialize the biblical account. Nor did the word "Creator" in the Declaration of Independence demean or trivialize God. Some secular meanings of religious language, images, and symbols are truly present, even though they do not exhaust or even really touch the full religious meaning that is also present, which is why Pope Benedict would not object to these secular uses of religious imagery.

This religiously based criticism of government use of religion is understandable, since politicians do like to claim divine approval for themselves and their policies. But applied rigorously to cleanse the public square of all such references, the criticism treats religion and society as separate realms, which they are not. The Bible, for example, presumably has lessons to teach to the most secular among us.

Nor is it true that the proposal in this book allows the government to use religious imagery for narrow, partisan purposes. Any narrow argument using religious language—such as, for example, God opposes global warming—would be an endorsement of one or more particular religions and thus would remain unconstitutional. The God of the Bible might endorse environmental stewardship, and evidence of that could be presented. But what would be the evidence that the God of Truth has such a position? Any such evidence would show that the God of the Bible, and not higher law, is being referred to by the government. That would be unconstitutional.

3. HIGHER LAW EXPRESSED THROUGH RELIGION IS STILL RELIGION

Some secularists are certain to complain that the word "God" is a religious word—or that the Ten Commandments are a religious image—and thus they simply have no business in an official public setting. But this criticism amounts to an ideological objection. To deny that religious symbols can carry deep secular meaning is foolish and represents an unmerited hostility to any hint of religion.

The richness of religious imagery was evident in the story in the introduction. Professor Cochran, not focusing on issues of religion as such, had no trouble understanding the nonreligious, jurisprudential point being made by the Ten Commandments display in the context in which he encountered it. The doctrine of higher law that he associated with the Ten Commandments display is not a religious doctrine. If a religious image can be used to express higher law principles without objection when the nonreligious meaning is very clear, as in the university building, there is no reason why a religious image cannot also be so used when the context is more ambiguous and both religious and nonreligious meanings are present.

Noah Feldman suggested in his book *Divided by God* that the minority religious observer, and perhaps by extension the nonbeliever, makes an "interpretive choice" whether to feel like an outsider when confronted by majority religious symbols in the public square.[23] That view seems unduly harsh and more than a little unrealistic. But in the context of a government commitment to higher law, in which the higher law secularist is being invited to participate in a commitment that she actually shares—the commitment to higher law—the decision to object to the use of a religious symbol does seem to be an interpretive choice. The only fair secular objection in such a context would be that a nonreligious interpretation of a particular religious symbol is impossible. In that instance the higher law justification would not be plausible, and there would in fact be a constitutional violation.

Other than that situation, the secularist is only objecting that although she can view the religious image in secular terms, religious believers see and hear something quite different, something genuinely religious. That does not seem to be a fair objection.

Admittedly, the secularist may feel she is simply presenting the other side of the criticism religious believers have often made against ceremonial deism. Some of the justices have said that certain uses of religious imagery have lost their religious authenticity through repetition in the public square. The believer who finds this same religious image quite authentic is offended at being told in effect she is wrong. Now, under my higher law proposal, the secularist is being told she should accept the proposition that plainly religious words have a nonreligious meaning. Why shouldn't the secularist be offended by that?

I am not denying the obviously religious meaning of religious language, images, and symbols in the public square. The higher law justification merely asserts that secular meanings are also present. When we say, for example, "one Nation under God," we are saying many things. That richness of meaning should satisfy secularists that religion is not being established.

Clearly it will not satisfy all secularists. Despite my hope for finding common ground, ill will may continue. The problem is the usual one in law: that we look for winners and losers. It will be a difficult change for the religious and nonreligious "sides" to admit that a kind of compromise between them is possible. Nevertheless, a meaningful compromise is possible.

4. THE HIGHER LAW JUSTIFICATION IS UNNECESSARY

Although there has been no convincing explanation as to why, Establishment Clause case law is obviously moving in the direction of allowing most of what my use of the government speech doctrine would permit the government to do. At least passive nonsectarian government religious expression is probably now going to be upheld by the Supreme Court as constitutional, even without a change in doctrine. So why bother with an elaborate justification of something that is already settled? Granted, Establishment Clause doctrine is incoherent, but why not just ignore that?

As the reader has already seen, there are many reasons why the Establishment Clause crisis is worth resolving. For one thing, the current movement on the Court toward a kind of consensus could change. What is settled could easily be unsettled, especially since no convincing explanation of the outcomes has been offered.

More important than this desire to forestall future disagreements on the Court is the need for a constitutional interpretation of the Establishment Clause that will win popular acceptance. Religious believers will not insist on the primacy of their religious commitments in the public square if they are given an interpretation of the Establishment Clause that does not endorse a fully separate secular state. I think religious believers will understand and accept higher law justifications for religious symbols in the public square and will be willing to abandon more grandiose religious claims, such as the claim that this is a Christian nation.

As for secularists, there is an even greater need for acceptance of the higher law justification. As the example of Steven Gey in chapter 5 shows, secularism in America has been drawn unthinkingly toward relativism. Part of the reflexive opposition to all things religious has included opposition to the theory of objective value. This unthinking relativism has been attacked by Austin Dacey, in his book *The Secular Conscience: Why Belief Belongs in Public Life.*[24] I have elsewhere also written about the need for a new kind of secularism as America grows more secular.[25] I will return to this theme in part 3 of this book.

What would adoption of my higher law proposal actually accomplish? In the short-run, I hope it would solve the Establishment Clause crisis by presenting the American people with a constitutional vision of the appropriate role of religious imagery in the public square around which a consensus could build. I would like to see the heat reduced in at least this one area of the culture wars.

In addition, I would like to see the competing, and in my view divisive, visions of the public square undermined and delegitimized. America is not now, if it ever was, a Christian nation, nor should any official, public effort be made to change that. I believe that most Christians share that commitment, that they wish Christianity to remain an important part of the weave of America, but not more than that. The attraction of something like Christian nationalist ideology stems in part from the absence of a constitutional vision in which religious imagery retains anything of its historic role. Once a constitutional interpretation is promulgated that is more embracing of religious imagery, it is my hope that more extreme religious formulations will be cast aside.

Nor is America a secular nation, if by that we mean one in which religion is to play no public role. It is my hope that secularists will eventually give up the effort to purge the public square of religious imagery. I believe they seek to do this now out of a mistaken constitutional understanding. If a better constitutional option were available, perhaps secularists could be convinced to abandon their effort.

One definite advantage of my proposal is that it would allow public embrace of the Declaration of Independence. Indeed, that document, our genuine founding document, would be able to occupy the paramount place in our national creed to which, by its content and history, it is entitled. Currently the use of religious imagery in the Declaration of Independence casts some cloud over its use. That is why Justice Black thought to refer to it as merely a historical or patriotic document. The Declaration of Independence can be unreservedly accepted only when its religious imagery can be unreservedly embraced.

Beyond these various short-run effects, I hope that acceptance of the higher law proposal will lead to a different kind of future for America. Although sociological experts disagree among themselves, the current growth of secularism in America may well continue. Eventually, by the end of the twenty-first century perhaps, America might see a secular majority. Unless current trends change, that majority could be quite hostile to religion. As such a majority grew toward political control, there might be increased political struggle over the use by the government of religious images, symbols, and language. One might well see express political campaigns during this coming century to rewrite the national motto and the Pledge of Allegiance. That would be a bleak future.

But under the higher law proposal, a very different future could unfold. Under that scenario, long before any such powerful political changes took place, the government would already have been reinterpreting religious imagery along secular lines. For years the government would have been proclaiming that higher law theory was being promoted by words like "under God" in the Pledge of Allegiance. Secularists would have gotten used to this explanation and religious believers would also have embraced it. Thus, when the day finally arrived that a newly emergent secular majority would finally have the votes to rewrite the Pledge of Allegiance, that same majority might find that it had no need to do so. What had begun, perhaps, as constitutional aspiration would have become constitutional reality. At least, that is my hope.

SEVEN

Applying Higher Law in Church/State Issues

Up to this point, I have treated the Establishment Clause as if symbolic government expressions, such as the Pledge of Allegiance, the national motto, and displays of the Ten Commandments, were the only issues that appear. But such cases are only a part of the history of litigation under the religion clauses of the Constitution. What about the rest of the legal issues that have arisen?

I proceeded in this way because all these other issues depend on the answer to a foundational question: religiously speaking, who are we as a people? As we saw in the introduction, Ronald Dworkin wrote that we have to decide whether we are a religious people tolerating nonbelief or a secular people tolerating religion. He was right that we must decide who we are before we can think intelligently about church/state issues. Once we come to a basic understanding, everything else will fall properly into place. In contrast, our current failure to do this is why an Establishment Clause crisis exists.

Fortunately there is a third possibility beyond the two choices offered by Dworkin. We are neither a religious people nor a secular people. We are instead a mix of believers and nonbelievers. We are also a mix of different kinds of beliefs, some of which are indistinguishable from nonbelief.

The false dualism between belief and nonbelief is keeping America from coming to a consensus about religion in the public square. It is keeping us from resolving deep matters of national identity, such as the

Pledge of Allegiance, that any healthy polity must be able to clarify. All nations must be able to say who they are, even if the claims are not universally acceptable.

Since church and state is a constitutional question, it is not unreasonable to expect the justices of the Supreme Court to help us resolve it. But instead of helping us clarify who we are, the Court currently seems determined to avoid Dworkin's fundamental challenge of identity. The justices seem unable either to choose between the alternatives Dworkin has presented or to go beyond his dualism to a more inclusive constitutional vision.

In lieu of genuine judicial statesmanship, the justices have refused to say anything definitive about the Establishment Clause. The justices found a lack of standing in *Elk Grove* and have not heard another Pledge of Allegiance case since. They split evenly in the two Ten Commandments cases. And they decided another Ten Commandments case—*Pleasant Grove*—by putting off the Establishment Clause issue through a refusal to ask the government to state plainly the meaning of its speech. And recently, in *Buono*, the justices decided a very narrow issue without adding any clarity to Establishment Clause analysis.

Some would disagree with this criticism and say this is judicial statesmanship. Years ago, Alexander Bickel wrote of the "passive virtues" in which the Supreme Court avoids cases it is best not to decide.[1] But we can now see the flaws in Bickel's approach. Perhaps we would have been better off if the Supreme Court had held in 1947 in *Everson* that the Establishment Clause only means that there is no one national religion and it has nothing to do with separation of church and state as such. That, however, would not have been avoiding the issue. It would have defined a Constitution that left the matter of church and state to political adjustment. Under this constitutional regime, in the years since 1947, we might have come to a national consensus about the place of religion in the public square.

Instead the Court gave us a very specific constitutional vision. The Court unanimously promised that the government would be neutral toward religion. No one should blame the ACLU and others for attempting to redeem that promise. Having given that promise, the Court cannot now walk away from church/state issues. If the justices avoid the issue of church and state now, they are leaving the American people in a morass that the justices created. It is too late for avoidance tactics like denials of standing.

Of course, my higher law proposal may not turn out to be helpful. It may be that the justices will end up endorsing Justice Scalia's official national monotheism. Or they may finally insist on genuine government neutrality. Or they may find some other way out, some description of God and religious symbols that is more satisfying than ceremonial deism. I don't know what the future will hold. I only know that the law's proper purpose is to bring reconciliation. Reconciliation must be the ultimate test of jurisprudence in this field as in any other field of law.

That is why, as important as are the other, more specific religion issues, they cannot be approached on their own. They can only be decided from within an overall context of who we are as a people.

So let us now look at a few of the implications of the higher law proposal as one possible constitutional future. If my attempt to retain government neutrality toward religion within a context of shared meaning were to become the Court's dominant overall interpretation of the Establishment Clause, what effect would that have on religion issues in general?

I won't bother here to note the many ways in which my proposal does not change the current law at all. For example, the government now sometimes grants to religion an exemption from generally applicable laws, as in the permitted use of wine during Prohibition. Since establishment of higher law is not religion, even when it uses religious imagery, the proposal has little to say about accommodation as such. Certainly accommodation of religion would not be restricted.

1. RELIGION IN THE PUBLIC SCHOOLS: DARWIN, THE BIBLE, THE TEN COMMANDMENTS, AND PRAYER

Many of the heated controversies that arise in the realm of church and state involve activities in the public schools. Of these, probably the most contentious issue is the teaching of evolution. The standard account by those who most favor separation of church and state is that people who oppose teaching evolution in the public schools object to it because evolutionary theory conflicts with the account of creation in Genesis. Thus efforts by parents and school board members to undermine evolutionary theory by pointing to gaps in the theory and by promoting alternative explanations for the origin and development of life are said to represent obviously unconstitutional establishments, or attempted establishments, of Christianity in particular and biblical religion in general. These alternatives to evolution used to be called creation science and now are referred to as intelligent design. But nothing important has changed with the change in terminology.

This standard model was the view of the Supreme Court in *Epperson v. Arkansas* in 1968,[2] in which the Court struck down an anti-evolution statute and *Edwards v. Aguillard* in 1987,[3] in which the Court struck down a balanced teaching statute that required the teaching of creation science along with any teaching of evolutionary theory. In both cases, a majority of the justices held that the state was attempting to protect and promote a particular religious doctrine—meaning some form of creation consistent with the Bible.

There is certainly some truth in the standard account of the struggle over evolution. In the Dover case that I discussed in chapter 1, Judge Jones cited numerous references to Christianity by board members and others who supported the disclaimer that was read to students in biology class. It was thus easy for Judge Jones to discount contradictory evidence that the concerns of the board were only to combat possible inaccuracies in evolutionary theory and a desire to expose students to a fuller and less biased account of the development of life. Judge Jones found that some witnesses for the school district had lied under oath and were not credible.

Of course, under the higher law approach proposed in this book, the government cannot teach school children that the Bible is true. Such an effort would not only be the establishment of religion, but an establishment of a particular religion—perhaps Christianity, probably Judeo-Christian belief, or, most inclusively, monotheism. But is the evolution controversy that simple?

The standard model assumes that evolutionary theory is religiously neutral and is not an attack on religion. That is not necessarily the case. Evolutionary theory is potentially more religiously threatening than Judge Jones, or others who criticize opponents of evolution, are willing to acknowledge. For one thing, as argued by Philip Kitcher in *Living with Darwin*,[4] evolution can be viewed as so messy and brutal that it could not possibly be the chosen technique of any God we might consider worshiping. For another, evolution is taught as a random process, not a directed one. If a random process created us, there could not have been a plan. As the Bible understands God, if there is no divine plan, there is no God. So, if evolution is true, God may well not exist. That is not a religiously neutral comportment.

Yet one might say, so what? It is not any school board's business whether students believe in a creator God. The promotion of belief in the biblical God would be an unconstitutional establishment of religion. If public school boards undermine evolutionary theory in order to make the world safe for the Bible, they violate the Constitution, just as the separationists maintain.

But evolutionary theory does not just have implications about a personal creator God. Judge Jones's opinion recounted the goals of a think tank that promotes intelligent design—the Discovery Institute—as "defeat[ing] scientific materialism and its destructive moral, cultural and political legacies" and "replac[ing] materialistic explanations with the theistic understanding that nature and human beings are created by God."[5]

Many people, not just opponents of evolution, agree that evolution implies scientific materialism. The journalist and author Robert Wright recently reported in an interview in the *New York Times Magazine* that he began to doubt his Baptist upbringing in his sophomore year in high school when he encountered evolutionary theory.[6] Nor is Wright's reported skeptical response either eccentric or merely a reaction against his parents' creationist religious commitment. Here is what Richard Dawkins, perhaps the best scientist among the New Atheist writers, said about evolution in 1995: "The universe we observe has precisely the properties we should expect if there is, at bottom, no design, no purpose, no evil and no good, nothing but blind pitiless indifference."[7]

According to Dawkins, it is not just God that goes out the evolutionary window, but "evil" and "good." This is an attack, and understood to be an attack, on the objectivity of values—an attack, in other words on higher law.

I am not suggesting that Dawkins's view of evolution is the only one possible. But it is not an idiosyncratic view among scientists either. In September 2008, the American physicist Steven Weinberg wrote in the

New York Review of Books about "the question of how it will be possible to live without God."[8] He admitted that living without God is not easy. He offered humor and the ordinary pleasures of life as compensations. But Weinberg acknowledged that "the worldview of science is rather chilling."

> Not only do we not find any point to life laid out for us in nature, no objective basis for our moral principles, no correspondence between what we think is the moral law and the laws of nature, of the sort imagined by philosophers from Anaximander and Plato to Emerson. We even learn that the emotions that we most treasure, our love for our wives and husbands and children, are made possible by chemical processes in our brains that are what they are as a result of natural selection acting on chance mutations over millions of years. And yet we must not sink into nihilism or stifle our emotions. At our best we live on a knife-edge, between wishful thinking on one hand and, on the other, despair.

I could give other examples of evolution-influenced reductionism of this kind. Certainly Dawkins's understanding of what evolution implies is an impression that a ninth grader could form in biology class.

That possibility—the demoralization of the ninth grader—is what is really behind the controversy in America over teaching evolution in the schools. It is a disagreement between atheists and religious believers over the ground of existence. For most religious believers, that fight is not about facts—although admittedly some mistakenly argue the facts of evolution—but about meaning. There are scientists who subtly, and, as we see, not so subtly, use the facts of evolution to assert not only that there is no God as understood in the Bible, but that the process of evolution—that is, life itself—has no meaning.

This is what is bothering most of the people who oppose evolution, whether they put it this way or not. For most opponents, evolution is not a problem because they want the literal truth of Genesis taught in school or don't believe an eye could come together naturally. The dispute is about whether the universe is mere mechanism. And, of course, the objectivity of values, the higher law, assumes that there is more to reality than mechanism.

The conclusion that life has no meaning is, of course, not science. The facts of evolutionary history show that over time and in a general way, the universe selected for beings with an increasing capacity for gratitude, for reverence, and for expanding the circle of empathy. And, as the work of Frans de Waal, and others, suggests, these moral traits did not pop up in humans but began to evolve in animals that are close to us on the evolutionary tree.[9] Why would that be? What kind of a universe selects for morality in such a comprehensive way? I would answer, one grounded in meaning.

I don't have any doubt about the facts of evolutionary theory, but I would not have wanted my children to conclude from biology class that life has no meaning. Since the presentation of evolutionary theory in school invariably emphasizes its randomness, biology class is likely to carry a hidden message of meaninglessness. That message is no more scientific than its opposite, but it tends to be there all the same. When I hear scientists frustrated over opposition to the teaching of Darwin, I wonder at their inability to appreciate what seems to be at stake for many parents.

I have a suggestion for a new disclaimer for biology class, which, unlike the disclaimer in the Dover case, could be viewed as constitutional even today and might reassure some of these parents. My disclaimer would begin as follows:

> Some people believe that evolution is a random process. Others believe that it is directed by God. Biology class is the place for you to see how evolution works. This class is not the place to judge whether evolution serves any larger purpose.

But I would like to go further. Schools should take a stand on the side of meaning. That is what it means to establish higher law. So I would like to add the following in a statement to biology students:

> Evolution is a messy process, with many dead-ends. But, in the end, evolution has produced beings with ever more curiosity and capacity for gratitude; ever more caring and capacity for self-sacrifice; ever more interiority and capacity for expanding the circle of empathy. You should reflect on that reality.

An introductory statement like this one might dilute the opposition to Darwin. And it would not be an establishment of religion. It would contribute to the establishment of higher law.

To come up with a statement like this one, however, school boards would have to be given the right to care whether their students become nihilists. Obviously, school board members care about this now, though they may feel they have to deny it. The fear of litigation based on the doctrine of religious neutrality sometimes turns school board members into liars. It would be far better to face the potential implications of evolutionary theory straightforwardly. To do that, we must allow government to establish, or try to establish, the objectivity of values.

Beyond simple disclaimers, a school board that is permitted openly to consider the demoralization that can come from relativism among students, and is permitted to promote alternative views of reality, might well encourage students to study new and broader understandings of science. I am referring in particular to new views of biology and evolution that are now being publicized by thinkers like Simon Conway Morris in *Life's Solution*[10] and Stuart Kauffman in *Reinventing the Sacred*.[11] I will return to these authors and related secular thought, in part 3 of this book.

This brings us to other aspects of religion in the public schools. For example, it is obvious that the Supreme Court was correct in *Schempp*[12] in holding that Bible reading in the public schools is a violation of the Establishment Clause. The Bible is a book of revelation. Reading only from it is obviously an endorsement of that revelation as uniquely reliable and true. So such reading is an endorsement of either Judaism or Christianity.

Probably most people now agree with the *Schempp* decision, which is always the best standard by which to evaluate a Supreme Court opinion—its acceptance by the people over time. Even those who wish to return prayer to the schools rarely mention reviving daily Bible reading there.

But something important was also lost when we stopped reading the Bible in school. The point of Bible reading was for students to hear something every day that could potentially be inspiring—some reading that might change a student's life. So something should be substituted for unconstitutional Bible reading.

That something could be a kind of "great thoughts" series of readings presented to all students. If government were free to establish the objectivity of values, the school board could select readings from all the religious traditions of humankind, as well as from secular sources, and have them read in school-wide assemblies as the great teachings in human history. In this way, students could be exposed to human wisdom from a variety of sources. It would not be necessary, if my higher law proposal were accepted, to purge these readings of their religious content.

The secular thought that the school board chooses would not have to include religion bashing, any more than it need include relativism, nihilism, or materialism. The readings would be presented as something along the lines of "great human thought on the good life" or "the purpose of life." The school board absolutely would make value judgments about the kinds of thought they wanted students to hear. As long as no particular religion was endorsed, and as long as organized religion itself was not endorsed, this would be constitutional. Indeed, without exposure like this, it is not clear that genuine education is even possible. Education properly understood is about learning from our history of collective human wisdom.

The Supreme Court was also right, and for similar reasons, to hold in *Stone v. Graham* in 1980[13] that the placement of the Ten Commandments in every classroom was a violation of the Establishment Clause. As I have argued in this book, Ten Commandments displays belong outside our courthouses and law schools. This makes sense because the Ten Commandments tell us something, or at least can be understood to tell us something, about the nature and meaning of secular law. Therefore, despite the opening statement of the Ten Commandments—"I am the Lord your God"—such a display is not an endorsement of Judaism or the biblical tradition. But in the setting of the public school classroom, such a display could only be taken to be an endorsement of the biblical God, which is what government is not permitted to do.

This leaves us with the various manifestations of prayer in the public schools, as the last important issue in terms of religion in the schools. The first question is, was the Supreme Court correct in ruling in *Engel v. Vitale* in 1962 that prayer in the public schools is unconstitutional? Even given my proposal for a greater openness to religion, the decision in *Engel* was probably the right one. Explicit public references to God always raise the possibility that the government is endorsing the Bible. That potentially unconstitutional endorsement is mitigated in the case of the Pledge of Allegiance for a number of reasons. For one thing, the word

"God" can have a broader meaning than just the monotheistic account in the Bible. For another, the Pledge of Allegiance is a political rather than a religious formulation.

But in *Engel,* the Court was dealing with a real prayer to God, although a banal one, as I suggested in chapter 1. This prayer had been written by the government and so it obviously represented the official line to impressionable school students. The prayer addressed "Almighty God," not just God, and it "beg[ged]" blessings from Almighty God in an attitude of submission, acknowledging "dependence upon" this God.

All of this is much more involved, much more detailed, and is presented in a much different context from the simple reference to God in the Pledge of Allegiance, even though the Pledge is also recited in public school every day. Such a prayer might be unconstitutional while the Pledge is not.

I don't mean to suggest that daily prayer in the public schools is necessarily unconstitutional. I can imagine a prayer more generic than the one in *Engel.* Indeed, I can imagine a prayer that gives thanks for parents and teachers and country without mentioning God at all. Such a prayer would certainly be constitutional. In that context, perhaps communal prayer could be returned to public schools.

The question is whether such a prayer would be worth it. There are people who regard *Engel* as wrongly decided and wish to reverse that decision. But I think they are a minority. Most Americans probably think that prayer in the public schools is a matter that is settled and not worth reopening. Yet even the people who want to reverse *Engel* would not be content with a prayer sufficiently "bleached" to satisfy the Establishment Clause, either as previously interpreted, or as I have proposed interpreting it. I have a feeling that daily prayer is probably not going to return to the public schools except as something akin to moments of silence.

Another context in which the Supreme Court has addressed prayer in the schools is prayer on special occasions. The two most important such cases are *Lee v. Weisman,*[14] which, in 1992 declared high school graduation prayers unconstitutional, and *Santa Fe Independent School District v. Doe,*[15] which in 2000 held unconstitutional a school-district-authorized election of a student to deliver a sanctioned invocation at varsity football games.

Most of the majority opinions in these cases discussed peripheral matters. In *Lee,* Justice Anthony Kennedy's majority opinion concentrated on whether coercion was present in the context of a high school graduation ceremony. In *Santa Fe,* Justice Stevens's majority opinion refuted the argument that the speech involved was the private speech of the student and therefore could not be attributed to the school district.

These arguments are beside the point. The determining question is whether there was in either case an establishment, or an attempted establishment, of religion in violation of the Constitution. If there was not, the coercion and private speech issues do not arise.

The high school graduation prayer in *Lee* was nonsectarian and did not even refer to the God of the Bible in any obvious way. The rabbi's term for the deity was "God of the Free, Hope of the Brave." The outcome in *Lee* would probably be reversed under my proposal. I can only say "probably" because, unlike legislative prayers that go on all the time, a high school graduation is a one-time event. Therefore, high school graduation prayer would have to be nonsectarian in order to be plausibly endorsing higher law. Alternatively, the school board might host a variety of prayer traditions, but then clearly someone on the list would have to be altogether nonreligious in the traditional sense and minority religions would probably also have to be represented.

The issue in *Lee* should not be thought of as whether something was said that any member of the audience disagreed with or found offensive; that obviously could be true in any talk by any speaker at any public event and is a hallmark of all government speech. The question should be whether the prayers in *Lee* were an establishment of a religion.

The question to put directly to Justice Kennedy's opinion in *Lee* is why the government cannot assert the "conviction that there is an ethic and a morality which transcend human invention"?[16] That assertion is the higher law tradition. Was he not aware that the Declaration of Independence asserts that very conviction? Is it just the religious form that invalidates the assertion? Surely the head of the school board could start the graduation ceremony with a simple statement: America stands for the proposition that there is a morality that is not a human invention. This is indeed the power of the higher law position. And it is a fully American creed.

Justice Stevens in *Santa Fe* was mostly concerned to show that the government was responsible for the content of the student's invocation. This is true but again does not change the standard for determining whether there is a violation of the Establishment Clause.

Once it is determined that the school board is responsible for the prayers that will be offered by students at football games, Justice Stevens's Establishment Clause objection in *Santa Fe* is the same as the one in *Jaffree:* the school board was endorsing prayer. That is why a facial challenge was permitted—the unconstitutional endorsement occurred once the school board attempted to bring prayer to football games. It is the positive attitude of the school board toward prayer that is unconstitutional, according to Justice Stevens.

Prayer would be a favored activity under my proposal, since the spiritual depth that it promotes goes beyond any one religious tradition. It is indeed possible to think of prayer as not necessarily religious at all, as in certain forms of meditation. The government speech approach recommended here allows government to be concerned about the spiritual condition of citizens, including school students.

This is a stark reminder of the difference between simple government neutrality toward religion—more or less the current official constitutional doctrine—and a modified form of such neutrality within the context of government endorsement of higher law, which I am proposing. In both *Jaffree* and *Santa Fe,* Justice Stevens's opinions have the effect of forcing government officials to act as if they are indifferent not only to whether public school students are religious or not religious, but to whether they are nihilists or not nihilists. No adult ought to be indifferent to that.

It would be a poor school board that did not care about the values of their students, understood in a broad sense. The board should be indifferent as to whether students are Jews or Buddhists. The board should be indifferent as to whether students belong to any organized religion, or whether students call themselves atheists or not. But no school board should be indifferent as to the moral implications of these choices. The atheist student may mean only that no supernatural being exists. To this student the board should have no reply. But if the atheist student believes that life is without meaning, that justice does not exist, and that there is no truth, the school board had better say, "You have the right to believe those things, but our curriculum and all our school practices make it clear that we do not agree with you." Justices Kennedy and Stevens are throwing into question the right of the school board to say this.

Granted, sporadic formal prayer at public events is not an effective way to transmit this message to students. I would like to see the public schools address the issue of meaning directly with required courses in what would once have been called comparative religion but should now be given a broader title, such as comparative wisdom. The schools should face up to the cultural threat of nihilism directly and expressly. Such a class would also be the ideal context to take up the question, in the words of Ted Peters and Martin Hewlett in the title of their book: *Can You Believe in God and Evolution?*[17] My impression is that school boards now avoid anything like this because it could be seen as partaking of religion.

This proposal is not the same as welcoming particular religions into the public schools to teach their doctrines to students. As we saw in chapter 1, in 1948, near the beginning of the era of required government religious neutrality, the Supreme Court banned teachers from holding religion classes in the public schools at a time when the children would otherwise be in school.[18] This was too close to having the government conducting the religious instruction. The Court held a few years later that a program that simply allowed students to leave school early in order to go to religion classes was permissible.[19]

No doubt the Court got the relationship of government and churches right in these cases. The reader should notice something else, though. With certain exceptions, institutional religion does not have this kind of community-wide power anymore. Already, since just the late 1940s, a palpable decline in religious affiliation is in evidence. In most places, released time issues today would concern piano and soccer practice and privately procured enrichment programs. This decline in religious institutions will accelerate. Secularists must begin to think of a world largely without religion and should no longer make judgments in reaction to the perspectives of all-powerful religious institutions that dominate the culture. By "fighting the last war," in effect, secularists are ignoring the new and more insidious threats of materialism, relativism, and nihilism to cultural health.

Prayer in public school is a difficult issue because children are susceptible to suggestion and peer pressure to actually be religious. Prayer
in public does not present such difficulty. While this book was being
finished, a federal judge found the National Day of Prayer to be an unconstitutional establishment of religion.[20] This decision will surely be
reversed, but in a sense it is a fair reading of the government neutrality
position. Under the higher law proposal offered here, the decision is
clearly wrong. Prayer is a practice shared by almost all religions. But it is
also easily understood in secular terms as deep self-reflection, including
radical self-criticism and confession. Because of this rich, shared meaning, the government may promote prayer.

2. FAITH-BASED SOCIAL SERVICE PROVIDERS

Another area of controversy, and this was especially so under the administration of President George W. Bush, is the use of faith-based providers
to deliver public services. Two questions have arisen in this context.
First, is it appropriate to use religious groups at all to provide government
services? Second, if it is appropriate to use such groups, may religious
providers of public services discriminate in favor of their co-religionists
in hiring staff?

The answer to the first question follows from the general approach
that government may benefit religious institutions when it is pursuing
secular goals. If a faith-based group, such as the YMCA,[21] is effective
in providing a particular service, such as smoking-cessation programs,
the government may use it and fund it. This conclusion assumes the
government goal in a particular program is secular and not religious.
Conversely, the government obviously may not use religious groups to
encourage people to go to church, for example. But the government may
certainly use religious groups to provide social welfare programs.

The constitutionality of government funding also assumes that
the religious groups in question deliver their services to all clients who
would benefit from the social service. There would be no secular reason for the government to limit the benefits it is paying for to members
of a particular religion. Current law makes this principle explicit, and
no religious organization is trying to get it changed to limit services to

members of its own religious group. Everyone is eligible for services from faith-based groups that receive government funds.

The more difficult question is not whether faith-based groups may be used by the government to deliver social services, but whether using religion itself in providing the service in question is permitted. When a client enters a typical YMCA, the client is likely to be confronted with passive references to the Christian tradition. In my own YMCA branch on the north side of Pittsburgh, there is a big sign referring to the Gospel of John, 17:21. If a client were intrigued by the reference, he or she might look it up and read the following: "that they may all be one; even as thou, Father, art in me, and I in thee, that they also may be in us, so that the world may believe that thou hath sent me."[22]

Theoretically, offering public services in a religious setting may cause some clients to convert to the religion of that group. The drug addict who reads the Gospel of John, for example, may become a Christian. Nor would this possible outcome be ameliorated by cleansing the premises of the faith-based group of all passive religious symbols. The addict who comes into the YMCA and is impressed with the commitment and compassion of the staff is going to know their commitment comes from their faith in Jesus Christ. Some clients are going to want to emulate that religious stance. Because this result is unavoidable (foreseeable, though not intended, by the government), it is still constitutional for government to use the faith-based group.

Then there is the further question of the more active use of religious instruction by the faith-based provider. The religious provider of addiction services, for example, may believe that the ultimate cause of addiction is spiritual rootlessness. The only way to break addiction, then, would be to recognize the power of God or, more specifically, to accept Jesus Christ as Lord and Savior. Under the principle that government may not establish religion, would public funding of this expressly religious approach to public services be constitutional?

Analysis of these issues is not easy, neither from the point of view of the current law of church and state nor from the perspective of my alternative approach. One problem in terms of challenging these programs in the federal courts is the decision in 2007 in *Hein v. Freedom From Religion Foundation, Inc.*[23] that taxpayers lack standing to challenge the executive orders that operationalized President Bush's Faith Based Initiative. Because of a lack of plaintiffs with standing, the constitutionality of faith-based provider programs may never be tested, or may create unusual challenges, such as those by competing service providers where available.

Another matter complicating analysis of these issues is the religious liberty of the potential clients. Whether the religious content of the faith-based provider is being presented more passively or actively, the potential client certainly should not have to choose between obtaining services to which he has a right as a citizen and the exercise of his undoubted constitutional right not to be forced into contact with religious symbols.

This concern is greater in the case of a client of faith-based providers of government services than is the case, for example, with having public voting in a church along with many other venues. In a faith-based service provider context, the client is indeed participating in the group's activities, whereas in voting, the voter is merely using a space owned by the religious institution. The activity of voting is itself entirely secular.

I assume that, whatever the answer to the question of the use of religion by service providers turns out to be, the government must provide reasonable access to nonreligious alternative service providers to those clients who want them. The permissibility of government establishment of religion in general should not be understood as permission to force people into unwanted contact with religion, organized or otherwise.

This principle of alternative service provision may be an insurmountable practical limit on the use of faith-based service providers. For one thing, a dissatisfied client presents a much more compelling case for standing to challenge the constitutionality of the use of religion by the service provider. For another, there is only so much money available for all these social services. Any kind of constitutionally required duplication might lead to intolerable inefficiency.

Assuming, however, that the problem of alternative providers can be solved, there is still the question of whether the use of religion by faith-based providers violates the Establishment Clause in and of itself, without regard to the unwilling client. As to passive religious symbols, the answer should be that by themselves they do not violate the Establishment Clause. If the publicly funded program does not actually use religion in the delivery of its services, these passive symbols amount merely to self-identification by the service provider with a church. Excluding such identification would effectively exclude faith-based providers altogether. Government funding in this context amounts only to implying that the government thinks that this religious group delivers the public service well. It does not imply endorsement by the government of the religion in question.

The situation changes, though, when a faith-based provider uses government funds to promote conversion, even though the ostensible purpose of the conversion is, for example, to break the power of addiction. That is what happens when a service provider explains to a client that the client needs God's help to break the addiction. Here the government funding seems to imply that the religious message of the group is actually true, or at least is effective. It seems to me that this cannot be constitutional.

If one were to call effectiveness of the program in question a "neutral" principle, it might be argued that the religious content of the service being provided by the religious group is irrelevant. Any effective service provider can apply for government funding. But if this rationale were actually accepted, government could seek directly to turn all children into Christians on the ground that they would then be better citizens because Christians are better citizens. There must be some limit on the use of religious means by the government as well as religious ends.

I conclude from all this that the government may fund faith-based providers but may not allow them to use government funds for even indirect religious indoctrination. It is not clear, however, the extent to which such indoctrination is going on now or the extent to which current federal and state regulations bar such direct use of religion to provide services.

Next we confront the second question raised at the beginning of this section. Assuming that the government may use faith-based providers of social services, should those same providers be permitted to hire only members of the group's own religious faith to provide the service in question? When Congress was considering legislation in this area, this matter was referred to by critics as federally subsidized employment discrimination.

Would it be a fair compromise if the government offered faith-based providers the following proposition—you can be eligible for federal funding, but only if you agree that you will not discriminate in your hiring practices? After all, it is already understood that such providers cannot discriminate among clients based on the religion of the client. So why not extend the practice of nondiscrimination to the hiring of the staff that provides the service?

It is not hard to understand the thinking that goes into a proposal like this. In attempting to procure public funding, faith-based providers are arguing that their services are just as good, and thus in essence of the same kind, as the services that nonreligious providers give. Faith-based providers claim that their outcomes will be just as effective in the sense that in dollars per client, they will treat more clients more successfully, or at least as successfully.

But if faith-based providers want to argue they are the same as nonreligious providers, then why should they not be subject to the same standards of nondiscrimination? Nonreligious providers cannot discriminate on the basis of religion when they hire staff, so why should faith-based providers be exempt from this requirement?

The argument that faith-based providers should not be allowed to have it both ways is not based on an allegation of unfair competition. If faith-based providers did not have to pay the minimum wage, for example, such providers would have an unfair competitive edge when it came to comparing cost effectiveness. The argument about nondiscrimination in employment is not based on that kind of objection, but on a notion of equal treatment. If faith-based providers are different because they are religious, then perhaps they should not be required to hire in a nondiscriminatory way. But if they are different because they are religious, perhaps they should not be applying for public funding in the first place.

This is an appealing argument. But it is ultimately unpersuasive because it does not fully take into account the nature of religious social service work. It fails to understand why religious organizations provide social services in the first place.

To explain this, let's start with two propositions that are apparently not very controversial. The first is that faith-based providers that do not accept public funding should be allowed to hire only members of their own religious denominations. The second is that faith-based providers that do accept public funding should not be permitted to serve only members of their own denominations. Admittedly, not all people accept these two propositions. Some critics of faith-based providers no doubt believe that even if such providers reject public funding, but still charge something for their services, they should not be permitted to discriminate in hiring. But many people intuitively do assent to these two propositions.

Both of these propositions imply that religiously provided services in all social welfare fields is a matter of religious witness to the truth of that particular religion's message. So, for example, a Christian group that helps addicts recover from addiction is testifying to the power of Christ to change lives. That does not necessarily mean that the addict must accept Christ to break the addiction, which as we saw earlier raises constitutional questions in terms of public funding. The power of Christ can simply mean that the Christian community defines itself as the agent of Christ in changing lives. The Christian faith-based provider is Christ's representative. And something similar would be the case with service providers in other religious traditions.

This explains why the faith-based provider does not object that services must be given to people who are not members of the faith. The faith-based provider is not attempting simply to provide services. If it were, it might prefer to keep these services among its own religious group. Instead, the provider is giving testimony to the power of Christ to intervene in the world and to require of Christians a certain kind of generosity toward others. Obviously, then, these non-Christian clients could potentially aid in presenting these messages to the non-Christian world. When the non-Christian world sees the power of Christ to change the lives of addicts through the actions of the followers of Christ, that world begins to understand better who Christ is.

The foundation of religious witness also explains why the faith-based provider might insist—I don't know whether they all insist, but some do—that the entire organization must consist of Christians. A non-Christian may, of course, be competent at providing social services, but by definition a non-Christian is not witness to the power of Christ. In fact, participation by non-Christians in the faith-based group would tend to undermine the claim of Christian witness because then it might be said that anyone, regardless of their belief or nonbelief in Christ, might behave the same way with the same power for good.

These claims of religious witness help resolve the issue of whether the faith-based provider should be permitted to discriminate based on religion in the hiring of staff when the group receives public funds. Rather than think of the matter as discrimination at all, it would be better to think of this hiring practice as similar to the need of the organization to identify itself as Christian. Just as there would be no religious point in providing the program if no one knew that it was Christ's representatives who were providing the service, the group could also not self-indentify as such if it were not composed exclusively of Christians. Since even with the receipt of public funds, faith-based providers are permitted to iden-tify passively as Christian, it ought to follow that even with the receipt of public funds, such groups may restrict hiring to Christians as well.

Another way of putting this is that discrimination in general is wrong because it is unfair and arbitrary. Discrimination is unnecessary and harms the person who is excluded. In contrast, in the context of a faith-based provider, the discrimination is not arbitrary at all but is crucial to the very purpose of the organization. While it is true that the person excluded is still harmed, that harm is at least in this context un-derstandable. This seems a reasonable basis to permit religiously based discrimination in hiring even when a group is receiving public funds.

3. POLITICS AND RELIGION: RUNNING FOR OFFICE AND VOTING

What exactly is the objection to a candidate running for public office on some kind of religious basis? In their book *The Godless Constitu-tion*,[24] Isaac Kramnick and R. Laurence Moore suggest that this kind of religious-political appeal would represent a "de facto . . . religious test for high political office."[25] They argue that under the "no religious test" clause of the Constitution "a person's religious faith, or lack thereof, should never be an issue in partisan politics."[26]

There is undoubtedly something right about this claim. But its for-mulation is overstated. The Religious Test Clause in the U. S. Constitution, article VI[27] has no direct application to voting. It is a prohibition only against government limitations on who may run for office.

Not only does the Clause not apply to voting in a technical sense, but voting for candidates on religious grounds arguably does not even violate the spirit of the Religious Test Clause viewed as a general constitutional principle. To see this, consider other prohibitions against government limitations on who may run for office. Although there is no clause in the Constitution prohibiting "ideological tests" for high public office, the First Amendment Free Speech Clause amounts to the same thing. Because of this right, the government may not, for example, bar socialists from running for high political office.

Voters, on the other hand, are not only free but are expected to cast votes depending in part on whether someone is or is not a socialist. Socialists have a constitutional right to run, and voters may accept or reject them on the basis that they are socialists. It might very well be the same for voters based on the religion of a candidate. Atheists or minority believers have a right to run for office, and voters might be entitled to accept or reject them on the basis of their religion or lack of religion.

It is certainly true, as Chief Justice Warren Burger wrote for the majority in *Lemon v. Kurtzman* in 1971, that "[o]rdinarily political debate and division, however vigorous or even partisan, are normal and healthy manifestations of our democratic system of government, but political division along religious lines was one of the principal evils against which the First Amendment was intended to protect."[28] While the framers of the Constitution famously hoped to avoid political parties altogether, they certainly would have been horrified to imagine an America with a Catholic political party or a Muslim or a Jewish one. To this extent, Kramnick and Moore are correct.

It is crucial to note, however, that this sort of religious identity politics is not what candidates associated with religion generally practice. For example, there is a dispute about whether former Arkansas governor Mike Huckabee's political ad that aired in December 2007 contained the suggestion of a Cross in the background. Governor Huckabee even joked at the time that the subliminal message of the ad was actually "Paul is dead" in reference to a famous rumor about a Beatles song.[29] But there is no question about the content of the advertisement, which ran at Christmas time. In the ad, Governor Huckabee said, "sometimes it's nice to pull aside" from politics and "remember that what really matters is the celebration of the birth of Christ and being with our family and our friends."[30]

So Governor Huckabee ran for president as a Christian in as explicit a way as one could. But this religious identification was not to attract Christians in general and not to ward off believers in other religions from voting for him. Governor Huckabee's version of Christianity was politicized. Everybody who watched his ads understood that Christianity here was a kind of shorthand for certain policies: anti-abortion, anti–gay marriage, for the expression of religion in public life, and so forth. The idea of the religious appeal was to attract a certain kind of religious conservative who would become convinced that Governor Huckabee shared that person's values. "Values" here does not mean theological values, but, primarily, political policy values.

To prove this point, just ask yourself what would happen if a liberal Christian—by which I mean in this context, someone who believes in the divinity of Christ but who favors gay marriage because "Jesus never condemned homosexuality" and abortion rights because "existing Jewish law in the time of Jesus allowed abortion"—ran an ad touting his belief in Christ. Would Huckabee supporters vote for such a candidate? The answer is obviously no. Governor Huckabee was making a religious pitch infused with political policy implications. As such, it did not threaten religious division of the sort the framers would necessarily have worried about.

Nor does religious motivation for constitutionally valid political action serve to invalidate that political action. This is a complex assertion. On one level, it simply upholds what religious leaders have often done in American history. Martin Luther King Jr., for example, felt that he was expressing God's will in preaching the liberation of African Americans. The Catholic bishops in opposing welfare reform also were expressing deep Catholic commitments to the poor and marginalized. Many people support capital punishment, or oppose it, based on religious commitments. Their motivations, though religious, have never been considered suspect.

The proper constitutional concern in this context is not the presence of religious motivation. The concern is that the underlying political action, which could be supporting a bill or voting for a candidate or any of a number of things, must itself be constitutional. So religious motivation behind a bill to force people to go to church would, of course, violate constitutional principles. In fact, the motivation for supporting any unconstitutional measure is usually irrelevant. Race and gender discrimination are important exceptions to that rule but they are the narrow exceptions. A law forcing people to go to church is unconstitutional simply because of its content.

So protestors were wrong to criticize the Mormon Church on the basis of the separation of church and state for the strong support that Mormons gave to Proposition 8 during the November 2008 election. Proposition 8 amended the Constitution of California to ban gay marriage after a court decision had earlier legalized it. According to the Associated Press, on Friday, November 7, 2008, three days after the election, protestors in Salt Lake City "marched around headquarters of the Mormon Church" chanting "Separate church and state."

There has been additional criticism of the Mormon Church by Proposition 8 opponents since that demonstration. On Monday, November 17, 2008, a story appeared in the *Los Angeles Times* in which Jim Key, a spokesman for the L.A. Gay & Lesbian Center, was quoted as follows: "We're making a statement that no one's religious beliefs should be used to deny fundamental rights to others." The story mentioned estimates, which could not be confirmed, that Mormons had given more than $20 million to support Proposition 8.

It should not be considered a violation of the separation of church and state for believers to express political goals they feel strongly about because of their religious beliefs. There were plenty of opponents of Proposition 8 who learned about the equality of all people from the Bible's claim that all people, including gays, are made in the image of God. Whatever content people want to put into the separation of church and state—assuming that they reject the higher law proposal in this book—separation still cannot mean that religiously motivated political actions violate constitutional principles. Citizens are motivated by many factors in politics. Deeply held views about the nature of reality, which is what religion is, cannot be excluded from political life.

There was one other aspect to the objections to Mormons' support of Proposition 8 and, in particular to the activity of the Church itself, in supporting it. Like all churches, the Church of Jesus Christ of Latter-Day Saints is a tax-exempt organization required to avoid certain kinds of political stands or risk loss of its tax-exempt status. Some opponents of Proposition 8 have suggested the Church's involvement in Proposition 8's adoption violated tax laws.

This objection echoed an earlier episode of partisan political activity from the pulpit during the 2008 presidential campaign. "Pulpit Freedom Day," Sunday, September 28, 2008, was the day that several pastors—reports stated that thirty-three ministers in twenty-two states participated—flouted federal tax law and delivered formal endorsements of political candidates.

But although this protest might have constituted an actual violation of tax-exempt status, our tax laws are quite ambiguous on the question of issue support and tax-exempt status. I doubt a tax violation can be shown in regard to support for Proposition 8. Other than that, critics are simply insisting inconsistently that religious organizations can be involved in other issues but not gay rights.

In November 2009 there was another example of dark intimations about the violation of the separation of church and state when representatives of a religious group entered a policy arena. It happened when the Catholic bishops played an obvious role in the healthcare debate, insisting that very severe restrictions be placed on the public funding of abortion before they would support any final reform proposal.

But, again, gaining the support of the bishops was a proper political goal of the proponents of healthcare reform. Sacrificing support for abortion choice to gain needed political support would not be different in principle from sacrificing the "public option" to gain a few needed conservative votes. Granted, it gave a minority view disproportionate power. But that is only because of the close divisions over healthcare. The fact that the motivation of some Catholic voters was religious, rather than socio/economic, is irrelevant.

The above examples and discussion probably serve well enough to give a sense of what might change and what would not change under the proposal of government speech establishing higher law through religious language, symbols, and images. What emerges is a public space much more open to religion in many senses than is true today. The government would regard religion more favorably in such a world because religion is one of the meaning-making institutions in society. A government that is concerned about meaning is going to be well-disposed toward institutions, secular or religious, that foster strong social morale.

We have seen, to this point, how establishing higher law through government speech using religious imagery could help end the Establishment Clause crisis. But that accomplishment would only be part of the potential benefits of this change in constitutional law. If secularism came to embrace this new interpretation of the Establishment Clause, then secularism itself would begin to change. Secularism would be enabled to grow closer to our religious traditions, to its betterment. Such a changed secularism, as we shall see in the next part, would be in a position to make a healthier contribution to American life than is currently possible.

PART THREE

Using the Higher Law Establishment Clause to Save Secularism

EIGHT

The Failure of Secularism
under the New Atheism

There are two forms of secularism in America, or at least there are two tendencies moving toward two ideal types. These two tendencies begin from the same secular starting point: natural laws identified by science are invariant; miracles, or any other supernatural interventions in the world, are impossible in principle. It is this rejection of the supernatural that defines secularism. Any notion of life after death, including the continuation of consciousness and identity, is ruled out. This secular position is incompatible with one or another beliefs of most of the world's religions, including Buddhism, which is usually regarded as nontheistic. I will introduce these two types of secularism here, before fleshing out their portraits in this chapter and the next.

The two forms of secularism I will present share the same starting point but diverge with respect to their relationship to religion. The form of secularism known as the New Atheism envisions religion and secularism as largely distinct from each other. One effect of that dualism is the controversial critique of religion by figures such as Richard Dawkins and Christopher Hitchens. In that critique, religion embodies negative traits, such as irrationalism and submission, while secularism embodies, at least in principle, positive traits, such as rationalism and autonomy. It is very important to this critique that there be a strong contrast between the two realms.

For the purposes of this book, the most important aspect of this distinction between the religious and the secular is that it supports, indeed makes possible, the strict separation of church and state and, more broadly, government neutrality toward religion. If the separation of church and state is to mean anything beyond merely institutional separation—that the government would not pay the salaries of clergy, for example—it must be possible to distinguish what is religious from what is not. Otherwise, it would not be clear what the government could do and could not do with regard to religious expression. Any attempt to merge or mix religion and secularism—by pointing out, for example, that all people pray in some sense or that all people experience transcendence—would undermine the separation of church and state and the foundation of this form of secularism. Government speech using religious imagery in support of higher law is one such mix of religious and nonreligious elements, which presumably the New Atheists would oppose.

The question for the future of secularism is, does this strong separation between religion and secularism have the effect of giving religion a monopoly on imbuing human life with depth of meaning? And does it then restrict secularism to mere materialism and relativism? As will be seen below, the New Atheists deny this.

Despite this denial, the other form of secularism, which I call the new New Secularism for reasons I will explain in the next chapter, arises out of criticism that the secularism of the New Atheism is flat and otherwise uninspiring. The new New Secularism tends either to embrace religion itself or to espouse practices and beliefs that are often associated with religion, such as nontheistic spiritual practices or endorsement of objective values. In another book, I set forth one proposed variety of this second form of secularism as "Hallowed Secularism."[1]

Although the constitutional theory of this second form of secularism is by no means yet worked out, there is at least the potential here for acceptance of religious imagery in the public square. Not all practitioners of the second form of secularism agree with that, however. Austin Dacey, for example, author of *The Secular Conscience*,[2] argues for openness to religion in public life so as better to criticize religion, and does not accept government use of religious imagery in the public square.

This general description of two trends in American secularism is meant only as a kind of map. It does not purport to describe in full the thinking of any particular secular thinker. Nor does it explore the entire

range of reasons to support or oppose separation of religion from government. For example, as we saw in chapter 6, it is sometimes argued
that government support of religion harms religion and inappropriately
aligns political authority with divine sanction. I do not deal fully with
concerns such as these in this book. Since I argue that the establishment
of higher law using religious symbols retains formal government neutrality toward religion and is not an endorsement of religion per se, these
concerns either would not arise or would be ameliorated. The question
here is the use of religious imagery to express the higher law.

Conversely, many religious believers fear that God will punish a
society that does not formally recognize God's sovereignty. This position requires formal endorsement of religion by the government, as
Justice Scalia has argued. My proposal is obviously insufficient from
this perspective.

The first of these two secular types, the New Atheism, is well known
to the public. But to tell the story of its failure to support a healthy secular way of life, we must begin with the dramatic growth of secularism
in America in recent years. Given the recent support for religion in the
public square by the justices on the Supreme Court, an observer could
be forgiven for thinking that religion must have an unshakeable grip
on American society. That conclusion is false and only arises because
of institutional governmental arrangements in the American system.
Because changes on the Supreme Court tend to lag changes in the political preferences of the American people, the current dominance on the
Court of what could be called "pro-religion" justices reflects the politics
of America circa 2004. The 2004 presidential election reflected a new
influence in America of religious, or values, voters. Weekly churchgoers, who represented 41 percent of the electorate in 2004, voted 61 percent for President Bush.[3] In such a close election, this was an enormous
advantage.

The Democratic Party reacted to this new dominance of religious
voters by attempting to reinvent the party as a more faith-friendly environment. This effort included personal faith confessions by party figures
—a sort of rebranding effort,[4]—successfully running more faith-ori-
ented candidates in the 2006 congressional elections[5] and highlighting
religious commitments by the presidential candidates during the 2008

presidential primary season.[6] Here is how Gary Scott Smith of Grove City College described this change in the Democratic Party on the conservative Christian blog, Crosswalk:

> After the 2004 election Democrats reassessed their strategy for reaching the nation's religious communities. Democratic leaders invited Jim Wallis, the editor of evangelical liberal Sojourners magazine, to advise them how to do this more effectively. The Democratic National Committee created the Faith in Action Initiative, which works to "strengthen and build relationships with members of the faith community ... based on our shared values and priorities." Democrats also launched a website—FaithfulDemocrats.com—to help persuade the religiously devout to support their candidates.[7]

The impact of religious voters in 2004 was a part of what appeared at the time to be a repudiation of the secularization thesis—the view, either as a prediction from the late nineteenth and early twentieth century that religion would decline with the spread of modernity[8] or as a description of a modern world in which this has come true.[9] While Europe secularized during the post–World War II period, religion in America seemed to become more entrenched and more significant politically. With the growth in the importance of Islam in the world in the early twenty-first century and the countering resurgence of worldwide Christianity, all of the assumptions behind the secularization thesis began to be questioned, perhaps most notably in the book, *God is Back*.[10]

But the announcement of the death of the secularization thesis may have been as premature as was the announcement of the end of religion. It appears in hindsight that while the influence of religious groups in the political process was growing, so too were the numbers of nonreligious or secular persons in American society.

One early indication of the growth of secularism during the period after the presidential election of 2004 was the influx of books on atheism. During the period 2004–2007, a phenomenon emerged in America that the *Atlantic* would later call "mass-market atheism."[11] Beginning with Sam Harris in *The End of Faith* in 2004,[12] continuing with Daniel Dennett's *Breaking the Spell*[13] and Richard Dawkins's *The God Delusion*[14] in 2006, and Victor Stenger's *God: The Failed Hypothesis* in 2007,[15] to the culminating best-selling blockbuster, *God Is Not Great,* by Christopher Hitchens, also in 2007,[16] this period saw the establishment of a muscular and assertively antireligious atheism that began to reach a popular market. These writers, and a few others similarly oriented, such as Mark Lilla, who wrote *The Stillborn God*,[17] are often referred to as the New Atheists.[18] And, amid these books, there were also less general critiques of the influence of religion on American political life, such as Kevin Phillips's *American Theocracy* in 2006.[19]

Not all of these books are purely critical of religion. Philip Kitcher's book *Living with Darwin*[20] was part of this eruption but was entirely respectful of the solace religion can bring to its adherents. Nevertheless, all of these books foresaw and promoted a less religious, or even a nonreligious, future.

Of course none of what these books had to say was new. Aside from their unacknowledged precursors, such as Nietzsche, Marx, and Freud, much of the biologically based religion critique had been laid out by Richard Dawkins in *The Blind Watchmaker* in 1986.[21] Nor is there any reason to believe that secularism actually grew in any sudden sense. The numbers of secularists may have been growing all along. What happened was suddenly a mass market existed for these books, which created the impression that there had been a kind of surge in secularism.

There was a climax to the perception that secularism had grown in the United States after the 2004 presidential election, but it only occurred after the Democratic Party ignored secularist trends. Despite the new assertiveness by secularists, most of whom no doubt identified with the Democratic Party, the Democratic presidential nomination contest in 2008 was perhaps the most religiously oriented in the party's history. In a typical story at the time, Peter Hamby wrote the following for CNN in October of 2007:

> Republicans no longer have a firm grip on religion in political discourse, Democratic presidential candidate Sen. Barack Obama told Sunday worshippers.
> The senator from Illinois delivered his campaign message to a multiracial evangelical congregation in traditionally conservative Greenville, South Carolina. "I think it's important, particularly for those of us in the Democratic Party, to not cede values and faith to any one party," Obama told reporters outside the Redemption World Outreach Center where he attended services.[22]

What was probably the religious highpoint of the Democratic nomination struggle came in the June 4, 2007, candidates forum on faith and values, televised by CNN and sponsored by Jim Wallis's Sojourners/

Call to Renewal organization. Hillary Clinton said in the debate, "Your faith guides you every day. Certainly, mine does." John Edwards spoke about how the death of his teenage son in 1996 helped rejuvenate his faith and declared, "I have a deep and abiding love for my lord, Jesus Christ." Barack Obama talked about the relationship of religious principles to his proposed policies: "Our starting point has to be based on the notion . . . that I am my brother's keeper, I am my sister's keeper, that we are connected as a people."[23]

The collapse of the economy during the summer and fall of 2008 dampened the religious tone of the actual presidential campaign in 2008. Nevertheless, Obama never ceased his courtship of the religious community. And even after President-elect Obama's faith-friendly presidential campaign ended, he continued to court religious voters, even conservative religious voters, by publicly inviting Rick Warren, the well-known evangelical Christian leader and author of the best-seller, *The Purpose Driven Life*,[24] to offer an invocation prayer at his inauguration.

Yet, after all that, President Obama seemingly changed course and electrified secularists by referring to nonbelievers in his inauguration address: "We are a nation of Christians and Muslims, Jews and Hindus—and non-believers." According to *USA Today*, this was the first time in American history that a presidential inaugural address had acknowledged nonbelievers.[25] This was the climax that the New Atheists had prepared.

Of course, there were good political reasons for President Obama's reference to nonbelievers. The Pew Forum on Religion and Public Life reported in preliminary figures that the religiously unaffiliated represented 12 percent of the 2008 electorate, up from 9 percent in 2000 and 10 percent in 2004.[26] To appreciate the size of this number, white nonevangelical Protestants made up 19 percent of the electorate, as did white Catholics.

This is how matters stood after the 2008 presidential election and inauguration. Secularism was widely regarded as having achieved something of a political breakthrough, but its extent was unclear. Then, in March 2009, the American Religious Identification Survey published results that emphasized two trends at once: America was more secular than ever and less Christian. Two figures may be said to have grabbed popular consciousness. First, 15 percent of respondents nationwide responded "none" when asked their religion. This figure is even larger than the corresponding figure concerning the 2008 electorate. The figure of the "nones" in 1990, in contrast, had been 8.2 percent.[27] Perhaps even more significant, however, was that the number of people calling themselves Christian fell to 76 percent of the population, from 86 percent in 1990. This is the figure that caused *Newsweek* to proclaim "The End of Christian America."[28]

There have been criticisms suggesting these findings may not reflect what is claimed for them. First, more than half of the "nones" say they believe in God or a higher power.[29] So it is not clear how secular the respondents actually are. Second, most of the growth in religious nonidentification actually took place between 1990 and 2001, while relatively little change occurred between 2001 and 2008.[30] Thus, the growth of this group may be slowing or may have stopped altogether. This is not the place to consider these critiques in any detail. Even if the growth in secularism has now permanently slowed, an American society that is 15 percent secular and slowly trending upward is a different place from the America we have previously been. The most recent data suggests that the growth in secularism is likely to continue.[31]

The question is, what way of life will this large and popular secularism manifest? In this context, secular refers to a way of life disconnected from organized religion. In terms of a secular way of life, it does not really matter that many of the "nones" retain a sense of God. Without any organized religious structure, they will still have to create a new, nonreligiously structured way of life.

I think it is fair to say that the New Atheist writers were not attempting to describe, even in a general way, a new secular way of life. As the titles of their works suggest, they were primarily interested in challenging religion, not in developing what might come next for secular people. In fact, as suggested by Sam Schulman in his review of *God Is Not Great* in *Commentary,* the upsurge of atheist writing after 9/11 could be viewed largely as an effort to blame religion for the attacks by militant Islamists and to reduce the influence of religion worldwide.[32] The challenge of the New Atheists against religion was, in other words, a predominantly negative effort. A secular way of life would then be just what falls out when religion is eliminated or weakened. A secular way of life would simply be the way people live when they do not have a religion.

Victor Stenger's book *God: The Failed Hypothesis*[33] is fairly representative of the New Atheist writings in this regard in that his main focus is to herald a postreligious future; only secondarily does he describe how to live in it. His view of religion, or at least of theism, is that it reflects a prescientific worldview that humanity has outgrown:

> Almost from the moment that modern humans appeared on the scene tens of thousands of years ago, they seem to have possessed a vague notion that they were more than the physical bodies that were born of women, grew and aged, eventually ceased to move and breathe, and finally disintegrated into a small pile of dusty bones. At some point in their development, people in almost every culture have imagined invisible spirits acting as agents for events around them, including the animation of living things such as themselves.
>
> Such thinking was perfectly reasonable during the childhood of humanity.[34]

According to Stenger, evolution did not need a designer in order to achieve life's complexity. Our morality, like everything else, has evolved. Evolutionary pressures have imparted to all human beings "a common set of moral standards. . . . [U]niversal norms do seem to exist."[35] Thus, Stenger seems to endorse something akin to the higher law position, though he would presumably object to using religious imagery to symbolize it. Stenger's challenge of religion is biologically driven, but he ends up supporting a universal morality for human beings.

When it comes, however, to actually living without God, Stenger is vague about what that would mean. He does try to confront the issue of meaning in a Godless universe. He acknowledges that even aside from immortality, "many people think that life is pointless unless they fit into some grand, cosmic scheme."[36] But Stenger concludes, quoting Peter Singer, that "[we] can live a meaningful life by working toward goals that are objectively worthwhile."[37] For example, one can lessen suffering in the world. Stenger also greatly admires the art and music that religion has inspired. He "cannot think of anything more beautiful or more touching (or amazing) than Michelangelo's *Pieta*" and other works of equal depth.[38] But he assures his readers that secular sources can be just as enriching as religious ones, including the feelings of awe and wonder that we experience as we ponder science's new understanding of the universe. Unfortunately, Stenger must concede that these insights into science are not available to most people. For the nonscientist, what remains after religious comfort is lost, is the pleasure in "art, music, literature, and the more mundane but equally important events of everyday life—family, work, and recreation."[39]

It would have to be admitted that many people could not live fulfilled lives based on Stenger's account of human life. Presumably, that does not bother Stenger because he doubts that religion has yielded much depth for most people either. The only particular practice of what one might call techniques of deeper living that Stenger mentions is "prayer or meditation," which leads to peace of mind. He links this practice to Buddhism but criticizes the Buddhist conception of nirvana on the ground that nirvana is nothingness and Stenger prefers the "joy and anguish of life."[40]

So, in the end, I'm not sure Stenger successfully answers his own question of how we are to live in a Godless universe. Stenger does not mean to criticize as false or an illusion the experience of depth in human life that many people have had. He claims that such experiences are "purely physical," but he does not seem to mean that they are therefore any less real. Our brains are wired to produce such experiences. He just cannot offer any hope that most of us will experience such depth in the new, postreligious world.

Why is it that Stenger fails to introduce a fulfilling secularism? He fails for the same reason that all the New Atheist writers fail in this regard. They all deny that human beings need to "fit into some grand, cosmic scheme." They deny that there is such a grand scheme, in the sense that the religions describe, and they deny that the highest and deepest human life needs one.

But Stenger's one example of genuine joy and fulfillment in life is Richard Dawkins, who plainly does "fit into some grand, cosmic scheme." Here is Stenger quoting from Dawkins's book *Unweaving the Rainbow*, in which Dawkins describes the meaning in his life:

> Isn't it a noble, an enlightened way of spending our brief time in the sun, to work at understanding the universe and how we have come to wake up in it? This is how I answer when I am asked—as I am surprisingly often—why I bother to get up in the mornings. To put it the other way round, isn't it sad to go to your grave without ever wondering why you were born?[41]

Why you were born? That question could just as well be stated as "what grand, cosmic scheme am I a part of?" Dawkins himself is part of a grand cosmic scheme and he knows it. In his scheme, humanity wakes from its pre-Enlightenment slumber and begins the adventure of understanding the universe through the natural sciences. It is an epic story. And it is a story that gives meaning and structure to the life of the scientist.

So does the story of John 3:16 for the religious believer: "For God so loved the world, that he gave his only begotten Son, that whosoever believeth in him should not perish, but have everlasting life." The point here is not to decide which story—the scientific or this religious one—is true. The point is to convince Stenger that a story is needed to live a fulfilling life. Humanity lives from such stories and ultimately cannot live without them. Our religions teach us such stories about human life. If secularism is to flourish, it must be able to do the same and not just for a scientific elite. Dawkins's story is a grand one, but it would have to be greatly modified to be accessible to most of us. And, in any event, people like Stenger, who presumably would be the ones doing the modifying, do not yet see the need to offer such a story to the mass of secularists.

Stenger is not the only New Atheist writer who ends up telling his readers little or nothing about a new secular way of life. In *God Is Not Great,* Christopher Hitchens, after 275 pages of antireligion jeremiad, felt the need to offer something positive for postreligious life. He titled his last chapter, "In Conclusion: The Need for a New Enlightenment." This new, or as he also put it, "renewed" Enlightenment "will base itself on the proposition that the proper study of mankind is man, and woman."[42] It will be "within the compass of the average person."[43] It will be a return to "Know yourself" from Greek philosophy.

And that is it. One page in his whole book. And I left out the sentences about a freer sex life, which is a frequent Hitchens theme. I don't think that the New Atheists have any idea what "this new humane civilization" will be like, except that it will lack our current organized religions.

As traditional religious belief has declined in America in recent years, I have not seen a corresponding growth in rational thinking, no matter how rationalism is defined. Instead, America seems to be sliding into forms of irrationalism that are even stranger than the supernaturalism of monotheism. Recently, the Pew Forum on Religion and Public

Life reported a poll showing that Americans now freely mix all sorts of religious beliefs. Around a quarter of the population say they believe in reincarnation and astrology and 30 percent "have felt in touch with someone who has already died."[44]

Perhaps most surprising is the report in the poll of intense religious experiences, despite rapid secularization in American life. In 1962, in answer to a Gallup poll question asking whether the subject has ever had a religious or mystical experience, defined as a "moment of sudden religious insight or awakening," 78 percent answered "no" and only 22 percent answered "yes." Yet, when the Pew organization repeated the question in December 2009, nearly half of Americans—49 percent—answered "yes." That is a remarkable change. Even among those unaffiliated with any religion, the "yes" response was 30 percent.

The New Atheists would probably consider all of this to represent a decline in popular rationality. Clearly, the decline in authoritative religious institutions has left people freer to experiment religiously. Unfortunately, people are also freer to latch on to what used to be called "enthusiasms." Perhaps there is some truth in the warning often attributed to G. K. Chesterton: "When people stop believing in God, they don't believe in nothing—they believe in anything."

In any event, there is obviously no guarantee that a secular society in the future will be a more rational one. Society might instead become more superstitious and less scientific. That possibility is why the New Atheists, who are so certain that religion is our problem, have an obligation to define and help bring about a secular way of life that is consonant with their values. Otherwise, as Hans Kung might say, that sky empty of God could be filled with things the New Atheists consider to be even worse than religion.

Surprisingly, there is a story, a sort of grand, cosmic scheme, that Stenger's account of reality could lead ordinary people to accept and celebrate. Furthermore, it is a story that would bring Stenger into close and fruitful connection with religious believers. It is exactly the kind of story that might help bring about a healthy secular way of life and prevent descent into the irrational. What is this story?

Stenger believes that there are objectively worthwhile goals for human beings to pursue in life. He points out that survey evidence shows that "human beings from all cultures and all religions or no religion agree on a common set of moral standards . . . universal norms."[45] Why not celebrate and deepen those universal norms? For that matter why not celebrate a universe that produces those universal norms? It should be a matter of great comfort to people that the universe has brought forth beings like us who are naturally drawn to goodness, truth, and beauty.

What is this description of the universe, after all, but C. S. Lewis's Tao? It is the higher law. And it is endorsed by atheists like Stenger as well as by all the world's religions. Looked at in this way, Stenger is part of a longstanding human account of the universe. And it would be possible for him to borrow from the traditional religions in order to strengthen and deepen the tradition of universal moral norms. He could show how human beings have responded to and invoked such universal norms.

Stenger would undoubtedly object at this point that it makes a great deal of difference whether a supernatural God revealed the nature of the good, the true, and the beautiful, or whether human beings have the innate capacity to recognize them through evolutionary development. But Stenger would be wrong to think that this is an ultimate distinction. This is just the old question of the ontological status of the good under theism. Does God will the good because it is good—that is, goodness is in some sense independent of God—or is something good only because God wills it? In the story of the destruction of Sodom and Gomorrah in the Bible, Abraham holds God up against what seems to be an independent standard of goodness to which God ought to respond: "Shall not the Judge of all the earth do right?"[46]

Many religious believers would agree with Stenger that there are common standards of right and wrong—the natural law—imprinted on every human heart. They would only disagree with Stenger about how the imprint got there. And they might not even disagree about that. Since evolution is a process of the universe, it could also reflect the hand of God.

In terms of the project of this book, the next step, and it is not a great leap, would be to allow the government to symbolically express the view that such universal norms exist. Once we are at that point, the argument would only be over whether religious symbols could be used to make the point. But, notwithstanding Stenger's criticisms of religion, if the religious traditions agree with him about the existence of universal norms, why not, at least sometimes, use religious symbols to make that point?

It is not only that religious symbols are just as good as secular ones to illustrate the higher law tradition. My goal here is to try to create a healthy secularism. That cannot happen without a grand cosmic story. The deeper the moral commonality between secularists and religious believers is, the greater the story of universal norms becomes. At a certain point, universal morality, as in for example the movement toward universal human rights, becomes humanity's great story, or at the very least, one of humanity's great stories. Thus drawing the connection between Stenger's norms and the norms of religion—not the specifics of religious teachings necessarily, although sometimes even those—is essential to give secularism the deep foundations in human history that will prevent secular civilization from beginning life as an orphan. Stenger should thus embrace an interpretation of the Establishment Clause that permits the government to use religious imagery when it is establishing, or trying to establish, the higher law.

While I have referred to Stenger as my major New Atheist model, this conclusion about higher law in the public square applies as well to other New Atheists, for example, Richard Dawkins. Dawkins, like the rest of the New Atheists, clearly objects to the use of religious symbols by government. He objects, on behalf of the framers of the Constitution, as well as on behalf of himself, to "ostentatious displays of the Ten Commandments in government-owned public spaces."[47] But should he?

For Dawkins, the capacity for human moral judgment arises from evolution, like everything else about humanity. He explains how our tendencies toward altruism and generosity might have served as an evolutionarily successful strategy. Today these tendencies remain even though, as in the case of adoption of a stranger's child, some actions resulting from these tendencies do not appear to serve an evolutionary purpose. As Dawkins puts it in the case of sexual arousal of a man by a woman he knows "is on the pill," "[i]t is a strong urge which exists independently of its ultimate rationale."[48]

For these deep biological reasons, there are in humanity "moral universals, crossing geographical and cultural barriers, and also, crucially, religious barriers."[49] But it would seem that with this conclusion by Dawkins, we are again back at the Tao of C. S. Lewis, right in the heart of the tradition of higher law. Dawkins seems to agree with Stenger and Lewis.

But at this point Dawkins tries to draw a contrary line. He rejects the concept of moral absolutes, or, as he calls it, absolute morality. Instead, Dawkins says that reason requires we judge morality solely by its consequences, as in utilitarianism. The other kind of morality, the absolute kind, is usually derived from religion: "a holy book of some kind, interpreted as having an authority far beyond its history's capacity to justify."[50] And this presumably would be why Dawkins objects, or would object, to illustrating the existence of higher law and doing so through the use of religious imagery.

It turns out, however, that history, and not consequentialist logic, is the actual source of moral authority for Dawkins. His most important moral category is a cultural and historical one, "The Moral *Zeitgeist*."[51] Dawkins tries to show that even the religious believers among us do not rely on revealed religious sources, many of which are now recognizably cruel and inhumane, to make moral judgments. How then do we decide what is right and what is wrong?

Dawkins answers that individuals reach moral conclusions in a variety of ways. No matter how individuals conclude, however, humanity in each historical epoch reaches a moral "consensus that prevails surprisingly widely."[52] That consensus is not formed by religion, and in fact most religious believers conform to this moral consensus even though they sincerely believe that their morals come from religion. Instead of religious sources, Dawkins identifies a moving moral zeitgeist as the source of most of our moral judgments.

Dawkins says that historically we can track the movement of humanity's moral consensus since biblical times. Slavery, which for most of human history was taken for granted, is now abolished, formally if not always effectively. The vote for women, and general civil equality for women, is another example, not yet fully effective. Another example is the dramatic decline in racism. And colonialism. And the movement to protect the environment. Dawkins even believes that the senseless brutality of the state was even worse in ancient times than in the time of Hitler. Certainly it is less so now.

But Dawkins has a problem. He regards these fundamental changes in human moral judgment as objectively positive and, barring catastrophe, irreversible: "There are local and temporary setbacks . . . [b]ut over the longer timescale, the progressive trend is unmistakeable and it will continue."[53] The problem for Dawkins is to answer the question of why all this has occurred through human history. C. S. Lewis would have no trouble answering that question. Lewis would say that these changes have occurred because these movements in morality are all closer to the truth of humanity and to the truth of the universe than are their opposites. For example, racism is wrong, given the kind of beings we are and the kind of thing the universe is. It was always wrong, and eventually human beings figured that out. That is exactly the kind of moral absolutist thinking that Dawkins purports to reject. In the absence of Lewis's simple answer, Dawkins flounders:

> Where, then have these concerted and steady changes in social consciousness come from? The onus is not on me to answer. For my purposes, it is sufficient that they certainly have not come from religion.[54]

Dawkins's attempts at an answer for the source of the moral zeitgeist are unsatisfactory. He writes vaguely of "the driving role of individual leaders," "improved education," and "natural extrapolation." But, of course, all of that could go just as easily in an opposite direction at any point. They are not grounds for a directional movement in history.

The higher law tradition answers this question directly. There is an irreversible reason for this movement in human history. The power of goodness is the power of truth. That is what explains the changes in human history that Dawkins notes.

Something like that is the reason why Justice O'Connor writes approvingly of the use of religious imagery in the public square to express "confidence in the future." She is also noting a kind of continuing movement in history in which humanity may have confidence. O'Connor believes that religious imagery expresses that idea.

Dawkins is so busy bashing religion that he fails to notice his deep agreement with believers and especially with monotheists about the movement of truth in history. The Jew, the Christian, and the Muslim all believe that God's will works in history. This is not a description of absolute moral progress because humanity also invents new moral challenges, as in the cases of aerial bombardment of civilians in war and the invention of the atomic bomb. But most religious believers would have no trouble agreeing with Dawkins that the moral zeitgeist moves, continually revealing new truth. Instead of zeitgeist, some believers would substitute the term, the Holy Spirit. Other religious traditions would use different terminology to describe a similar insight.

Dawkins cannot see his similarity to the religious believer and his deep debt to the Bible, because he imagines that religion sees itself as settled. But that is not the case. It is true that the text of the Bible, for example, does not change. But our understanding of it certainly does change. This is no different from the guarantee of Equal Protection in the Fourteenth Amendment. That text is also set. But originally it did not protect women from discrimination and now it does.

Thus, Dawkins should not oppose a Ten Commandments display in the public square. Such a display could represent the insight that our rights are not gifts from other human beings. Dawkins presumably agrees that when slavery was commonly accepted, humanity was morally mistaken. Slavery was always wrong, even when that was not recognized. I am sure that Dawkins would agree that the movement of the zeitgeist did not change the actual nature of the institution of slavery. Thus, a human being has a right and always had a right, independent of the opinion of others, not to be a slave. That right never depended for its rightness on the opinion of others. This is an example of what a display of the Ten Commandments can mean apart from its religious message.

Unfortunately for Dawkins's desire for separation of church and state, if one believes that the moral zeitgeist represents the movement of truth in human history, and believes also that the word "God" stands for truth, and finally believes that truth is a matter of public policy (on such issues as slavery, the rights of women, and the health of the environment), then there cannot be the kind of separation between religion and government that Dawkins says he favors. The moral zeitgeist he describes cannot be separated from religious claims that tell the same story. The movement of truth that he describes is both religious and not religious; it is public and private; it is an affair of government and also not an affair of government.

Thus far I have tried to show that the New Atheists might not have grounds for objecting to the use of religious imagery to illustrate government support for the higher law. I could have used other New Atheists as examples. As we saw in chapter 5, Sam Harris also endorses the concept of absolute right and wrong that religious believers endorse and that the Ten Commandments could illustrate. And Christopher Hitchens excoriated the left at the time of the invasion of Iraq for its relativism in refusing to condemn Saddam Hussein as "evil."[55] Obviously, religious images could be used to express the concept of evil.

Daniel Dennett, however, is a harder case. Like Dawkins, he criticizes moral absolutes and associates them with religion.[56] He is especially critical of people who accept the moral teachings of their religion simply because they are "the will of God." The rest of us should not give any credence to such faith-based opinions because they are not conscientiously maintained.

But who exactly is Dennett criticizing? In the American public square, religious believers are constantly making their arguments from nonreligious sources. The abortion issue is the best example of this. Abortion is said by most religious believers who oppose it to be wrong because it takes a human life. And even in the case of opposition to gay marriage, where specifically religious sources are often heavily relied upon, the feeling that gay marriage weakens the institution of marriage, which is clearly a this-worldly concern, is passionately argued by religious believers. Concern about weakening heterosexual marriage might be foolish as a reason for opposing gay marriage, but it is not a religious reason per se.

But even aside from the fact that religious believers defend their views in universal, nonreligious terms, Dennett's argument against moral absolutism fails more fundamentally. Dennett, again like Dawkins, but with less exuberance, demonstrates that he also believes in moral absolutes. When Dennett disputes the notion that materialists like himself are not morally good people, he falls back on the same sort of common moral sense that Dawkins and Stenger say human beings share:

> The misalignment of goodness with the denial of scientific materialism has a long history, but it *is* a misalignment. There is *no reason at all* why a disbelief in the immateriality or immortality of the soul should make a person less caring,

less moral, less committed to the well-being of everybody on Earth than some-
body who believes in "the spirit."[57]

Conversely, Dennett adds, there are plenty of religious types who
act immorally in accordance with similar widely held standards of universal morality: they "are cruel, arrogant, self-centered, and utterly unconcerned about the moral problems of the world."[58]

Despite all his protestations against moral absolutes, Dennett believes he is speaking here in an utterly accessible, universally applicable
and objectively reliable moral language. And he is. But since the world's
religions agree with him about that, why not emphasize that commonality by allowing government to represent our common moral commitments through the use of religious imagery?

I hope the reader now sees why I believe that the New Atheists by
and large would agree with the higher law position, at least as a theoretical concept, and why I think they should be open to the interpretation
of the Establishment Clause that I offer in this book. But, of course, as
the reader undoubtedly suspects, all of the New Atheists would certainly
object to my proposal for government use of religious imagery to illustrate the higher law. Among other objections, they would deny that these
religious symbols represent universal truths. They would point out that
the Ten Commandments, for example, begin with the recognition and
worship of a tribal God whose commandments are by no means universal but are aimed at one tribe.

What is disappointing about the New Atheists is not just this reflexive opposition to religion, but their indifference to the consequences of
the removal of religious concerns and emphases from the public square.
Granted, the New Atheists would not want the Pledge of Allegiance to
say "one Nation under God," but what would they want it to say? Would
they recommend that the Pledge say that we are "one Nation under Truth
and Reason"? Or, as seems more likely, would they urge that the Pledge
say nothing fundamental at all?

This is an important question because the main criticism of the New
Atheists is that they offer very little by way of describing and defending a
healthy nonreligious way of life. They do not offer a story through which
we can live. But if there is a moral zeitgeist marching through history,
as Dawkins urges, then America and other nations should endeavor to
live up to it. Indeed, we should endeavor to anticipate it and cooperate

with it, though not of course through violence imposed on other nations. Certainly the Pledge of Allegiance should say something about it.

I am referring to the notion of theonomy. According to Richard John Neuhaus, a theonomous culture is one that acknowledges accountability of a society to transcendent truth.[59] As Dawkins notes, a local group or nation that, like the American South in its institution of slavery, stands against the moral zeitgeist is courting disaster.

But this idea of theonomy does not spread by itself. It needs a cultural space in which it can be regarded as credible. If life is just one thing after another—a series of biological accidents—and everything is really the same, ethically speaking, the sense of moral movement in history is lost. Dawkins at least, and the other New Atheists perhaps as well, should agree that the idea of binding and developing moral improvement can permissibly be spread by the government, in public displays, in the public schools, and in any other ways.

Therefore, at least let us agree that dedication to truth should be taught, that generosity and empathy should be taught, that self-sacrifice should be taught. And that these should be taught not as mere possibilities among other possibilities, but as ultimate human fulfillments that are consonant with the sort of beings we humans are and the sort of universe we live in. That is what the proposal for a higher law secularism aims to accomplish.

I don't believe that the New Atheists will actually accept this proposal or any part of it. All of it would have too much of the smell of religion to be acceptable to them. This is why I titled this chapter the failure of secularism under the New Atheists. They certainly do nothing to prevent such failure. For all their contrary assurances, in practice the New Atheists come down on the side of relativism. And their prescriptions for secular life therefore fall flat.

The impact of the New Atheists, however, has by no means been completely negative. There has arisen a new form of secularism somewhat in opposition to the project of the New Atheism. This new New Secularism is more open to meaning in human life, and often more open to religion as well, than the New Atheists have been. We now turn to these secularists and their potential to define a different kind of secular life.

NINE

The New New Secularism and the Higher Law

Where does the term "new New Secularists" come from? It comes from a somewhat altered term in a newspaper column. Peter Steinfels, a professor at Fordham University and co-director of the Fordham Center on Religion and Culture, writes a biweekly column, called "Beliefs," for the *New York Times*. In a February 2009 column entitled "The New Atheism, and Something More,"[1] Steinfels wrote about atheist thinkers who, he thought, were going beyond the New Atheism that I discussed in the last chapter. If the "New Atheists" are "polemicists who set out to counter in-your-face-religion with in-your-face atheism," wrote Steinfels, Ronald Aronson and André Comte-Sponville are perhaps examples of a "new new atheism."

According to Steinfels, what sets the two types of atheist thinkers apart is that the project of the new New Atheists is not to reject religion as such but, as Aronson says, to present "a coherent popular philosophy that answers vital questions about how to live one's life" without God and thus "affirm a secular basis for morality, point to ways of coming to terms with death and explore what hope might mean today."[2] Steinfels also quotes Aronson's characterization of today's nonbelief as manifesting "incompleteness or tentativeness . . . thinness or emptiness." *Living without God*—the title of Aronson's recent book[3]—does not just mean living without something, as in living without traditional religious dogmas, but must "mean . . . turning toward something."

Just what that "something" could be is elusive. While Aronson's substitute for religion is mostly what one might expect—leftist politics and a commitment to an interdependent humankind—Steinfels points out that he adds "gratitude" to his recipe for secular life: "Giving thanks . . . has been central to religion, and secular culture needs to be enriched with an equivalent." Gratitude for what we have been given is a religiously saturated comportment toward reality. It is not how any of the New Atheists would describe a secular way of life.

Steinfels's other new New Atheist is Comte-Sponville, who has written *The Little Book of Atheist Spirituality.*[4] Comte-Sponville comes to his atheism through the same kind of spiritual experiences—he refers to Freud's "oceanic feeling"—that have led many believers into close connection with God. Comte-Sponville describes his own experience of interconnection with all reality that is common in religious literature, "a state of timelessness and bliss, a plenitude of reality rendering both life and death inconsequential." But for Comte-Sponville this experience led not to God, but away from theism—"it removed all need of dogma, hope, eternity, salvation, 'even the longing for God.'"[5]

Comte-Sponville's approach to life is consonant with that of many religious believers, although obviously not all, as is also the case with Aronson. To put the matter simply, these two atheist thinkers seem to be describing experiences and ideals with which religious believers are also familiar and engaged. While there are important differences between religious belief and nonbelief, anyone as close to religion as are Aronson and Comte-Sponville, would have to be respectful toward organized religion, at least insofar as that person is borrowing some of religion's very themes. It comes as no surprise that neither Aronson nor Comte-Sponville opposes religion as such—they are simply not believers. Both utilize their religious training and experience to enrich their atheism. Comte-Sponville even expresses a doubt that whole societies can flourish without religious belief. In other words, he acknowledges that his atheism might not be healthy for an entire society. All this is a very different starting point from that of the New Atheists.

In his column, Steinfels was describing two individuals. He was not announcing the formation of a new movement—a new New Atheism.

And it is true that there is not yet in America or the West any organization of thinking around the themes that Aronson and Comte-Sponville emphasize. There are no academic forums yet in the new trends in secularism. But at one point in the column, Steinfels calls them "example[s]." That is in fact what they are. These two thinkers are part of a loose collection of nonbelievers whose main focus is secularism itself—and its capacity to flourish in the future—rather than focusing on the shortcomings of religion. Some of these other writers are antireligion, while others are not, but all of them are concerned with how to live a nonbelieving life well. As secularism continues to grow, it seems to be inevitable that voices whose main concern is the future of secularism will multiply. I will describe a few of these voices below.

Before discussing these other nonbelievers, however, I need to note a change in terminology. Steinfels calls these thinkers the "new new atheists," whereas I refer to them as the new New Secularists. The reason for this change is that while Aronson and Comte-Sponville eschew the word "God," not all of these nonbelievers do. Nontheistic use of the word "God" is not a new phenomenon. As I mentioned in chapter 6, John Dewey exasperated some of his fellow humanists by refusing to abandon the word "God" when he abandoned Christian dogma. In Dewey's view, "[u]se of the words 'God' or 'divine' to convey the union of actual with ideal may protect man from a sense of isolation and from consequent despair or defiance."[6] Indeed, there are current religious thinkers within the Judeo-Christian tradition who also reject the personal creator God of some versions of biblical religion—the same type of God that the new New Secularists reject.[7] The use of the word "God" is a fraught and important issue that I will return to in the next chapter. By calling these thinkers secular rather than atheistic I mean merely that some of these thinkers use the word "God."

There are a number of persons who might be included within the category of the new New Secularists. But two tendencies must be especially emphasized: a scientific emphasis in building secularism and a political approach to the same end. The former is important because science is often portrayed today as antithetical to religion and as allowing, if not requiring, a strictly materialistic understanding of reality. Science, or at least a popular image of science, is the foundation of all modern secular thinking in the United States. The political approach is significant because the secular/religious divide is of enormous political significance in this society. It was shock in the face of the obvious political power of conservative Christianity that gave the New Atheism its vitality after the 2004 presidential election, for example. Every attempt to define the proper role of religion in the American public square yields enormous political fallout on all sides.

One scientist who can obviously be placed in the new New Secularist category is Stuart Kauffman, the founding director of the Institute for Biocomplexity and Informatics and the author of the book *Reinventing the Sacred*.[8] Kauffman is a biologist and researcher in complex systems. His controversial arguments about the relationship of biological complexity to natural selection are frankly beyond me. His importance for our purposes is that, on strictly scientific and naturalistic grounds, Kauffman rejects the reductionism that grounds the natural world solely in physics—a rejection of what we might call a strictly materialist account of reality. For Kauffman, organisms, including human beings and all their acts and values, are "real entities in the universe."[9]

According to Kauffman, the creativity of the universe cannot be reduced to the unfolding of invariant natural laws, but rests in indeterminacy. Thus, the very quality of the universe that so frightened Einstein—that in quantum theory God might be playing dice with the universe[10]—exhilarates Kauffman. He writes that the capacity of the universe to create without fixed rules "is so stunning, so overwhelming, so worthy of awe, gratitude, and respect that it is God enough for many of us. God, a fully natural God, is the very creativity in the universe."[11]

Kauffman believes that this way of thinking about, and experiencing, reality holds the promise of a new human solidarity:

> If we are members of a universe in which emergence and ceaseless creativity abound, if we take that creativity as a sense of God we can share, the resulting sense of the sacredness of all of life and the planet can help orient our lives beyond the consumerism and commodification the industrialized world now lives, heal the split between reason and faith, heal the split between science and the humanities, heal the want of spirituality, heal the wound derived from the false reductionist belief that we live in a world of fact without values, and help us jointly build a global ethic.[12]

I will return in chapter 11 to the possibilities of coalition building among believers and higher law secularists. Aronson and Comte-Sponville could obviously be engaged in such an effort, while the New Atheists realistically could not be. Kauffman sees such coalition building, in a general if not a specifically political sense, as an important goal.

Kauffman is not alone among scientists in seeing a kind of transcendence in reality without any suggestion of the supernatural. The British paleontologist Simon Conway Morris would certainly agree with Kauffman that reality is not reducible to physics and materialism—that is, not reducible to particles and forces. But whereas Kauffman emphasizes surprise at the heart of reality, Conway Morris sees a kind of ultimate inevitability, although with plenty of open-ended creativity mixed in. In *Life's Solution*[13] Conway Morris argues that there is a strangeness and mystery about the universe. One such mystery is evolutionary convergence, in which the same kinds of appropriate solutions emerge in different contexts. Thus, in a very simple example, wings in birds and bats evolved separately but convergently. Because of this tendency to convergence, there might be similarity and familiarity for us in any kind of life anywhere in the universe that life has emerged.

The other great mystery for Conway Morris is "how it might be that we, a product of evolution, possess an overwhelming sense of purpose and moral identity yet arose by processes that were seemingly without meaning."[14] These two mysteries of convergence and purpose are related. For the first—convergence—suggests that the second—purpose—is no contingency. In other words, our sense of purpose is no accident regardless of how contingent the processes of evolution may seem. Conway Morris concludes that "the universe is strangely fit to purpose."[15] Reading Conway Morris, admittedly as a nonscientist, I would not say that God "put" these potentials—or inherencies—into matter (neither would he), but I might conclude that the word "God" is the word we use when we mean that the potentialities for consciousness, self-consciousness, and purpose *are* built into—that is, inherent in—matter.

It is very significant that serious and accepted scientists such as Kauffman and Conway Morris are engaged with themes of obvious religious import. There is an assumption among many secularists, few of whom are actually trained in the sciences, that religious concerns are unscientific, even childish. That is precisely what Victor Stenger wrote, for example. So it is important that the prestige of science not be hijacked into polemically antireligion channels. When the rest of us see scientists taking religious themes seriously, it is akin to a permission-slip for us to do the same.

Even as religiously authoritative a figure as Pope Benedict acknowledges the importance of reconciling religion and science for the sake of the legitimacy of religion: "Both the collapse of the religions of antiquity and the crisis of Christianity in modern times show us this: if a religion can no longer be reconciled with the elementary certainties of a given view of the world, it collapses."[16] The predominant worldview of America and the West today is scientific rationalism. While that does not mean we are in fact rational, as I noted in the last chapter, it does mean that no perspective contrary to that of scientific rationality can serve as a foundation of our society. Religion must not be understood as inherently antiscientific or antirational. This is why believers who find current evolutionary theory contrary to the revealed wisdom of the Bible have begun to reinterpret the natural sciences—in a creation museum in Kentucky, for example—to explain how biblical truth and scientific truth might be reconciled. While their efforts are not convincing, the fact that such an effort is felt to be necessary demonstrates the power of science in all phases of our culture and among almost all groups. No mass religious movement in America is going to feel it can contradict clear scientific evidence. Obviously there will be disputes concerning how clear the scientific evidence is about a particular matter. For example, some conservative Christians claim that global warming has not been proven by clear scientific evidence.

On the political side of the new New Secularism, Austin Dacey's book *The Secular Conscience: Why Belief Belongs in Public Life*[17] came as something of a shock when it arrived in 2008. Dacey may be regarded as a fully committed atheist, and even a critic of religion, because of his association with the Center for Inquiry, which is an organization that debunks paranormal claims and defends evidence-based inquiry into all aspects of the human condition. Thus, when Dacey accuses secularism as having "[l]ost its [s]oul"[18] in moral relativism, something significant is happening in terms of secularism's self-understanding. Dacey maintains that not only are values not private, but they are not ultimately subjective. For Dacey, there is a sense in which values are true or untrue. Although Dacey does not state this expressly, he clearly shares the view of Martin Luther King Jr. that there is a moral arc in the universe and the view of Richard Dawkins about a moving moral zeitgeist. Dacey's examples of the rights of women and of animals are clearly meant to illustrate a one-way process of genuine moral development. In discussing all this, Dacey neatly turns a claim associated with Richard Rorty against itself by attributing conversation-stopping not to religion and religious claims but to the unwillingness of secularists to debate moral assertions.[19]

The objectivity of values is, as Dacey notes, not a uniquely religious position. As I have shown, for C. S. Lewis the theory of objective value— "the belief that certain attitudes are really true, and others really false, to the kind of thing the universe is and the kind of things we are"[20]—serves as an overall ground for all religion and indeed for all classical philosophy. Thus, if secularism were to adopt the kind of objective comportment toward reality that Dacey champions, it would, in accordance with Lewis's view, share many common features with our religious traditions.

Dacey himself is an ardent critic of organized religion and a defender of a strict separation of church and state. So are a number of the New Secularists. Aronson, for example, is strongly identified with such separation.[21] My point here is that a form of secularism may be developing toward starting points and assumptions that it shares with religious understandings of reality, whatever its currently stated view of the interpretation of the Establishment Clause. Eventually that connection with religion may lead to a softening of the commitment to a strict separation of church and state.

The thinkers discussed above are just examples. In the realms where secularism and religion might most obviously overlap or come together—philosophy and ethics, broadly defined—there are many other thinkers who could define a common ground between believers and nonbelievers. Chet Raymo is an example of a thoroughly religious naturalist, and his recent book *When God Is Gone Everything Is Holy*[22] is precisely what the title says: a description of how to live "religiously" without God. Susan Neiman's recent book *Moral Clarity*[23] describes how to live ethically without God. And there is a somewhat earlier work by James C. Edwards, *The Plain Sense of Things: The Fate of Religion in an Age of Normal Nihilism*[24] that suggests how to live poetically and philosophically without God. All these works can be read by believers and nonbelievers to similar effect. These books suggest how close some forms of secularism and our religious traditions have come to each other in recent years.

Lately, the recognition of a newer kind of atheism that is closer to religion than was the earlier New Atheism seems to have gained even more currency. In an October 2009 article for the Religion News Service, Daniel Burke called it Atheism 3.0, in addition to referring to the "new 'New Atheists.'"[25] Burke contrasted this newer group with older atheist orientations: "The old atheists said there was no God. The so-called 'New Atheists' said there was no God, and they were vocally vicious about it. Now, the new 'New Atheists'—call it Atheism 3.0—say there's still no God, but maybe religion isn't all that bad." Specifically, Burke says that this newer group of nonbelievers sees "little reason to belittle believers or push religion out of the public square."

One of the new New Atheists whom Burke describes is Greg Epstein, the Humanist Chaplain at Harvard University. Epstein's emphasis is on what nonbelievers believe, as in his new book *Good Without God*.[26] Epstein says that nonbelievers should learn from people like Rick Warren, whose bestseller *The Purpose Driven Life* argues that "you have to have a purpose in life bigger than yourself, and that not everything is about you. . . . And he's absolutely right about that."[27]

Burke notes that this new group of nonbelievers still criticizes religion. Epstein, for example, criticizes Warren for insisting that if you don't believe in Jesus Christ, "you're going to hell for eternity." And Burke also refers to Austin Dacey, who wants religion to be free to remain in the public square, in part at least, "to criticize it."

Why is this ferment concerning religion and religious themes occurring in secularism? The reason may be the growth of secularism itself. It now seems conceivable that by the end of this century, most Americans will not be Christians. Perhaps they will not even be religious believers. Given such numbers, it is inevitable that secularists will begin to ask about the ways in which such a secular culture can sustain meaningful human life on its own. There has never been in human history a really secular culture, in the sense that we mean it today, here and in parts of Europe. No one actually knows whether such a culture can work in the long term. So it makes sense to ask how religion might contribute to it.

Besides, as Dacey told Burke, the moment in the sun in which the New Atheists challenged religion is over. It has been done. Now people who are not a part of organized religion want a "balance," a "happy medium" between religion and secularism.

Having shown the growth of a different kind of secularism, we finally arrive at the most important question for our purposes. If secularism has changed, or is changing, in ways that bring it into closer relationship with traditionally religious concerns and perspectives, what, if anything, does that suggest for the law of separation of church and state? What does it say about the establishment by government of the higher law perspective through the use of traditional religious imagery?

The new New Secular thinking undermines the strict separation of church and state because it mixes traditional religious categories with secular categories. This is clear when we think of government endorsement of objective values. Steven Gey, for example, expressly associates separation of church and state with "modernist" value skepticism, which he contrasts with "collective determinations of ultimate truths."[28] For Gey, the religiously neutral state would necessarily be representative of some form of relativism as well, as compared to a state that endorses religion. But, as we have seen, at least some of the new New Secularists, such as Dacey, want to challenge relativism in the name of a newly resurgent, substantively grounded secularism. Dacey wants to return us, if return is even the right word, to the view that human rights are rooted in some kind of objective truth. Rights are absolute, in other words.

There is a sense in which Dacey is here recapitulating the Declaration of Independence's commitment to the idea that we are endowed by our Creator with certain unalienable rights. These words represented a political, rather than a theological, claim. The point was not the nature of the Creator, but the nature of rights. The Declaration was affirming that human rights are not gifts from government, in this case not a gift of the King.

The public display of the Ten Commandments might be one way of endorsing Dacey's view of objective values. Granted that religious believers today, and most people in the eighteenth century, thought the revelation of the law from God is what gave the law its supra-human quality of truth. Obviously Dacey would deny that. But the question is not, how is it that rights are objectively grounded? The question is whether rights *are* objectively grounded. Not only Dacey, but the entire tradition of universal human rights, assumes that the foundation of human rights goes beyond majority or individual will. As long as that message of objectivity can be gleaned from a display of the Ten Commandments, such a display would seem a perfectly acceptable symbol for such expression, even though the Ten Commandments are a religious symbol. In this context, the point being represented in a display of the Ten Commandments would be political rather than theological. Earlier generations understood this political truth about rights in religious terms, and many people still do, but the government expression would be made to endorse the political truth alone.

Even the use of the word "God" by government looks different from the perspective of the new New Secularism. The challenge to the use of the word "God" in the Pledge of Allegiance, for example, is straightforward in terms of the assumptions of the traditional view of government neutrality toward religion. As the Ninth Circuit Court of Appeals held, the words "under God" express government endorsement of the biblical Creator.

Many religious believers agree with the Ninth Circuit that the Pledge is an endorsement of the God of the Bible, though some of them, in opposition to the Ninth Circuit, support this religious expression as a form of public worship. Many secularists also accept the description of the Pledge as endorsing the God of the Bible, though undoubtedly most of them agree with the Ninth Circuit that the words "under God" should be removed. These secularists recognize the word "God" as a form of public worship and oppose such worship when sponsored by government. If these conflicting political positions remain the same, eventually, as secularism grows in influence, the words "under God" might be removed from the Pledge of Allegiance through an intense political struggle.

But if God were reconceptualized by secularists as a "symbol of something true," as Jack Call, another of the new New Secularists puts it in the title of his new book,[29] then the words "under God" might be understood to express a view of human experience—that reality is creative and beneficent, for example—that many secularists share. Then we would have a situation in which the Pledge of Allegiance did endorse biblical religion in the minds of some but also expressed an endorsement of a worldview shared by both believers and nonbelievers in the minds of others.

This changed semantic context for the words "under God" would then be seen as applicable not just to issues of church and state, but, more generally, to the public expression of shared meaning—a common commitment to the significance and purposefulness of life.

Not everyone, of course, would share this view of the meaningfulness of human life. It must be remembered that under the government speech doctrine, government may endorse messages that are not universally accepted. Materialists, humanists, relativists, and nihilists have never been viewed as having the right to prevent government endorsements of a worldview they oppose. Thus, the government might be permitted to use the word "God" to express a nonreligious, but still controversial view of reality, whether Kauffman's view of the universe or some related government message.

This use of the word "God" would not be mere ceremonial deism or vague civil religion. It would be a commitment to a particular way of encountering the world. It would be both religious and nonreligious. I will return to this theme in the next chapter.

As I pointed out in chapter 7, the fight over evolutionary theory in the public schools might change its terms when looked at through the lens of someone like Simon Conway Morris. Not unexpectedly, Conway Morris opposes teaching creationism or intelligent design as bad science. But he appreciates in a way that many secularists today do not that the apparent meaninglessness of the processes of evolution presents a serious issue of cultural morale. It is not wrong for parents to fear that ninth-grade biology class might indirectly endorse a kind of nihilism. One point of Conway Morris's work is to combat just that implication of the purposelessness of life. And so I suppose that instead of insisting on the bad science of intelligent design, school boards could just assign Life's Solution along with the theory of evolution.

If a school board were to do that, and were to do it expressly to combat the specter of meaninglessness, of nihilism, there should not be a challenge to the policy in the name of the separation of church and state.

This is a good illustration of how a new New Secularism might lead to the end of the current law of church and state and might substitute a new and much richer approach, which might be called "higher law secularism." That new approach could include not just government endorsement of the theory of objective values, but of all of the substantive commitments of the new New Secularists.

There is nothing particularly surprising in the observation that a secularism more open to religion would probably be less likely to object to the use by government of religious imagery in the public square. Whereas the New Atheists are engaged in a critique of religion as their primary task, the new New Secularists are by and large not interested in the faults of religion as their main focus. Even if government use of religious imagery were thought to advance religion as such, there might be a general feeling among the new New Secularists that fights over such matters are not worth the enmity they would generate. Thus the Establishment Clause controversies described earlier in this book might be greatly affected by this change to a new New Secularism.

But in this part of the book, we are asking not just about harmony in the relationship between believers and nonbelievers, as important as that is. We are also asking how the use by government of religious imagery in the public square under the rubric of higher law might strengthen secularism, or "save" it in my more challenging formulation. How could that be? What would government endorsement of the higher law through religious imagery be saving the new New Secularism from?

I noted before that as secularism achieves a greater self-confidence based on its vision of a predominantly nonreligious culture in the future, secularists are beginning to think about what that future might be. How will secularists live when they are not trained in religion as young people and do not rely on largely religious traditions for social ceremonies and a general societal outlook? Though rapidly secularizing, America still lives in the shadow of Christian values and commitments. In the words of John Maynard Keynes, describing an earlier period of secularization, "We destroyed Xty & yet had its benefits."[30] What happens, however, when that is no longer the case?

This question was raised in an October 2009 article in the online magazine *Religion Dispatches.* Anthony Pinn, professor of religious studies at Rice University, wrote the piece after attending the Atheist Alliance International 2009 as an invited humanist speaker. Pinn described the gathering's aggressive tone toward religion in the same terms as the new New Secularist critique of the New Atheism:

> The main topic? The great harm done throughout history by religion: the single most dangerous human creation. The welfare of humanity, it was argued, depends on the dismantling of religion and all of its delusions. The possibility of collaboration, of compromise, of any shared ethical commitments between theists and non-theists, was not on the table.[31]

As to what atheism should promote, Pinn suggested the same kinds of orientations that we saw above in other secularist thinkers:

> Atheists must more carefully present a system of ethics meant to enhance quality of life, both through scientific advancement and rigorous struggle against irrational modes of destruction such as racism, sexism, and homophobia. What is necessary is the application of practices that speak clearly to atheism's concern for life within the context of a fragile environment.

Although there was nothing new in these observations, Austin Dacey reacted strongly to the story in one of his own, entitled "Decomposing Humanism: Why Replace Religion?"[32] Dacey accuses Pinn, and by extension, other humanists, of seeking "to organize a replacement" for religion.

The issue Dacey raises is how secularists will live in the future and even in the very near future. Dacey denies that, as religion declines, there will "be a single new institution that . . . arises to serve the same social functions it served—that the social space vacated by religion must be filled by a religion-shaped object. Instead, it could be that in the lot once occupied by faith there springs up a variegated garden, a patchwork of independent institutions, each of which fulfills one of those functions." Specifically, secularists will not be going to humanist services, a la those of Greg Epstein at Harvard, whom Dacey singles out, humorously, as "a lovely person, but I've heard him sing, and I think I'll stick to Bach, Arvo Pärt, and Kirk Franklin for my spiritual uplift. Do we really need an institution for people who find Reform Judaism and Unitarian Universalism too rigid? Yes. It's called the weekend." There will not be in the future an organized secular civilization, but a "disorganized" one. Dacey expects and hopes that the mainstream culture itself will become more secular. Secularism will not be a separate activity in the future.

The question about the future of secularism is a serious one, but not in the way Dacey thinks. The question is not what particular social structures will characterize an American secularism, but whether secularism will be able to support strong social structures at all. In other words, will secularism become just another American manifestation of individualism?

One can easily predict that Americans will not start joining humanist organizations en masse. But the specter of the open weekend is not as funny as Dacey supposes. Since I ceased attending synagogue out of loyalty to my newly formed secularist beliefs, I have felt the emptiness of American culture. My weekends are free, but they lack the connection to a community that I had before. They lack the spiritual refreshment that I experienced in synagogue. I have wondered what my funeral will be like, and have watched with a touch of envy the funerals of others who were still involved with their religious communities at the end of their lives. Those funerals have a fittingness about them. I have also wondered who will officiate at the weddings of my children.

Certainly these are all pedestrian and conventional concerns. One would expect a new secular society to create new social forms and practices, not just substitute secular ones that are in the same basic shape as the religious ones they are replacing. I am guilty of looking for old wine in new bottles. That is the point that Dacey is making.

But these secular forms of the future, whatever they are, will be *social* forms. They will not be choices made by individuals or by individual families. That is not how culture works. These forms will not just happen, as Dacey seems to think, along with free weekends. So secularists had better be thinking about social forms of the future.

And secularists had also better be thinking about social formation in the secular young. My children were raised in a liberal Jewish tradition, even though they, like I, seem now to have put that tradition aside. But liberal Judaism was there in my life, and theirs, when it was needed. Dennett may suggest that raising a child within a religion is akin to child abuse,[33] but he is just reaching to be provocative. It really does take a village to raise a child and religious traditions in America provide just such social structures. This is not only a matter of social solidarity and a feeling of belonging, though it is that; it is also a question of beliefs and structures of meaning. Certainly children can be raised well within a secular tradition. But I don't think children can be raised well without any tradition.

The danger is a kind of rootless individualism that could end up taking the place of religious orientations in America. Dacey claims there should not be in secular culture "any unitary philosophy or community." But it is more likely that there will be precisely such unitary structures in a more secular America: the philosophy of relativist materialism and the community of shoppers at the mall.

It will not do to wave off the serious prospect of a secular desert in America with vague references to Western Europe and its largely successful secularism, as Dacey and others do. A destructive and aggressive individualism is the American curse, not the curse of Europe. At least not yet. Just to pick one recent example, there might not be one country in Western Europe that would greet the call for universal health insurance as a threat of "socialism," as it has been called in America. America may use its religious traditions to promote social solidarity in ways Western Europe does not need. What happens when those religious traditions are gone or are so greatly weakened that they no longer undergird the entire culture?

The doctrine of government speech referred to in this book is one form of social practice that can help to counter such extreme individualism. All government expression is inherently social. All such expression binds us together. The nation "under God," for example, is a communal form of meaning whatever its substance turns out to be. The same is true of displays of the Ten Commandments and of secular displays of government speech as well. Government speech of all kinds maintains a public space for socially shared meaning in the face of the individualism that the decline of religion threatens to unleash. Granted, these forms of government speech are not very effective by themselves, but they do help keep the expression of shared meaning as an activity in the center of the culture. Government speech is not an answer to the challenge of the future of secularism, but it is perhaps a part of an answer.

The use in government speech of religious symbols to express shared meaning is beneficial in this context of combating individualism for two reasons. First, these religious symbols have a cohering history. They are inherently expressions of community, whether the Church, the Jewish people, or the Umma. Thus they lend themselves to the countering of individualism. They are reminders of the possibility of social solidarity.

The second advantage of the use of religious symbols is that they are not nationalistic, or at least they can easily shed a nationalist context. While the formula "one Nation under God" can represent an idolatrous worship of the nation, that same formula can also invite a prophetic critique of the nation. Conversely, secular symbols, like the flag, pose a much greater threat of supporting hyper-nationalism. Religious symbols always contain at least the seed of universality.

Government speech is not the only form of social expression available to a secularism cast adrift from the universal social structures of religion. Public practices and holidays abound that can be reformulated to serve the needs of a growing secularism. As a banal example, Halloween in America is just such a social practice. Halloween is not something that the individual controls. Its meaning is a shared social one. Every parent in America has learned this lesson. Participation in Halloween—and even refusal to participate is a form of participation—carries with it very particular customs and expectations.

Thanksgiving, of course, is another example. Compared to Halloween it is an ethically and morally richer social occasion. As in the case of government speech using religious images, it is undoubtedly Thanksgiving's particular religious heritage that gives the holiday its socially healthy meaning of giving thanks for our blessings.

Other public occasions are also capable of expressing shared social meaning, but they run the risk of encouraging worship of the state. Presidential inaugurations are great public occasions as are holidays such as Memorial Day and Veterans Day. Those occasions, however, inevitably lead to praise for America. Perhaps public occasions such as Independence Day and the birthdays of Abraham Lincoln and Martin Luther King Jr. might be recast as genuinely universal celebrations. Independence Day might mark the beginning of liberal democratic government in the world. Abraham Lincoln and Martin Luther King Jr. might stand for human liberation from all forms of tyranny. But none of this can happen if religion is banished from the public square. Any such universal occasions are going to at least be touched by religious images and traditions as well as secular ones.

As long as the new New Secularism affirms substantive truths, government speech and public holidays should be viewed as potential supports for the dissemination of such truths. For example, despite Dacey's criticism that secularism should not seek a "unitary philosophy," his insistence on an anti-relativist position for secularism is precisely such a unitary philosophy. Government speech that promotes the higher law supports that anti-relativism in a broad social context.

Beyond government speech, and beyond government-sponsored public holidays, there is the role of government as educator of many of the young that also serves as a foundation of shared meaning in society. Government will particularly be educating many of the secular young, who presumably will be attending public schools rather than the mostly religious private schools. In the context of educator, government will be teaching, or trying to teach, a philosophy that combats the social acid of relativism, materialism, and nihilism. Forms of religious imagery are needed here as well.

In addition to the promotion of objective values, which is supported by the establishment of higher law, the new New Secularists are also promoting related, but somewhat different, ultimate commitments. For Kauffman, for example, there is appreciation of the beneficent creativity of the universe. For Aronson there is gratitude for what we have been given. And, of course, there are many other examples. But all of these expressions share in the foundational commitments of America's religious heritage. Religious believers could, and have, emphasized the very same kinds of values and commitments that the new New Secularists are experimenting with.

And beyond particular value commitments, it is the commitment to truth itself that it most clearly shares with organized religion. Government use of religious imagery, therefore, can promote not only the particular values of the new New Secularism but, by reminding secularists of the shared history of secular and religious commitments, it can also foster human solidarity across the religion/nonreligion boundary.

In a recent interview with Mark Juergensmeyer, Robert Bellah put the need for truth at the social level very well: "The question is whether you can have a society without anything important in common. I'm arguing . . . that such a society is impossible."[34] Government speech is going to be part of the expression of that something we will always have to have "in common" and religious imagery can represent one way of expressing it.

To what extent will secularism be open to this kind of sharing of social space with religion? Caught between the new New Secularism and the "old" New Atheism, which is still very much with us, secularism is coming to a crossroads. Anthony Pinn, above, for example, was writing of collaboration and compromise between believers and secularists. It is easy to imagine Pinn accepting the proposal in this book to reinterpret religious imagery in the public square—the Pledge of Allegiance, for example, or prayer before legislative sessions—in a kind of live-and-let-live way, so that religious meaning is communicated to the believer and secular values are communicated to both the secularist and the religious believer. But it is just as clear that such compromises would be vehemently rejected by the New Atheists. Thus secularism will soon have to choose.

A recent vignette suggests how divisive this choice is going to be. In August 2009, Robert Wright, author of *The Evolution of God*,[35] offered in the op-ed pages of the *New York Times* what he called "A Grand Bargain Over Evolution."[36] Wright pointed out that C. S. Lewis inferred from the universal human apprehension of morality that the moral law does exist, that it is "out there." Lewis took this to be evidence that God exists as well. Since Lewis's time, evolutionary psychologists have developed a plausible account of how this human moral sense evolved and how it served as a successful evolutionary strategy. But, argued Wright, this evolutionary account is not only compatible with a God who works through evolutionary processes—and thus evolution does not rule God out—but aside from God, this evolutionary account is entirely consistent with the kind of beneficent unseen order of higher purpose that theology has classically presented.

Now obviously Wright was not contesting any of the "facts" of evolution; he was pointing to potential disagreements in the interpretation of those facts. In all of this, Wright was speaking like the new New Secularists, in the same key as Stuart Kauffman and Simon Conway Morris above.

A few months later, Nicholas Wade, the science writer for the *New York Times* and the author of *The Faith Instinct*[37] would trip over the wire separating the New Atheism from the new New Secularism in trying to make a similar point about evolution. Wade was reviewing Richard

Dawkins's book *The Greatest Show on Earth*, which defends evolution.[38] Wade, like Wright, doubts none of the facts of descent from a common ancestor, nor does he doubt the theory of evolution. He begins his review with this declaration: "The theory of evolution really does explain everything in biology." In the review, however, Wade chided Dawkins for calling evolution a "fact" as opposed to a "theory": "When Dawkins asserts that evolution 'is a fact in the same sense as it is a fact that Paris is in the Northern Hemisphere,' it seems he doesn't know what a theory is."

This was not really a fundamental point. Wade understood that Dawkins was calling evolution a fact in order to "refute the creationists" who mean by theory something that can easily be called into doubt. Wade has no doubt about the claims of evolutionary theory and he does not think anyone else should have doubts either. Wade is pointing out a flaw that might be "a fault just of tone." Dawkins's misuse of the fact/ theory distinction is part of his becoming "as dogmatic as his opponents," and no longer speaking the language of science or even "civility."

The surprise was what came next. Two of the New Atheists, Daniel Dennett and Philip Kitcher, responded, in letters to the *New York Times*.[39] In fact so many other scientists and philosophers responded that the *New York Times* organized the other letters into blog form.[40]

Dennett objected to Wade's breezy and easygoing tone. Dawkins is right to be upset, Dennett maintained. The "worldwide campaign of disinformation" that creationism represents is much more of a threat than Wade or the *New York Times* seems willing to admit. For his part, Kitcher claimed that Dawkins is justified in calling evolution a "fact" because it is so well supported, so amply confirmed by the evidence, "that it may be accepted without [further] debate."

Since Wade did not support creationism, nor cast doubt on evolution, and since Wade himself acknowledged the very use of the word "fact" that Kitcher pointed to, the vehemence of their responses, and the fact that such eminent thinkers went to the trouble of responding at all, seems surprising. It can only be explained, as can the volume of other responses the *New York Times* received, by the desire not to give any aid and comfort to the "enemy" creationists.

It seems sensible to predict that the same kind of angry secular response will greet any attempt by some secularists to find common ground with believers over the use of religious imagery in the public square. Any such attempt is going to run into a buzz saw of criticism from fellow secularists not so much because acceptance of the position will mean acceptance of the actual religious imagery itself. That imagery, after all, is present in the public square already and no court at the moment seems willing to order its removal. No, the objection is more of the "nose of the camel" sort that is unwilling to concede any ground for fear that such a first step will just embolden opponents to make more and greater demands for the public expression of religion.

On my part, this is not mere prediction. I presented a version of the ideas contained in this book at the very secular Netroots Nation convention in Pittsburgh in August 2009, and I saw the negative reaction there, as well as the negative comments that greeted a further development of the ideas in the online magazine *Religion Dispatches*.[41] Even allowing for the flaws in my presentation, one must assume that at least part of the problem is opposition to the goal of finding common ground with religious believers in a way that does not banish or diminish the presence of religion in society. Many secularists currently oppose that goal.

Thus the division within secularism in the end is going to center around something like the proposal to interpret the Establishment Clause as allowing the use of higher law imagery—that is, around the acceptance in law of the use of religious imagery by government to make nonreligious claims. Undoubtedly all secularists agree that today's crisis in Establishment Clause jurisprudence must be resolved. But the New Atheists want to see it resolved not by a grand compromise and common ground but by a rededication to the strict separation of church and state and either the removal of religiously oriented symbols from the public square or, at least, a ban on further such expressions in the future.

As we will see in the last chapter in this book, such secular insistence would have the effect of preventing the formation of a new progressive political coalition. Before reaching that pragmatic point, however, one more theoretical issue must be resolved. Granted that secularists will divide over the use of religious imagery in the public square, is there any sense in which the use of the word "God," in and of itself, might be a special case? Is there any way in which the word "God" may be considered a universal symbol acceptable even in a secular society?

TEN

Is God a Universal Symbol?

Secularists will be surprised to hear that America is much closer to resolving at least a part of its religious culture wars than they might have thought. Despite all of the concern about Christian nationalism and the undoubted desire of a substantial number of Americans that Christianity be recognized as America's official religion, in fact if not in name, the Supreme Court has been quite clear that the government may not endorse any one religion, including Christianity, and that a Pledge of Allegiance, for example, that referred to America as "one Nation under Christ" would be unconstitutional. Even Justice Scalia has stated that the view held by some in the "founding generation" that the Establishment Clause "permitted government invocation of Christianity" has been "clearly rejected" in our subsequent history. All important government acknowledgments of religion "have invoked God, but not Jesus Christ."[1] This interpretation of the Establishment Clause has been settled since the Court invalidated a courthouse crèche in the Allegheny County case in 1989 on the ground that the placement and context of the crèche seemed to endorse Christianity.

So it is already the law that any use by government of a sectarian religious symbol must be justified in some nonsectarian way. That is why the following exchange took place in oral argument in fall 2009 in *Buono*, the case challenging the erection of a cross on what had been public land as a war memorial to those fallen in World War I:

JUSTICE SCALIA It's erected as a war memorial. I assume it is erected in honor of all of the war dead. It's the—the cross is the—is the most common symbol of—of—of the resting place of the dead, and it doesn't seem to me—what would you have them erect? A cross—some conglomerate of a cross, a Star of David, and you know, a Moslem half moon and star?

MR. ELIASBERG Well, Justice Scalia, if I may go to your first point. The cross is the most common symbol of the resting place of Christians. I have been in Jewish cemeteries. There is never a cross on a tombstone of a Jew.

(laughter)

MR. ELIASBERG So it is the most common symbol to honor Christians.

JUSTICE SCALIA I don't think you can leap from that to the conclusion that the only war dead that that cross honors are the Christian war dead. I think that's an outrageous conclusion.[2]

The point of this exchange for our purposes is that Justice Scalia is assuming that the cross must serve a nonsectarian purpose if it is to be upheld. That secular purpose is the representation of all the war dead. Justice Scalia agrees that the cross would be unconstitutional if it represented an endorsement of Christianity.

The doctrine of nonpreferentialism—that the government at least may not prefer one religion to another—is accepted by all the justices on the Court. The operating assumption of all of the justices in the Ten Commandments cases, *McCreary County* and *Van Orden*, was that the Ten Commandments displays at issue could not be endorsements of Judaism or Christianity. And there is already case law in the lower courts to the effect that legislative prayers that are systematically and predominantly addressed to Jesus Christ are unconstitutional.

Granted, for some of the justices, nonpreferentialism has served as the counterpoint to the government neutrality doctrine. When then-Justice Rehnquist began his assault on the government neutrality doctrine in his dissent in *Wallace v. Jaffree* in 1985, he did so on behalf of the doctrine of nonpreferentialism. Nevertheless, the constitutional requirement of at least nonpreferentialism is not itself controversial.

But if all of this is settled, what is the continuing very real struggle in church/state symbolic representation about? It is at its base about the continuing use by the government of the word "God" or implied references to God. As controversial as Ten Commandments displays may be, they could all be banned and the disputes over the use of the word "God" would remain unchanged.

The two assertions—that the government may not prefer one religion over another and that the public use of the word "God", in the Pledge of Allegiance and our national motto, for example, and in countless other ways, is constitutional—may strike the reader as contradictory. Even aside from the beliefs of sincere atheists, who are discounted by the several justices who maintain that the government may prefer religion over irreligion, there are many Americans who practice religions that do not share a belief in the God of monotheism. Indeed, in defending the public display of the Ten Commandments in his *McCreary County* dissent in 2005, Justice Scalia even mentioned a percentage for American monotheists, which he defined as practitioners of "Christianity, Judaism and Islam": "97.7%."[3] By extrapolation, therefore, non-monotheists comprised 2.3 percent of American believers. In his dissent in the companion Ten Commandments case, *Van Orden,* Justice Stevens put the number of non-monotheistic American religious believers at "more than 7 million,"[4] which is not an insignificant number of people. So how can their religious beliefs be marginalized by the use of the word "God" without violating the Establishment Clause if the government may not prefer one religion over another?

The main response to this apparent contradiction is that the use by government of the word "God" is, for a variety of reasons—depending on the particular justice and the facts of the case—not really religious. One line of this approach is the assertion that such uses of the word as in the Pledge of Allegiance are instances of "ceremonial deism," robbed of any genuine religious content. Another version is that the Pledge of Allegiance and, by extension, the national motto, and much else, are patriotic and historical rather than religious, or even represent a mere acknowledgment that, originally, the American people had a belief in God and that most Americans retain that belief. A variant of these positions asserts that the word "God" is as close as language can get to pure religion, free from the dogmas of particular religious sects, and is not an endorsement of the biblical tradition itself. All of these arguments, and their variants, are present in numerous places in the case law. All of them are buttressed by the undeniable fact that God has been publicly and officially addressed throughout American history.

The problem with this is that our political life makes it plain that many American monotheists do regard these public governmental expressions as endorsements of the God of monotheism, and maybe even the God of the Bible. That is why these expressions are fought for in the public square as upholding the honor of God. Since many Christian, Jewish, and Muslim believers see these references to God as in fact manifestations of their own religious beliefs, nonbelievers and non-monotheistic believers may be forgiven for also disputing the assertions that these displays and references are really not religious. Contrary judicial rhetoric is just not believable.

The other approach to upholding government use of the word "God" is that of Justice Scalia. Justice Scalia does not deny that government references to God are religious. As we saw in part 1 of this book, he refers to such government usage as "honoring God through public prayer and acknowledgment."[5]

Justice Scalia is not entirely clear about why honoring God the Creator is not a denigration of religions that reject such a concept. Part of his reason is a theory of interpretation of the Constitution that takes long established practices as uniquely normative. Thus the fact that the American government has always acknowledged and honored God means that acknowledging and honoring God cannot easily be unconstitutional. Part of the reason is that the honoring of God does not disparage non-monotheistic religion, nor expressly proselytize on behalf of monotheism. Honoring God is not an active rejection of polytheist religion, but expressly disparaging polytheism presumably would be unconstitutional. But perhaps the most poignant reason for allowing God to be honored publicly is that monotheist believers cannot thank God publicly, *as a people,* unless the occasion to do so is government sponsored. So to remove all public references to God would be to take a side against a form of religious belief. It would not be a neutral act by a court. Thus it is not entirely true that Justice Scalia accepts the principle that the government may not prefer one religion over another. The government may apparently prefer monotheism. For Justice Scalia, this may simply be a necessity. It may be that there is an inherent commitment in monotheism, at least in biblical monotheism, that requires some kind of public, indeed official, acknowledgment of God.

There is something very refreshing about Justice Scalia's description. His position is a much more accurate representation of what most people think is actually going on, whether or not they agree with his conclusion that honoring God is constitutional. Only the notion that what is at stake is the honor of God, and the right of believers to worship God, can account for the political resonance of the current wording of the Pledge of Allegiance and the national motto. If these kinds of references to God were as religiously bland, even meaningless, as some of the justices assert, the Supreme Court could remove them from the public square without suffering serious political damage. Instead, as everyone can see, even the justices who believe such references to God are unconstitutional, are loath to act on that conclusion for political reasons. As Justice Scalia says, to so act would be foolhardy: "[Government neutrality] is discredited because the Court has not had the courage (or the foolhardiness) to apply the neutrality principle consistently."[6]

Assuming that Justice Scalia is right that something meaningful, rather than merely formal and empty, is being asserted through government use of the word "God," is there any way for nonbelievers and non-monotheistic believers to engage and appropriate that meaning without sacrificing their beliefs? Any positive answer to that question must recognize that monotheistic believers will not alter their belief that public acknowledgment of God constitutes a form of public worship of the God of the biblical tradition. So the question is, even given that "God" represents the traditional God to the monotheist believer, can "God" mean something else to others in a way that maintains everyone's dignity and sincerity? The answer to that question may determine the tone of American politics for many years, perhaps even to the end of this century.

We must begin by asking what God Justice Scalia is invoking. We can get a sense of what he means by his reference in *Lee v. Weisman* in 1992, the high school graduation case, to something the government may not do under the Establishment Clause. In his dissent in that case, Justice

Scalia conceded that "our constitutional tradition . . . [has] ruled out of order . . . government-sponsored endorsement of religion . . . where the endorsement is sectarian. . . ." "Sectarian" has a very particular meaning for Justice Scalia that reveals his understanding of the God who may be honored, indeed worshiped, in a public American setting. The government is violating the Constitution when, even without coercion and even without proselytizing, it "specif[ies] details upon which men and women who believe in a benevolent, omnipotent Creator and Ruler of the world are known to differ (for example, the divinity of Christ)."[7] In Justice Scalia's mind, the God of the Pledge of Allegiance is the "benevolent, omnipotent Creator and Ruler." That understanding of God is why it makes sense to think of public worship as having real world effect—that this God is capable of "watch[ing] over . . . the United States of America."[8]

This formulation of the meaning of God contradicts the beliefs of some in the founding generation. Justice Souter tried to make that point in the *McCreary County* majority opinion by referring to George Washington as a "deist." David Holmes describes the classic five points of deism as follows: "(1) there is a God; (2) he ought to be worshipped; (3) virtue is the principal element in this worship; (4) humans should repent of their sins; (5) there is a life after death, where the evil will be punished, and the good rewarded."[9]

By our current standards, deism is a very religious orientation, nothing like the various forms of secularism I have been describing in this part of the book. Nevertheless, the God of deism is not the omnipotent Ruler. Nothing in the above list suggests the kind of active rewarding and punishing here on earth that the biblical God, who is clearly the God Justice Scalia has in mind, engages in. There would thus be no point in the kind of public ceremonial worship of the God of deism that Justice Scalia is championing. The God of deism does not watch over the United States as a result of our worshiping him.

It is clear that Justice Scalia does not understand this difference between deism and biblical monotheism. He was exasperated at Justice Souter's implied criticism:

> This reaction would be more comprehensible if the Court could suggest what other God (in the singular, and with a capital G) there *is*, other than "the God

of monotheism." This is not *necessarily* the Christian God (though if it were, one would expect Christ regularly to be invoked, which He is not); but it is *inescapably* the God of monotheism.[10]

Because they reject the God of deism, the Pledge and the national motto are actually sectarian in Scalia's terms, and thus ought to be considered unconstitutional. If the national motto stated plainly "We trust in God, the omnipotent Creator and Ruler of the universe," there would be many practitioners of Christianity, Judaism, and Islam who would realize that this is not their God, along with the atheists and non-monotheistic believers who already know that.

In other words, some of the very believers that Justice Scalia invokes in claiming that "97.7% of all believers are monotheists" reject, or at least reinterpret, the single Creator God. Yes, they may say, "God created the universe," but that is a metaphor for a mysterious activity that has no name. Mordecai Kaplan, the founder of Reconstructionist Judaism, for example, would have said something like that. He wrote in *The Meaning of God in Modern Jewish Religion* that the belief in creation from nothing has only a "remote, if not altogether irrelevant" relationship to spiritual life in the "modern way of thinking."

> Only the moral aspect of that belief is nowadays of vital import. *The moral implication of the traditional teaching that God created the world is that creativity, or the continuous emergence of aspects of life not prepared for or determined by the past, constitutes the most divine phase of reality.*[11]

Admittedly, Kaplan would be regarded as a very liberal Jewish voice. Many Jews who are more traditional in their religious practices would agree with Justice Scalia's understanding of God. On the other hand, there are also liberal Christian views similar to those of Kaplan. I could add on the Christian side, for example, Michael Hampson, who writes in *God Without God*[12] that the church's proof of the existence of God from creation "points to a mystery" that anything exists at all. The word "God" "means only the ultimate mystery of existence itself."[13]

One doesn't have to go to the liberal edge of the traditions, however, to find thoughtful questioning about the meaning of the concept of God. That can be found in the very heart of the Christian tradition. In *United States v. Seeger*,[14] the Supreme Court extended conscientious-objector status to claimants who did not believe in a traditional conception of God. In coming to that conclusion, Justice Clark's unanimous opinion quoted Paul Tillich as one who "identifies God not as a projection 'out there' or beyond the skies but as the ground of our very being." Justice Clark then quoted from Tillich's *Systematic Theology:*

> I have written of the God above the God of theism. . . . In such a state [of self-affirmation] the God of both religious and theological language disappears. But something remains, namely, the seriousness of that doubt in which meaning within meaninglessness is affirmed. The source of this affirmation of meaning within meaninglessness, of certitude within doubt, is not the God of traditional theism but the "God above God," the power of being, which works through those who have no name for it, not even the name God.[15]

Or, more simply and yet profoundly ungraspable, "to argue that God exists is to deny him."[16] In Tillich's terms, Justice Scalia wrongly assumes not only that the God of theism is God, but that no other conception of God is conceivable.

Tillich was a Protestant, but this is not a matter of Protestant theology. In the Roman Catholic tradition, Karl Rahner expressed a similar criticism of a being-like God: "*that* God really does not exist who operates and functions as an individual existent alongside of other existents, and who would thus as it were be a member of a larger household of all reality." Instead, says Rahner, God is "the most radical, the most original, and in a certain sense the most self-evident reality."[17]

Also on the Roman Catholic side is a different approach to God, one solidly set in the realm of secular humanity, by Bernard Lonergan:

> The question of God . . . lies within man's horizon. Man's transcendental subjectivity is mutilated or abolished, unless he is stretching forth towards the intelligible, the unconditioned, the good of value. . . . There lies within his horizon a region for the divine, a shrine for ultimate holiness. It cannot be ignored. The atheist may pronounce it empty. The agnostic may urge that he finds his investigation has been inconclusive. The contemporary humanist will refuse to allow the question to arise. But their negations presuppose the spark in our clod, our native orientation to the divine.[18]

We can take this disagreement among monotheists as to the nature of God as the starting point of a different appreciation of the word "God." Secularists can come to an understanding and perhaps an appropriation of the word, first by seeing the wide range of meanings that have been attached to God within monotheism itself. Then secularists need to appreciate the way that religious traditions that do not use the word "God" can be viewed as communicating the same experience of reality that monotheists use the word "God" to express.

Given the breadth of meaning attributed to the word "God" by theologians, it is not clear that the usual assumption about nontheistic religions is actually true. Yes, there are religions that reject the omnipotent Creator/Ruler God, but, as we have seen, so do some monotheists. If God is taken to mean something other than that being-like entity, the border between monotheism and non-monotheistic belief becomes permeable.

One of my favorite quotes supporting this view of the all-encompassing nature of the concept of God, including nontheistic religion, is that of Huston Smith in *Why Religion Matters*:

> Making due allowance not only for differences in terminology but for differences in nuances, in East Asia we find Confucianism's shang ti, the supreme ancestor, and beyond him Tien, or Heaven. In Taoism, there is the tao that can be spoken, and the Tao that transcends speech.
>
> In South Asia, Hinduism presents us with sanguna brahman—God with attributes or qualities, among which sat, chit, and amanda (infinite being, awareness, and bliss) are primary—and Nirguna Brahman, the neti, neti (not this, not this) of the Brahman who is beyond all qualities. Buddhism presents a special case because of its ambiguous stance toward God, but though the personal God is absent in early Buddhism, it could not be excluded indefinitely and came pouring in through the Mahayana.... The transpersonal God is, of course, solidly ensconced in Buddhism's sunyata—emptiness—and Nirvana.[19]

Hampson makes a similar point:

> In acknowledging God who is the ground of all being, we find ourselves in profound communion with the whole human race, for there is only one humankind, only one creation and only one ground of all being. The Hindu faith recognizes Brahman, the limitless one, ultimate being, beyond all the icons and incarnations. The Buddhist kneels in silence seeking to disconnect from the pain of this world and to connect instead with an essence or non-essence far more profound that lies beyond. The Sikh reaches out for the one God of all humankind, known in all authentic faiths, in meditation, worship and selfless service. The Buddhist seeks Buddha nature within each human soul, the Hindu faith speaks of *atman*, the presence of God in each individual, and our own tradition sees the image

of God as the very essence of humankind. All who seek to understand what it means to be human in the world, and who seek the potential for good in every human being, are reaching out for the same mystery.[20]

The concept of God is simply too great and mysterious to be cabined as the God of monotheism unknown to Buddhists, Hindus, and other minority believers.

Of course, there is an objection to this broader way of looking at the word "God." As the previous quotations show, religions outside the monotheistic tradition have their own terms for what could be understood as a universal religious reality. Just as clearly, the use of the word "God" in the American tradition was not originally intended to include their understandings. It was intended to name only the biblical experience of the divine. How can such a sectarian beginning yield universal results?

This is certainly a fair objection. But it is reminiscent of the decision to name Sunday as a society-wide day of rest earlier in American history. The desire for one day free from commerce perhaps transcended the Christian community that wished to protect Sunday per se. But if one day were to be selected for rest, it only made sense for that day to be the one that a significant portion of the community already regarded as the appropriate one. A predominantly Christian country like the United States should not have to choose Wednesday for a day of rest just because Sunday is a Christian holy day.

For example, if the government placed a monument in the courthouse honoring the Hindu lawgivers Manu, Yajnavalkya, and Parasara, I suppose no one would think the government was endorsing Hinduism. In a theoretical sense, therefore, that exhibit would accomplish the same purpose as a display of the Ten Commandments without the potentially unconstitutional message of endorsement or preference of a particular religion.

This hypothetical suggestion, however, just shows how silly is the idea of requiring the government to utilize a non-Christian religious symbol. In a country overwhelmingly Christian in numbers and tradition, only a relative handful of citizens would have any idea who Manu, Yajnavalkya, and Parasara are or what they have to do with law. In this country, if you want to communicate a general nonsectarian religious message using a sectarian symbol, you have to use Christian symbols. Certainly, you don't avoid them.

We can look in the same way at the words "under God" in the Pledge of Allegiance. The word "God" is not the word that a Hindu or Buddhist, for example, wishing to express the transcendence that underlies all reality would choose. But the question is whether the word "God" can be translated into terms that are not antithetical to Hindu or Buddhist belief. Smith and Hampson think that it can.

In another culture, it would be the monotheist who would be doing the translating. There is a famous story in the book of Acts in which Paul calls the pagans to whom he is speaking "very religious" and tells them he can proclaim to them the god they know as "an unknown god."[21] This story shows that fundamental religious reality is shared among believers though they express their understandings differently and in some ways they disagree with each other. As the great Indian student of religion, Sarvepalli Radhakrishnan, explains, "Something is directly experienced, but it is unconsciously interpreted in terms of the tradition in which the individual is trained."[22]

It is but one more step to say the same of secularists and the word "God." Granted, the point of being a nonbeliever is that one does not believe in God. It would be said by most secularists that they are specifically excluded by the public use of a phrase like "under God."

But as we saw above, in chapter 9, there is a growing recognition among some secularists that values are absolute and that science and religion are not necessarily antagonists. Some of these secularists use the term "God," or other traditional religious terminology, without surrendering a secular worldview. Stuart Kauffman, for example, uses the term "God" to name the ceaseless creativity in the universe. Nor is Kauffman particularly unusual in this regard. Jerome Stone defines an entire category of religious naturalists as "those who conceive of God as the creative process within the universe. . . ."[23] Another category that uses the term "God" consists of "those who think of God as the totality of the universe considered religiously."[24] The point is that there are commitments expressed in religious imagery that secularism may be able to appreciate and even appropriate through the reinterpretation of traditional religious language.

This possibility is not a new phenomenon. In *A Common Faith,* John Dewey refers to "God" as "a unification of ideal values that is essentially imaginative in origin." As we saw in chapter 6, Dewey did not mean by imaginative, unreal. Dewey was thus still using the word "God" though by this time he rejected all forms of supernaturalism. So the phrase "under God" might be much more inclusive than is usually thought.

Aside from theology, there is also a mixed political/theological aspect to the word "God" that is very much supported by some secularists. This applies, for example, to the claim in the Declaration of Independence that we are endowed by our "Creator with certain unalienable Rights." This assertion in the Declaration is probably not a claim about the nature of God but about the nature of rights. Rights are not given by other human beings. Rights are more inherent than that. Many secularists would assent to this claim.

As I mentioned in chapter 8, the Bible itself suggests that political or ethical claims might have a reality that is binding even on God. Susan Neiman, in her book *Moral Clarity* loves the Old Testament story of Abraham arguing with God over the fate of the cities Sodom and Gomorrah.[25] Abraham says to God, "Shall not the Judge of all the earth do right?"[26] As Neiman puts it, "Abraham dares to remind the King of Kings that He's about to trespass on moral law."[27] Since the source of the moral law must also be God, because God is the creator of everything, this means that even God is "under God." And to be "under God" is to live in accordance with the moral law of the universe.

It is common for those who favor a strict separation of church and state to misinterpret God-language in a theologically wooden way. One well-known example of this tendency is the book *The Godless Constitution,* in which Isaac Kramnick and R. Laurence Moore argue that the Constitution differs from the Declaration of Independence in that the Declaration mentions God, that is, the Creator, whereas the Constitution is Godless and thus secular.[28]

On the face of it, this suggestion is dubious because it presumes that there was a great change in thinking about the proper role of religion in public life between 1776 and 1787. Considering the large role of Thomas Jefferson in drafting the Declaration, the idea that it is more pro-religion than the Constitution is silly. But more fundamentally, the argument mistakes the role of the Creator-language in the Declaration.

That language served to ground rights as transcending positive law. In other words, the reference to the Creator served a higher law/natural law purpose.

But the Constitution clearly shares precisely this commitment to natural rights. That is the point of the Ninth Amendment, which states, "The enumeration in the Constitution, of certain rights, shall not be construed to deny or disparage others retained by the people." Although there is controversy in American jurisprudence about whether the Ninth Amendment should be judicially enforceable, there is no question that its purpose is to render explicit the proposition that there are "unalienable rights" that exist independently of positive law, in this case independently of their enumeration in the Bill of Rights. The absence of a word like "God" as the source of these rights does not render the Constitution atheistic any more than the presence of such a word renders the Declaration theistic. These are political documents and their political worldview is the same. The addition of the word "God" or "Creator" to the Ninth Amendment would have changed nothing.

Religious symbols and language often play important political roles, especially in confronting the tyranny of the state. For example, the Polish labor union "Solidarity" drew much of its strength from its Roman Catholic foundation and Pope John Paul II's visit to Poland in 1979. Similarly, but more controversially, the Catholic Church has been involved in liberation movements all over South America. Moreover, this role of religion is not just a Western phenomenon. Pankaj Mishra describes in just these terms the role of Buddhism in resistance to the dictatorship in Burma, officially the Union of Myanmar:

> The real center of Rangoon, however, is still the Shwedagon Pagoda, Burma's holiest site, whose gilded spire is visible from much of the low-rise city. More than a millennium old, the Buddhist temple is not only an enduring symbol of the principal Burmese faith. Standing on a hill in the middle of the colonial city, it also appears to be a higher court of appeal than the modern government buildings that signify, to most Burmese, the state's brutal and arbitrary power.[29]

This is precisely what it means in a political sense for a nation to be "under God." As Neiman puts it, "[w]hatever else the idea of God may be, or not be, it's above all the idea that human beings have limits."[30]

Neither secularists nor minority believers are necessarily excluded by the phrase "one Nation under God" when those words are understood as a bulwark against arbitrary human power. As secular a thinker as Austin Dacey argues that values are objective and real. This means real apart from the will of human beings. The word "God" in this context stands as a placeholder for, as John Dewey would say, the power of the ideal.

The question then becomes whether the use of the word "God" is an acceptable shorthand for a fuller expression of this kind of political commitment. Certainly the word "God" brings with it all sorts of baggage that is inappropriate in the context of the Establishment Clause. The word "God" is open to the narrowest sectarian abuse. All that is true.

But what would be gained by a reference in the Pledge of Allegiance that substituted for the word "God," the phrase "one Nation under the mystery of existence" or under "the ground of being" or made reference to "the ontological status of rights"? God may just be the deepest and most inclusive word we have for the expression of the objectivity of meaning.

I don't mean here to echo Justice O'Connor's and Justice Brennan's view that only religious language can adequately express some secular sentiments. Rather, the secular sentiments being expressed in the Pledge have always been a part of the particularly religious meaning of the word "God." Understandings of God have always played a political role. They did so during the Revolutionary War and during the creation of our constitutional republic. They continue to do so even as we enter a more secular time.

The growth of secularism is the final context in which to consider the role of religious language, such as "one Nation under God." Religion has been dominant in America since its founding and it will continue to exert in the short-run a strong political influence in American elections. Secularists may be excused therefore if they push back against religion every chance they get.

But this period of religious domination is ending. It is either already necessary to think about the needs of a secular world, or it will be soon. My purpose in insisting on the use of the word "God," and other instances of religious symbols and language, is to keep a certain kind of cultural space open. This is akin to what Judge Ferdinand Fernandez wrote in his partial dissent in the Ninth Circuit in *Elk Grove*. Removing the word "God" from public expression, "remove[s] a vestige of the awe all of us, including our children, must feel at the immenseness of the universe and our own small place within it, as well as the wonder we must feel at the good fortune of our country."[31]

This is not a concern only for religious people. Susan Neiman has written that the Enlightenment created natural religion, and used the term God, to "express . . . the breath of wonder that the age of Enlightenment exhaled."[32] When the word "God" is gone, the sense of wonder may go with it.

It may be true that we do not need religion to experience reverence for existence. But if that is true, it is because we have the example of religion. I am afraid that prematurely jettisoning religious language, including the word "God," might expose humankind to profound demoralization.

I have seen suggestions of such demoralization. In chapter 7, I noted the impact that evolutionary theory could have on notions of right and wrong, and I used the physicist Steven Weinberg as an example. It is worth remembering, however, that Weinberg's main point was not about evolution but, as he put it, "the question of how it will be possible to live without God."[33] Weinberg knew that living without God is not easy. And he placed responsibility for the death of God directly in "the worldview of science" that he maintained "is rather chilling." It is worth recalling his words here:

> Not only do we not find any point to life laid out for us in nature, no objective basis for our moral principles, no correspondence between what we think is the moral law and the laws of nature, of the sort imagined by philosophers from Anaximander and Plato to Emerson. We even learn that the emotions that we most treasure, our love for our wives and husbands and children, are made possible by chemical processes in our brains that are what they are as a result of natural selection acting on chance mutations over millions of years. And yet we must not sink into nihilism or stifle our emotions. At our best we live on a knife-edge, between wishful thinking on one hand and, on the other, despair.

Not all scientists agree with Weinberg about the implications of the scientific worldview, of course. I am quoting him not because I think he is right about that, but merely to demonstrate the stakes that he acknowledges in living without God. Living without God is no doubt the direction in which we are headed. But we should not rush ahead without careful preparation. We may eventually have adequate substitutes for expressions like "one Nation under God." But we do not have them yet.

Until we do, we are better off reinterpreting the language we have to offer the deepest and most inclusive reality we can yet express.

When scientists do use the word "God," it seems to me they do so to express an attitude toward the universe quite different from that of Weinberg. Certainly that was true of Albert Einstein in his famous comment about God playing dice with the universe in relation to aspects of quantum theory. He did not mean a personal God, a being, apart from space and time, who could and did intervene to set aside the natural order according to his will. He meant that the universe was an orderly place, with an intelligible structure, one that welcomed human investigation.[34] Einstein may just have been wrong about quantum theory suggesting otherwise.

It is not a "fact" that the universe is a cold, indifferent place in which humans happen to be, by accident. Beings like us, thinking, loving beings, may instead be "inevitable," as Conway Morris puts it, given the natural processes we know and sufficient time. And if humanity is alone, in the sense that there is no God to talk to, then we are alone in a home well suited to us. That is not a bad place to be.

Scientists are tempted to think of the orderly structure of nature as planned. And even to think in God-like terms. Here is how the great physicist Werner Heisenberg put it, with full recognition of the pitfalls of such thinking:

> Was it utterly absurd to seek behind the ordering structures of this world a "consciousness" whose "intentions" were these very structures? Of course, even to put this question was an anthropomorphic lapse, since the word "consciousness" was, after all, based purely on human experience, and ought therefore to be restricted to the human realm. But in that case we would also be wrong to speak of animal consciousness, when we have a strong feeling that we can do so significantly. We sense that the meaning of "consciousness" becomes wider and at the same time vaguer if we try to apply it outside the human realm.[35]

And why restrict this sense of fitting order to nature in a physical sense? This is how Pope Benedict, writing before becoming Pope, described the movement from the natural order to the order of natural rights:

> If "nature" is being talked about here, then what is meant is not just a system of biological processes.... Being is not blindly material, so that one might shape

it in accordance with sheer utilitarian aims. Nature bears spirit within it, bears ethical value and dignity, and thus at the same time constitutes the legal claim to our liberation and the standard for this.[36]

All of this relates to the question before us, the use of the term "God." God does not just mean Justice Scalia's Creator/Ruler. God consists of a family of meanings, of which the Creator/Ruler is certainly one aspect. But just as important, and as historically grounded, is a much vaguer sense of order and welcome and hope. These notions are also expressed in the word "God." Justice O'Connor was not wrong to say that religious language can be used to express confidence in the future. She was just wrong to be so dismissive of it. She was wrong to denigrate its current power. She was wrong to reduce it to Hallmark-card sentimentality.

Does that render God a universal symbol? No. These understandings of God clearly do not include those of Steven Weinberg. They do not include nihilists, relativists, pure materialists, some humanists, postmodernists, and on and on. But they do include many nonreligious, nonbelieving persons. They do include many formal atheists, who mean by their atheism only that the supernatural Creator/Ruler God does not exist, not that the universe is alien to us.

So the word "God" can be used in formulations like "In God We Trust," not to indicate that Justice Scalia's God exists, but that radical trust is the proper comportment of humanity toward reality.

When I presented ideas along these lines at the highly secular Netroots Nation convention in Pittsburgh in 2009, I was met by two quite thoughtful objections, among others. The first was that once government could legally use the term "God" to express contested ideas, as I was suggesting, then why would the government not sponsor billboards proclaiming that "God hates abortion"? After all, the noxious placard "God hates fags" is proudly proclaimed at demonstrations organized by Westboro Baptist Church, along with "The Jews Killed Christ" and other loving examples of Christianity.[37] So why not government use of God to oppose abortion?

My answer is that there is a reason current government usage of the word "God" is restricted to general attitude, such as "In God We Trust." Any more specific usage, and certainly any programmatic usage by the government, would require reliance on particular texts from specific religious traditions, like the Bible. And of course any such use would be sectarian and thus unconstitutional under any Establishment Clause formulation.

Naturally the next criticism would be that such a use of the word "God" is so vague and general as to be useless. The usage is vague and general, but it is not by extension useless. It is quite enough if the word "God" occupies a space that would otherwise be occupied by Steven Weinberg's cold description of the universe. That is approximately why John Dewey did not abandon the use of the word "God" when he no longer believed in the Christian God.

The other objection that was leveled in Pittsburgh was that even if all of this discussion about the word "God" were true in some general sense, the discussion omits the political context in which the demand for the use of the word "God" takes place. That demand takes place in a highly contested political context. It is clear, for example, that the push to place the Pledge of Allegiance and the national motto in the Capitol Visitor Center was a partisan pitch on behalf of the Creator/Ruler God. It was understood by everyone to be such a pitch. The Republicans wanted to be identified with this God and the Democrats were afraid not to be. My fellow panelist Fred Clarkson said it succinctly—any other understanding was "baloney": "God means God."

There is a sense in which this objection is correct. The great majority of Americans are believers, in fact, Christians. Whenever the word "God" is used, many of them will hear a reference to the biblical God, the Creator/Ruler. And they will feel at home and they will feel public affirmation of their identity as believers. Not only that, but the government officials who propose and use the word "God" may, and often will, also be thinking of the God of Genesis. They may even be thinking of Jesus Christ.

It also follows that nonbelievers will tend to react with similar understanding and hear in the word "God" a denigration of their identity, which is why there is such opposition to something as otherwise innocuous as the Pledge of Allegiance and the national motto. There are deep politics here and the existing parties supporting and opposing God-usage are not being silly or wasting time. It is important to a diverse nation to get identity issues right.

That is why the public—governmental—justification of the use of the word "God," as well as the use of any other religious symbol, must affirm that secular values, in particular the higher law in these contexts, are being promoted. It seems to me churlish of the nonbeliever to object that religious language comforts the believers as long as values that believers and nonbelievers share—or at least nonreligious values that they might share—are being officially promoted. As long as the relevant government officials affirm that the higher law is being endorsed, the use of religious imagery does not seem to undercut the secularist position whatever the religious believer hears. In a country as diverse as America it is valuable when symbols can be affirmed in different ways by the vast majority of the citizenry.

It should be added here that there is a reason why Einstein and Heisenberg speak of God and consciousness and intention. They were harkening to the monotheistic usage, borrowing its meaning in part. They were using the shorthand word "God" offered without endorsing the Creator/Ruler God. We can do the same.

Secularism should not be afraid of the word "God." It can be used to express a secular hope for the future. It can be used to ward off the nihilism and relativism that secularism can be prey to. In an earlier work, I wrote, "The starting point for secular hope is that the ways of freedom, justice, and peace have power to change the world."[38] Religious believers have been expressing that hope through the use of the word "God" for thousands of years. Secularism can also hear that promise whenever the word "God" is spoken.

ELEVEN

The New Politics of
Higher Law Secularism

Could America ever produce a dominant progressive political coalition? Maybe I should say, reproduce such a coalition, since we may have had such a coalition of forces during the early years of FDR. But we don't have such a coalition now, as witnessed by the simple fact that during the debate over healthcare reform, a single-payer system was never a serious possibility. I am going to suggest in this chapter that higher law secularism, that is, a secularism that accepts higher law in the public square expressed in part through religious imagery, might serve as a basis for the creation of just such a new progressive coalition.

It is important that this suggestion not be misunderstood. Only a sincere higher law secularism could possibly be part of such a coalition. A merely pragmatic concession by secularists grudgingly accepting religious imagery in the public square would be something different, though undoubtedly a good thing in its own way. Such a compromise is not the higher law secularism I am proposing.

Nor am I suggesting that secularists should surrender their principles in return for temporary political gain, trading a Pledge of Allegiance they really oppose but can't repeal, for example, for religious support to combat global warming. Such cynical plays for power never work in the long run. Only if secularism were convinced by the truth of higher law secularism could the political effects I will describe in this chapter come about.

I am asking in this chapter whether a genuine higher law secularism, one that has actually come into closer and meaningful relationship with religious imagery, might open up new political possibilities. If it turns out that no such secularism will exist, or even could exist, the suggestions in this chapter will be irrelevant. I believe that such a secularism is possible, even likely. But only history will decide that question, one way or the other.

As important as coalition building is, however, the main political attribute of a higher law secularism is not that capacity. Rather, the new politics suggested in the title of this chapter has more to do with secular political life itself. A higher law secularism might answer the question of the nature of political life, that is, the proper goals of politics, differently from the answers given by a more antireligion, relativistic secularism. There might be different available sources to learn from. There might be a different approach to American history. And there might be differences in tone. I will look at all this below, albeit briefly.

We should start with the question of what American politics is like now, from the point of view of the secularist–believer relationship. It is well known that religion was a key factor in the 2004 reelection of George W. Bush. Roughly speaking, among whites, the more often you went to church, the more likely you were to vote for Bush. In fact, the tendency that the more religious the voter the more likely that voter was to vote for President Bush actually applied across all groups and not just among whites; it just applied to whites to a much more dramatic extent. According to John Green, a senior fellow in religion and American politics at the Pew Forum, "There wasn't a single religious group where there weren't political differences by worship attendance."[1] And it is also well known that a major Republican campaign strategy in 2004, this one particularly authored by Karl Rove, was to emphasize that electoral advantage.[2]

But what is not as much appreciated is that in the 2008 presidential election, despite the emphasis on economic issues because of the recession and the corresponding downplay of religious themes, and despite the enormous efforts by the Democratic Party to become more faith-friendly in both the 2006 and 2008 elections, the same basic relationships of religion and politics held. Weekly attending evangelical Protestants, weekly attending mainline Protestants, and weekly attending white Catholics voted overwhelmingly for John McCain, over 80 percent, over 60 percent, and nearly 60 percent, respectively.

The converse was also true. The Pew Forum separates voters without a religious affiliation into two groups, the seculars and the unaffiliated believers, depending on whether the person responding gives some indication of religious belief. Both groups voted overwhelmingly for Barack Obama, 70 percent and close to 70 percent, respectively.

Granted, the strong tendency to vote Republican among religious voters is primarily a white Christian phenomenon. Black Protestants, Jews, Hispanic and other minority Catholics, and other non-Christians —essentially this group includes Hindus, Buddhists, and Muslims— voted for Barack Obama to an even greater extent than did persons without a religious affiliation. In other words, these religious believers voted Democratic by a larger percentage than did secularists. Nevertheless, that caveat, in a country still predominantly Christian and white, does not alter the basic equation. Minority religious believers and racial minorities have particular reasons to vote contrary to a Republican coalition comprising—overwhelmingly comprising—white Christians. Even among these groups, however, as the greater Republican leaning among Orthodox Jews than among less observant Jews suggests, the relationship of religious belief and Republican Party support still tends to hold.

So the statement that religion in America is partisan remains a basic political reality. Believers tend to vote Republican. Nonbelievers tend to vote Democratic. What lies behind this trend?

The answer to that question is that many things lie behind it and most of them have nothing or little to do with religion. As a group, weekly churchgoers are undoubtedly conservative in a general sense, whether or not they are also conservative in a theological sense. To the extent they are socially conservative, they may be hostile to gay marriage or feminism or immigration, without much, or indeed without any regard, for the religious implications of these positions. To the extent they are economically conservative, they may oppose government intervention

into the private market. In other words, weekly churchgoers might re-
semble other conservatives who do not go to church and who also tend
to support the Republican Party.

But most of these issues *do* have a religious resonance. Obviously,
abortion and gay marriage have sparked specifically religious opposition.
That is why an economic conservative like former House majority leader
Dick Armey was portrayed in a *New York Times Magazine* profile as opposing an emphasis on social issues of that kind: "When Republicans are
fighting against the power of the state, we win. When we are trying to
advance it, we lose."[3] The decline in influence of the social issues versus
concerns about government involvement in the economy is said to "signal... the rise of economic conservatives in the Republican Party—and
a decline in influence of the religious right."[4] So, while there is overlap,
there are also differences between religious and nonreligious conservatives on issues. There are specifically religious grounds for some of the
support religious voters give to the Republican Party.

Even a pro-market stance can have a kind of religious foundation,
though this seems counterintuitive as a religious position, especially
a Christian one. Bill McKibben pointed out this irony in an article in
Harper's Magazine in 2005:

> Three quarters of Americans believe the Bible teaches that "God helps those
> who help themselves." That is, three out of four Americans believe that this
> uber-American idea, a notion at the core of our current individualist politics
> and culture, which was in fact uttered by Ben Franklin, actually appears in Holy
> Scripture. The thing is, not only is Franklin's wisdom not biblical; it's counter-
> biblical. Few ideas could be further from the gospel message, with its radical
> summons to love of neighbor.[5]

Some religious conservatives who favor the free market may assume that
this is a religious, indeed a biblically justified position.

The specifically religious aspect of a conservative social agenda can
also be seen by the one issue that splits Protestants and Catholics to a
further extent than any other: immigration. Nonreligious conservatives
may largely support restrictions on immigration and sanctions for illegal
immigrants already here, but the issue has not been clearly identified as
a religious issue because the Catholic Bishops and many lay Catholics
oppose such measures.

THE NEW POLITICS OF HIGHER LAW SECULARISM

The importance of these religious foundations to political positions is that even if weekly churchgoers viewed the Democratic Party
as equally grounded in religion as the Republican Party, the religious
voting divide would not alter if the Democratic Party took the "wrong"
stance on issues like abortion and gay marriage. A higher law secularism
that was open to religion but still retained certain policy commitments
that weekly churchgoers oppose, like support for the right to choose, or
gay marriage, or even government regulation of the market, would still
alienate these religious voters. No broad coalition on these religiously
divisive issues is currently possible.

But not all of the support for the Republican Party is based on issue disagreement. Some of it is premised on supposed or real hostility
to religion on the part of secularists who are then viewed as part of the
base of the Democratic Party. That identification of secularists and the
Democratic Party, as we saw above, is basically true. Secular voters do
overwhelmingly vote Democratic. It is in this realm, as opposed to issue
specific divisions, that new possibilities for coalition are present.

To see this, consider the coverage of the healthcare reform debate in
the pages of *World Magazine,* a popular Christian news magazine. The
magazine considers itself to be committed to biblical values. As such, edi-
torially, *World* strongly supports the goal of extending health insurance
to the uninsured. But the magazine is suspicious of a federal government
takeover of healthcare and prefers alternative policies such as expansion
of the "more than 1,200 free medical clinics around the country, serving
more than 3 million patients each year,"[6] to be supported in part by extending free medical malpractice insurance to doctors.

That suspicion of government control is not simply a matter of anti-
government ideology. *World* fears that government will be hostile to
religious institutions. At the height of the healthcare debate in the House
of Representatives, on November 7, 2009, *World*'s cover story told of
the gender discrimination complaint brought against Belmont Abbey
College, "the 1,600-student, Catholic college connected to the [Belmont
Benedictine] monastery."[7] Based on Catholic teaching, the school re-
fuses to cover contraceptives, abortion, or sterilization in its healthcare
coverage for employees. Earlier in 2009, eight faculty members filed a
gender bias complaint over this practice with the Equal Employment

Opportunity Commission. The EEOC district office dismissed the complaint in March 2009 but then reinstated it: "A July 30 letter from District Office Director Reuben Daniels claimed the college is discriminating against women by refusing to pay for birth control, despite the school's religious objection to the practice. The implication was clear: In this case, an accusation of gender discrimination trumps religious freedom."[8]

The magazine story was not subtle about drawing a lesson from what happened to Belmont Abbey College to what might happen to other religious institutions under government controlled healthcare: "What if the proposed public option that Congress is considering eventually crowds out the private healthcare plans that religious organizations often use? That's a scenario that could leave some religious organizations—and individuals of faith—with few choices for balancing healthcare plans with moral convictions."

This coverage in *World* helps explain why trying to satisfy, or even genuinely satisfying, pro-life objections to healthcare reform, will not necessarily bring many religious voters to support healthcare reform as the Democrats are formulating it. The objection in the magazine story is to government control, not just to the particular policies that a government plan might include, such as abortion funding.

The assumption behind the claim in the story that even *alleged* gender bias trumps religious freedom, is that the government officials charged with designing and carrying out any government healthcare plan will be hostile to religious practices and commitments. This is probably not true. None of the current healthcare proposals drop the conscience clauses that now exist to protect religious institutions. Nor, of course, does the story deal with a federal healthcare program. Nor has the college finally been decreed to have discriminated.

An ironic aspect of the story is that Belmont Abbey College would have had an argument under the Free Exercise Clause before *Employment Division v. Smith*[9] excluded generally applicable laws from Free Exercise scrutiny. The *Smith* opinion was written not by a secularist judge but by the religious-right favorite, Antonin Scalia. In any event, since the anti-discrimination law in question is federal, the college should still be able to rely on the Religious Freedom Restoration Act of 1993, which, although struck down vis-à-vis state and local governments,[10] can apparently still bind the federal government.[11] So the college should be fine in the end. Nevertheless, this story illustrates the suspicion on the part of religious believers of what they consider to be the secular Obama government. Is this suspicion justified?

If that question were asked about the New Atheists described in chapter 8, the answer would clearly be yes. The New Atheists specifically want to restrict religion as much as possible because of religion's negative impact on people. There is no secret about their hostility.

But even if the focus is on more moderate secularists, as long as the stated aim of secularism is to remove religious imagery, and the word "God" in particular, from the public square, believers are going to be justifiably suspicious that their interests will not be protected by a sec-ular-dominated government. Thus religious believers generally support the Republican Party, which although it may pursue policies with which committed Christians disagree, is much less likely to be dominated by a secular, antireligion agenda.

Given this description, it is clear that a higher law secularism would be much more palatable to the audience of *World Magazine* than are cur-rent forms of secularism. For one thing, a higher law secularism would not be pursuing the particular goal of banishing religious imagery from the public square. For another, a higher law secularism would have come to appreciate the values that it shares with the religious traditions. Thus its sensitivity to the legitimate needs of religious believers would not be feigned or grudging but would be open and generous.

But would a new political coalition actually result from such changed attitudes? The only answer one can give is, maybe. There are a variety of obstacles potentially in the way. For one thing, there really are a lot of issues on which weekly attending believers and secularists disagree. So, for example, while abortion can perhaps be temporarily set aside in a healthcare debate, it obviously cannot be put aside in a debate about abortion. The same is true of stem-cell research, gay marriage, global warming, and all the rest. Even if everyone concedes good will and non-hostility, there is still honest policy disagreement.

Resolving those kinds of policy disagreements requires rapproche-ment, not between believers and secularists, but among believers who disagree about the religious implications of these issues. Secularists will by definition lack credibility in arguing whether the religious traditions should be interpreted to oppose abortion. Rather, liberal religious believers will have to be much more willing to take on their more conservative brethren to make the case for a new set of policy commitments. This actually is already occurring with regard to global warming and may occur with regard to other issues. Of course, though this is never seriously considered in secular circles, it might also be that the religious believers who disagree with secularists are right about some or all of these issues. That possibility has to be considered as well.

Outside issue disagreement, let me set forth two instances in which the potential of new political formations can be seen. The first has to do with practical politics and the second with political theory. Both are just small seeds. But they point toward much greater potential.

The first instance concerns the lighthearted claim by Democrats that the healthcare reform bill originally passed by the House in November 2009 was bipartisan because it had Republican support. It did—exactly one Republican voted for the bill, Joe Cao of Louisiana. The *New York Times* reported that House Majority leader Steny Hoyer of Maryland made that claim of bipartisanship "teasingly" at the news conference to celebrate the bill's passage.[12]

Despite the levity, it was apparently important to the White House that at least one Republican vote for the bill. After the very restrictive anti-abortion amendment by Bart Stupak was adopted by the House, thus satisfying the demands of pro-life Democrats and infuriating the much larger pro-choice bloc, there was apparently widespread pressure on Cao to support the final bill. *Time* described the pressure this way: "The sole vote for the bill came from Cao, a former Jesuit priest who represents a heavily Democratic district and who was leaned upon by the Catholic Bishops and the White House after the Stupak amendment passed."[13] Cao's vote was, in a sense, a religiously oriented vote.

Although the actual effect on voting was small, both the White House and the Bishops were obviously interested in sending a signal that the disagreement over the healthcare bill was premised on a particular issue—abortion—rather than either general hostility by the Catholic Church toward healthcare reform or partisan opposition by the Church

against anything the Democrats might do. The latter point was important to the Democrats as well. This small event could represent a beginning of the creation of a new coalition.

The more general theoretical issue concerns private religious speech
in the public square. For a long time, secularists have argued that religious language in the public square is inappropriate—a conversation
stopper, as Richard Rorty once put it.[14] Rorty later claimed to have
changed his position on that matter[15] and others did as well. Still, as late
as 2006, then-candidate Obama was continuing to tell believers to translate their religious beliefs into secular language before offering those
beliefs as grounds for political action:

> Democracy demands that the religiously motivated translate their concerns into
> universal, rather than religion-specific, values. It requires that their proposals be
> subject to argument, and amenable to reason. I may be opposed to abortion for
> religious reasons, but if I seek to pass a law banning the practice, I cannot simply
> point to the teachings of my church or evoke God's will. I have to explain why
> abortion violates some principle that is accessible to people of all faiths, includ-
> ing those with no faith at all.[16]

Religious believers would be right to ridicule this position as undemocratic in practice and unconstitutional in principle. Believers have
the right to speak in their own language in the public square. And, as
the United States Supreme Court pointed out in the famous "Fuck the
Draft" case, *Cohen v. California*,[17] the form of words can convey as much
as the "ideas" they can be said to embody. The phrase, "I don't agree with
the draft" would just not be the same thing. Translating "God loves the
unborn" into something else would also not convey the message the
believer intends to communicate.

Is religious language undemocratic? Insofar as the insistence on religious grounding costs a speaker political support, no one suffers but
the speaker. That would be a consideration for the speaker and for no
one else. There are no speech monitors in a democratic society who get
to decide who is allowed to say what. For that matter, in a society still
three-fourths Christian, maybe references to the will of God are an excellent democratic strategy.

Is religious language irrational? Who is Barack Obama to declare
that religious claims are not amenable to reason? Many religious believ-

ers think that religious claims are the heart of reason, that God's plan for humanity and creation is plain to see and reflect upon.

In his book *Between Naturalism and Religion*,[18] the German philosopher Jürgen Habermas treats this issue of translation in a subtle way that is helpful to understanding what the role of higher law secularism in politics might be. Habermas treads a difficult line in the book. On the one hand, the "necessary *institutional* separation between religion and politics" must not become "an unreasonable *mental and psychological* burden" for the believer.[19] On the other hand, "[e]very citizen must know and accept that only secular reasons count beyond the institutional threshold separating the informal public sphere from parliaments, courts, ministries, and administrations." Habermas seems to be saying that Obama-like translation is best in the liberal state but concludes that believers "should . . . be allowed to express and justify their convictions in a religious language . . . when they cannot find secular 'translations' for them." I will leave for another time Habermas's contemptuous tone of "allowing" religious believers to speak. Overall, this is a good starting point for politics in a still-religious society.

What is crucial for higher law secularism is what comes next. According to Habermas, all citizens have a democratic obligation to "cooperate in producing a translation" of religious arguments about policies. Both the believers and the secularists have this responsibility. According to Habermas, religious commitments have a particular value in modern politics: "Religious traditions have a special power to articulate moral intuitions, especially with regard to vulnerable forms of communal life."[20] Without a willingness to translate, this content might be lost, which imposes a responsibility and an opportunity on secularists as well as believers: "secular citizens must open their minds to the possible truth content of those presentations and enter into dialogues from which religious reasons might well emerge in the transformed guise of generally accessible arguments."[21]

Whether or not Habermas is a species of higher law secularist, the proposal in this book for higher law secularism is certainly consistent with his vision. Higher law secularism supports an ongoing translation of religious imagery in the public square through government appropriation of religious terms and symbols—and this project of translation is to be justified on purely secular grounds. Higher law secularism is "open" to the secular truth that is expressed in a phrase like "In God We Trust" and does not resist the religious formulation of that truth just because it is expressed in religious terms. The secularist accepts that the believer can only use this kind of religious language to express what she means, but does not consider that fact as constituting an end to dialogue about the meaning that is present.

Higher law secularism agrees with Habermas that the state must be neutral toward religion. But it perhaps goes beyond Habermas in seeing that neutrality means neutral whenever the state is giving reasons for policies, but not necessarily religiously neutral in all of the government's language. While both religious and secular truths are present in religious formulations such as "In God We Trust," the state mines the religious truth for its universal message, a message that is not at all hostile to its specifically religious meaning. Support for this project is precisely the democratic obligation the secular citizen owes to the religious citizen. And the reverse is also true. The believer has an obligation to hear secular reason in its fullness and to try to find the common ground between it and the believer's religious commitments.

Habermas does not speak of a coalition, but of the requirements of citizenship. Nevertheless, it is obvious that a secularism that accepts Habermas's proposal would be able to reach out to religious believers and form healthy political associations that do not currently exist.

All of this requires an understanding that religious believers and secularists are not really speaking languages alien to each other when they speak in the political realm. Secularists understand in a general way the claims that religious believers make concerning the kingdom of God. Religious believers, in their turn, understand the secular hope of universal human rights. Higher law secularism is fundamentally a way to encapsulate common ground between believers and secularists in visual and creed-like form.

There is one important way in which Habermas points beyond political meaning shared by religious and secular citizens, as important as such mutual understanding is. In referring to the "special power" of religion to express moral intuition, Habermas seems to be saying that secularism has something to *learn* from expressions of religious truth. In other words, higher law secularism is not just more open to the coalition building that allows religious and secular citizens to retain their integrity while participating in inclusive political activities. Higher law secularism would actually be willing to consider religious insights for their political merit. Thus higher law secularism might come to represent a different kind of secular politics than secularism does now.

Let me be more specific and contentious about this point. Some religious believers maintain that, either at the moment of conception, or at some other point before birth, the human fetus should be considered a human person, with all the protections that such a status would confer. By and large, secularists have been contemptuous of this claim. In his 1989 dissent in *Webster v. Reproductive Health Services*,[22] for example, Justice Stevens went so far as to claim that he was "not aware of any secular basis for differentiating between contraceptive procedures that are effective immediately before and those that are effective immediately after fertilization," as if fertilization did not have any biological effect and did not create new human DNA. For Justice Stevens only religious people could think that human life begins at conception.

But if at some point prior to birth a human being exists, that point of human personhood must begin sometime. And with the rapid increase in sophistication of prenatal imaging, with some imaging centers now offering "keepsake DVDs," it is going to become impossible to maintain that human life begins at birth and that abortion is purely a private choice. It may even become impossible to be totally indifferent, as secularism surely has been up to now, to the moral implication of stem-cell research.

That does not mean that secularism will change its general commitments in these fields. I am reminded of the observation by one of the leading feminist thinkers in America, Catharine MacKinnon, who acknowledges that "many pregnant women" experience the fetus within them "as a human form of life." The reason for defining personhood at the point of live birth is not because of the nature of unborn life, but because of the reality of "sex inequality in society,"[23] a reality to which, in my view, the pro-life movement has been as indifferent as secularism has been to unborn life.

A higher law secularism that is listening to, and learning from, religion might rethink some of its policy commitments and if not change them, at least better understand religious opposition to them. A more sensitive secularism might emerge.

This leads to the final question of this chapter: what is the nature of politics under higher law secularism? The title of this chapter refers to a "new" politics. In what ways might the politics of higher law secularism be new, compared to those of secularism now?

We can see an example of possible differences in a secular politics open to religion if we ask why the housing market imploded so spectacularly in 2008. Among the many reasons, including the fact that bubbles just happen under capitalism, lies a breakdown in social discipline. As illustrated in the long-term, dramatic decline in the savings rate, Americans are no longer content to wait and save but want to be rich now. This impatience extends to both the borrowers and the lenders.

As a number of observers have noted, this trend can be described in specifically religious terms. In a recent article, Steven Malanga, senior editor of *City Journal* and a senior fellow at the Manhattan Institute, describes the balance of religion and materialism that Alexis de Tocqueville thought imparted morality to America's quest for wealth. Max Weber would later refer to this as the "Protestant ethic" that lies behind the success of capitalism. Malanga then notes the recent decline of these attributes in America:

> What would Tocqueville or Weber think of America today? In place of thrift, they would find a nation of debtors, staggering beneath loans obtained under false pretenses. In place of a steady, patient accumulation of wealth, they would find bankers and financiers with such a short-term perspective that they never pause to consider the consequences or risks of selling securities they don't understand. . . . They would find what Tocqueville described as the "fatal circle" of materialism—the cycle of acquisition and gratification that drives people back to ever more frenetic acquisition and that ultimately undermines prosperous democracies.
>
> And they would understand why. After flourishing for three centuries in America, the Protestant ethic began to disintegrate, with key elements slowly disappearing from modern American society, vanishing from schools, from business, from popular culture, and leaving us with an economic system unmoored from the restraints of civic virtue. Not even Adam Smith—who was a moral philosopher, after all—imagined capitalism operating in such an ethical vacuum.[24]

It is not inevitable that secularism, even as currently formulated, must lead to a politics of destructive individualism. Evolutionary theory can explain the growth in our history of empathy, generosity, altruism, and all the elements necessary for a healthy and flourishing society. Secular politics could be built along those themes instead of being built on the interests of the individual.

But secularism, because it lacks an after-life or other obvious hope that transcends an individual human life, can easily descend into a narrow and selfish quest to satisfy one's own desires here and now. And because the New Atheism describes itself as the alternative to religious enthusiasm, it is particularly susceptible to defining the goal of politics as simply leaving people alone as long as they don't harm each other, as Mark Lilla, who is sort of the political theorist of the New Atheism, puts it.[25]

In contrast, the politics of higher law secularism, because it is by definition open to religious insight, is also open to the idea that there might be more to human life than just earning and shopping. And it is also open to the insight that this "something more" might not just be a matter of individual choice but might have something to do with the nature of the human being and the nature of the universe.

American political life has certainly become more and more a matter of "what's in it for me?" Instead of a challenge to go to the moon or create a new, environmentally sustainable world, we get debates on healthcare, which is the ultimate narcissism.

But how exactly would the politics of higher law secularism come to be different? The change would lie in a different approach to history, sources, tone, and meaning. In terms of American history, higher law secularism could be open in a way that current secular thought, beset by its preoccupation with the separation of church and state, cannot. As I mentioned in the last chapter, current secularism is nervous about our genuinely founding document, The Declaration of Independence, because it, unlike the Constitution, refers to a Creator. Secularists would actually prefer that the Declaration of Independence not be on the walls of every schoolhouse. They prefer the Constitution.

But secularists who feel this way do not understand that the Constitution is primarily a procedural document. There is very little to live for in the Constitution. The Declaration of Independence is about *why* political life is important. The Constitution is about the arrangements that allow politics to go forward without tyranny. The latter is not insignificant by any means, but you don't read the Constitution for inspiration on the Fourth of July.

Secularists are also nervous about perhaps the greatest statement of political morality in our history, Lincoln's Second Inaugural Address, and the reason is the same. There is too much divinity in it. But these references to divinity, including all the other such references in American political history, define the greatness of America, not in the sense that Justice Scalia thinks—declaring a winner in the culture wars—but in the political understanding of reality that they represent. The point of learning from American history is to appropriate the meaning of these references for us here and now, not to delete them or cast them onto the ash heap of history as merely something patriotic and historical. The Declaration of Independence and Abraham Lincoln are still speaking to us, secular as we have become.

Higher law secularism is also open to the depth of great sources of political thinking in a way that current secularism is not. The best example of this is the current enthusiasm for Reinhold Niebuhr. Peter Beinhart led that enthusiasm during the Bush Administration as a kind of counter-weight to the triumphal American exceptionalism of those years.[26] But the enthusiasm for Niebuhr has continued even as the Bush administration has ended. It is symbolically significant that there is a quote from then-Senator Barack Obama on the back cover of the recently republished edition of *The Irony of American History*.[27] Obama is quoted as taking these lessons away from Niebuhr: "there's serious evil in the world, and hardship and pain. And we should be humble and modest in our belief we can eliminate those things. But we shouldn't use that as an excuse for cynicism and inaction."

The problem with this understanding of Niebuhr is that a secularist cannot just put Niebuhr on, like a coat. He is a whole suit of clothes, including underwear. Niebuhr was first and foremost, at all times, in all subjects, a Protestant theologian. For a secularist to learn from Niebuhr requires the same kind of translation that Habermas was talking about. As Brian Urquhart puts it, Niebuhr wrote in the "prophetic style."[28] There is no other way to read Niebuhr except within a biblical framework.

That task of translating Niebuhr is not insurmountable. In fact, it is done with Niebuhr by secularists almost seamlessly, without any apparent difficulty at all. But that just shows the potential of higher law secularism. Secularism already borrows from the religious traditions, but it does so without acknowledgment of the sources of some of its wisdom.

In terms of tone, we have already seen that the new New Secularists, such as Ronald Aronson, are able to define secularism in positive terms. In Aronson's case, for example, the operative tone is one of gratitude. And more generally, I think the reader can detect the spirit of celebration throughout the thinkers discussed in chapter 9. There is a hopeful spirit in the new New Secularism that is absent in the New Atheism. There may in fact be something to hope for in human life, after all. Obviously a politics rooted in that commitment is different from a politics that is not.

This is not the same as the secular utopianism that characterized the French Revolution and the Communist revolutions of the twentieth century. That utopianism probably had a lot in common with certain forms of religion and may in fact have represented a mere substitution of a secular for a Christian eschatology and apocalypticism.

I am speaking here, instead, of hopefulness and a kind of positive spirit that is appreciative of what we have in life and looks to improve the human condition while not limiting the good life to economic accumulation. That is the kind of politics that higher law secularism might be capable of practicing.

The final category of difference between the politics of higher law secularism and current secularism lies in meaning, specifically in the idea that there is meaning in the human condition in the universe. This is a real question for people today and one that we tend to think of in terms of religion versus secularism. That is why the Templeton Foundation, which probes the relationship of religion and science, posed as one of its big questions, "Does the Universe Have a Purpose?" and asked scientists and theologians to answer.[29] Not all the scientists answered no, either.

We have not gotten to the point where the answers to these kinds of questions are really helpful. But that is partly because something like higher law secularism has not yet fully developed. We still tend to divide reality dualistically, into matter and spirit. The former then becomes the secular realm and the latter the religious realm. No secularism can accept such a division.

In higher law secularism, "spirit" would have to be part of matter. If rights are in some sense real, for example, then there is more to the world than the matter that can be measured. This is not a category of the supernatural but an affirmation that there is more to the world than is ordinarily apparent. Purpose would then be one of the invisible attributes with which matter is imbued.

When four leading thinkers came together in October 2009 to address the question "Rethinking Secularism," the central problem for two of the speakers, Charles Taylor and Jürgen Habermas, was characterized as "the challenge of inhabiting a common world without universally shared absolutes."[30] This question is one that secularism currently sees as the outcome of the decline of religion. It is thus secularism's core question. It is normally answered by some form of humanist, relativistic ethics.

Higher law secularism questions this premise. The acceptance of the use of the word "God" in government speech is an assertion that even without supernaturalism, it is still meaningful to speak of shared absolutes. As we have seen, even as atheistic a thinker as Richard Dawkins can point to a moving moral zeitgeist that takes as its premise an absolute toward which morality can move.

This book has not been an argument trying to justify the assertion that there are universally shared absolutes even in the absence of God. Charles Taylor has suggested that secularism lacks the ontology to make such a claim coherent. It is possible that he is right. But it is by no means certain. The acceptance by secularism of religious imagery in the public square represents a commitment, not an argument. It is a commitment to the assertion that absolutes exist that are by their nature universal. Because of that commitment, a common world for the believer and the secularist can be inhabited. That is the place of the new politics of higher law secularism.

CONCLUSION:
PERFECTING DEMOCRACY

Jeffrey Stout's American Academy of Religion's 2007 presidential address concerned the relationship among secularism, religion, and democracy.[1] He claimed that some secularists believe that religion must be removed from the public square in order to safeguard democracy. To the extent that religion must be privatized, however, it is clear that ordinary democratic processes are unlikely to accomplish the goal. Americans are much too religious for that. Thus one is left either with some form of coercion—even if accomplished through the courts rather than the Gulag—or an unperfected democracy.

Stout then went on to argue that democracy open to religion yields better democracy. He pointed to the great reform movements in American history, such as the antislavery movement, that included religious support as well as what today would be called secular support. And Stout does not believe that this is only an American phenomenon. He also invoked the example of South Africa.

The relationship of religion and secularism is the fundamental question of American political and legal life today. It is not always the question on the surface. But, like racial relations, it is often the question below the surface.

In the name of the Constitution, the United States Supreme Court has promised to the American people a public square in which government will be neutral toward religion. That promise has been understood to mean the eradication of religion in that official space. Since that eradication has not occurred and, as Stout points out, is not likely to occur, the Court may be thought to have failed in its obligation to democratic life.

The point of this book is to suggest that the Supreme Court was right in its promise but wrong—deeply wrong—in its understanding of the implication of that promise. A government neutral toward religion is what is needed in an era of growing secularism. But that government need not avoid religion, including its images, language, and symbols. Secularism does not need to banish religion from the public square in order to redeem the promise of neutrality. Instead, secularism needs to find the common ground with religion that will enable a real common-wealth to emerge. Such common ground is available only if we change our frame of reference to seek the secular meaning of religious claims.

As Abraham Lincoln said in his first inaugural address, "We are not enemies, but friends. We must not be enemies." Nor, as I hope this book shows, is there any reason for us to be enemies. We can all share this democracy in order to form a more perfect one.

NOTES

INTRODUCTION

1. 330 U.S. 1 (1947).
2. Robert F. Cochran, "Is There a Higher Law? Does it Matter?" *Pepperdine Law Review* 36 (2009): i.
3. This was Justice Breyer's approach in *Van Orden v. Perry,* 545 U.S. 677, 699 (2005) (J. Breyer, concurring in the judgment): "the Establishment Clause seeks to avoid . . . social conflict. . . ."
4. "Benedict XVI reflects on U.S. visit, recalls highlights," *Catholic News Agency,* April 4, 2008, at http://www.catholic newsagency.com/new.php?n=12499 (accessed April 25, 2010).
5. Ronald Dworkin, *Is Democracy Possible Here?* (Princeton, N.J.: Princeton University Press, 2006).
6. Ibid., 57.
7. Ibid., 58.

1. WHAT WE SAY

1. 330 U.S. 1 (1947).
2. Ibid., 11.
3. *Reynolds v. United States,* 98 U.S. 145, 164 (1878).
4. 330 U.S. at 18.
5. 370 U.S. 421 (1962).
6. 374 U.S. 203 (1963).

7. 370 U.S. at 432 (quoting Madison's *Memorial and Remonstrance against Religious Assessments*).
8. 374 U.S. at 217 (quoting from Justice Rutledge's dissent in *Everson,* 330 U.S. at 31–32).
9. Ibid., 218 (quoting from Justice Jackson's dissent in *Everson,* 330 U.S. at 23–24).
10. Ibid., 279 (J. Brennan, concurring).
11. Ibid., 222.
12. 403 U.S. 602 (1971).
13. 403 U.S. at 612–13.
14. 397 U.S. 664 (1970).
15. Michael W. McConnell, John H. Garvey, and Thomas C. Berg, *Religion and the Constitution* (New York: Aspen Law & Business, 2002), 495.
16. 473 U.S. 373 (1985).
17. 473 U.S. 402 (1985).
18. 472 U.S. 38 (1985).
19. 472 U.S. at 56 (emphasis in original).
20. Ibid., 60.
21. 465 U.S. 668 (1984).
22. 465 U.S. at 687–88.
23. 472 U.S. at 70.
24. 530 U.S. 290 (2000).
25. 472 U.S. at 113 (J. Rehnquist, dissenting).

26. Ibid., 98.

27. 545 U.S. 677 (2005).

28. 545 U.S. 844 (2005).

29. 545 U.S. at 700.

30. Justice Breyer distinguished *McCreary County* from *Van Orden* on the ground, in part, of the "short (and stormy) history" of "a government effort substantially to promote religion. . . ." 545 U.S. at 703 (J. Breyer, concurring in the judgment).

31. 545 U.S. at 869.

32. 400 F. Supp. 2d 707 (M. D. Pa. 2005).

33. Ibid., 727, n. 7, 747 and 748, n. 21.

34. 505 U.S. 577 (1992).

35. See, e.g., *Adler v. Duval County School Bd.*, 250 F.3d 1330 (11th Cir. 2001) (en banc).

36. Douglas Laycock, "Formal, Substantive, and Disaggregated Neutrality Toward Religion," *DePaul Law Review* 39 (1990): 993.

37. 536 U.S. 639 (2002).

38. Ibid., 653.

39. Ibid.

40. *Corporation of the Presiding Bishop of the Church of Jesus Christ of Latter-Day Saints v. Amos*, 483 U.S. 327 (1987).

41. 489 U.S. 1 (1989).

42. 472 U.S. 703 (1985).

43. Ibid., 708–709.

44. 512 U.S. 687 (1994).

45. Ibid., 703.

46. Philip B. Kurland, "Of Church and State and the Supreme Court," *University of Chicago Law Review* 29 (1961): 1.

47. Ibid., 96.

48. *Hobbie v. Unemployment Appeals Comm'n of Fla.*, 480 U.S. 136, 144–45 (1987).

49. 494 U.S. 872 (1990).

50. 333 U.S. 203 (1948).

51. Ibid., 210.

52. Ibid., 212.

53. 343 U.S. 306 (1952).

54. Ibid., 316 (J. Black, dissenting).

2. WHAT WE DO

1. Will Herberg, *Protestant, Catholic, Jew: an Essay in American Religious Sociology* (Garden City, N.Y.: Doubleday, 1955).

2. "Judge doesn't ban 'God' in inaugural oath," *Associated Press* (January 15, 2009), http://www.msnbc.msn.com/id/28663712/ (accessed November 23, 2009).

3. 333 U.S. 203 (1948).

4. Ibid., 256 (J. Reed, dissenting).

5. 343 U.S. 306 (1952).

6. Ibid., 313–14.

7. 343 U.S. at 312–13.

8. 370 U.S. at 435, n. 21.

9. 374 U.S. at 235 (J. Brennan, concurring).

10. Ibid., 237–38.

11. Ibid., 258, n. 24.

12. Ibid., 271.

13. *Marsh*, 463 U.S. at 796 (J. Brennan, dissenting).

14. 374 U.S. at 303–304.

15. 542 U.S. 1 (2004).

16. *Newdow v. U.S. Congress*, 328 F.3d 466 (9th Cir. 2003). Judgment reversed by *Elk Grove Unified School District v. Newdow*, 542 U.S. 1 (2004).

17. "Poll: Keep 'under God' in Pledge of Allegiance," *Associated Press*, March 24, 2004, http://www.firstamendmentcenter.org/news.aspx?id=12989 (accessed April 26, 2010).

18. Steven H. Shiffrin, "The Pluralistic Foundations of the Religion Clauses," *Cornell Law Review* 90 (2004): 9, 65.

19. *McCreary County of Ky. v. American Civil Liberties Union of Ky.*, 545 U.S. 844, 892 (2005), pointing out that the Court occasionally ignores the government neutrality principle in Establishment Clause cases without legitimate justification (J. Scalia, dissenting).

20. Steven G. Gey, "'Under God,' The Pledge of Allegiance, and Other Constitutional Trivia," *North Carolina Law Review* 81 (2003): 1865.

21. *Newdow*, 328 F.3d at 487.

22. *Elk Grove*, 542 U.S. at 12–18. A later California Superior Court decision stated that the two parents have "joint legal custody" but that the mother "makes the final decisions if the two . . . disagree." Ibid., 14.

23. Ibid., 18 (C. J., Rehnquist, concurring in the judgment).

24. Ibid., 45 (J. Thomas, concurring in the judgment).

25. Ibid., 48 (J. Thomas, concurring in the judgment) (quoting from *County of Allegheny v. American Civil Liberties Union, Greater Pittsburgh Chapter*, 492 U.S. 573, 594 [1989]).

26. Ibid., 45.

27. Ibid., 52.

28. Ibid., 26 (C. J. Rehnquist, concurring in the judgment).

29. Ibid., 30 (C. J. Rehnquist, concurring in the judgment).

30. Ibid., 36 (J. O'Connor concurring in the judgment) (quoting concurring opinion in *Lynch v. Donnelly*, 465 U.S. 668, 692–93 [1984]).

31. Ibid., 40 (J. O'Connor concurring in the judgment).

32. Ibid., 42 (J. O'Connor concurring in the judgment).

33. Ibid.

34. Ibid., 40 (J. O'Connor concurring in the judgment).

35. 129 S. Ct. 1125 (2009).

36. 545 U.S. at 869.

37. Ibid., 888–89 (J. Scalia, dissenting).

38. 545 U.S. at 683–84 (C. J. Rehnquist, announcing judgment of the Court).

39. Ibid., 692 (J. Scalia, concurring).

40. Justice Alito's majority opinion in *Pleasant Grove* set forth the Church's account as follows: "The Summum church incorporates elements of Gnostic Christianity [. . . .] According to Summum doctrine, the Seven Aphorisms were inscribed on the original tablets handed down by God to Moses on Mount Sinai. . . . Be-

cause Moses believed that the Israelites were not ready to receive the Aphorisms, he shared them only with a select group of people. In the Summum Exodus account, Moses then destroyed the original tablets, traveled back to Mount Sinai, and returned with a second set of tablets containing the Ten Commandments." 129 S. Ct. at 1129–1130, n. 1 (quoting Respondent's brief).

41. *Pleasant Grove City, Utah v. Summum*, 483 F.3d 1044 (10th Cir. 2007).

42. 129 S. Ct. at 1139 (J. Scalia, concurring).

43. Ibid., 1134.

44. 545 U.S. at 885 (J. Scalia, dissenting).

45. Justice Scalia's *McCreary County* dissent on this point was joined by only Chief Justice Rehnquist and Justice Thomas.

46. 129 S. Ct., at 1135.

47. Ibid.

48. That is how the Ten Commandments monument began in litigation between the City of Ogden, Utah, and Summum. *Summum v. Ogden*, 297 F.3d 995, 997 (10th Cir. 2002).

49. *Van Orden v. Perry*, 545 U.S. 677 (2005).

50. *Marsh v. Chambers*, 463 U.S. 783 (1983).

51. John M. Bickers, "Of Non-Horses, Quantum Mechanics, and the Establishment Clause," *Kansas Law Review* 57 (2009): 405.

52. 410 U.S. 113 (1973).

53. 505 U.S. 833 (1992).

54. 347 U.S. 483 (1954).

55. 349 U.S. 294, 301 (1955).

56. *District of Columbia v. Heller*, 128 S. Ct. 2783 (2008).

57. 545 U.S. at 698 (2005) (J. Breyer, concurring in the judgment). Chief Justice Rehnquist, joined by Justices Scalia, Kennedy, and Thomas voted to uphold a Ten Commandments display in the case.

Justices Stevens, O'Connor, Souter, and Ginsburg dissented.

58. Ibid., 699.

59. Ibid.

60. Ibid., 703.

61. Ibid., 704.

62. Although not precisely the same, this suggestion of essentially political choices by the justices and the people is a kind of "political jurisprudence" along the lines suggested by L. Scott Smith, "Religion, Politics, and the Establishment Clause: Does God Belong in American Public Life?" *Chapman Law Review* 10 (2006): 355.

3. WHY ONLY THE PEOPLE AND NOT HISTORY CAN RESOLVE THE ESTABLISHMENT CLAUSE CRISIS

1. 410 U.S. 113 (1971).

2. Merrill D. Peterson, ed. *Thomas Jefferson: Writings* (New York: The Library of America, 1984), 285.

3. *Jefferson's Letter to the Danbury Baptists* (1802), http://www.loc.gov/loc/lcib/9806/danpre.html (accessed November 10, 2009).

4. Peterson, *Thomas Jefferson: Writings,* 1186–1187 (Thomas Jefferson, letter to Rev. Samuel Miller, from Washington, January 23, 1808).

5. The best presentation of this argument remains, Isaac Kramnick and R. Laurence Moore, *The Godless Constitution,* 2nd ed. (New York: W. W. Norton, 2005).

6. 330 U.S. at 12.

7. C. S. Lewis, *They Asked for a Paper* (London: G. Bles, 1962), 160.

8. 330 U.S. at 11.

9. Ibid., 15.

10. 472 U.S. 38 (1985).

11. Ibid., 92 (J. Rehnquist, dissenting).

12. Ibid., 98.

13. Ibid.

14. Ibid., 114.

15. 545 U.S. at 893 (J. Scalia, dissenting).

16. 463 U.S. 783 (1983).

17. 492 U.S. 573 (1989).

18. 492 U.S. at 670 (Kennedy, J., concurring in the judgment in part and dissenting in part).

19. 545 U.S. 844 (2005).

20. 545 U.S. at 892 (J. Scalia, dissenting).

21. 347 U.S. 483 (1954).

22. 472 U.S. at 98.

23. Catharine Cookson, ed., *Encyclopedia of Religious Freedom* (New York: Routledge, 2003), 436: "It is in the nineteenth century that the thread is taken forward again and the term secularism begins to be used...."

24. The constitutionality of such searches was determined in *Kyllo v. United States,* 533 U.S. 27 (2001). While the Court considered the degree of intrusion possible during the common-law period, no one asked what the framers thought of such technology, nor indeed what they thought the relationship should be in general between privacy and enhanced technology. While the justices found such an intrusion to be a search, no one I suppose would have referred to the opposite result as "demonstrably false."

25. 545 U.S. at 885 and 890 (J. Scalia, dissenting).

26. Ibid., 886.

27. "I do solemnly swear (or affirm) that I will faithfully execute the Office of President of the United States, and will to the best of my Ability, preserve, protect and defend the Constitution of the United States."

28. Kramnick and Moore, *The Godless Constitution.*

29. 545 U.S. at 887 (J. Scalia, dissenting).

30. 494 U.S. 872 (1990).

31. 545 U.S. at 887 (J. Scalia, dissenting).

32. Ibid., 893.

33. Ibid., 894.

34. 545 U.S. at 894 (J. Scalia, dissenting).

35. Ibid., 877.

36. Ibid., 879.

37. Ibid., 881, n. 26.

38. 545 U.S. at 712 and 717 (J. Stevens, dissenting).

39. Ibid., 687 (C. J. Rehnquist, announcing the judgment of the Court).

40. Ibid., 723 (J. Stevens, dissenting).

41. Ibid.

42. 143 U.S. 457, 471 (1892).

43. 545 U.S. at 894-900 (J. Scalia, dissenting).

44. http://www.pilgrimhall.org/GivingThanks3c.htm (capitals in original) (accessed November 12, 2009).

45. 545 U.S. at 897 (J. Scalia, dissenting).

46. Ibid., 897 (italics in the original).

47. Ibid., 896–97.

48. Ibid., 900.

49. Ibid., 893.

50. Andrew Koppelman, "Phony Originalism and the Establishment Clause," *Northwestern University Law Review* 103 (2009): 727.

51. Charles L. Black, Jr., *The People and The Court: Judicial Review in a Democracy* (New York: Macmillan, 1960).

52. Ibid., 2.

53. Larry D. Kramer, *The People Themselves* (New York: Oxford University Press, 2004); and Mark V. Tushnet, *Taking The Constitution Away From the Courts* (Princeton, N.J.: Princeton University Press, 1999). For a recent account of the influence of public opinion on the Supreme Court, see Barry Friedman, *The Will of the People* (New York: Farrar, Straus and Giroux, 2009).

54. *Debs v. United States*, 249 U.S. 211 (1919).

55. Anthony Lewis, "Justice Holmes and the Splendid Prisoner," *New York Review of Books*, Vol. 56 Number 11, July 2, 2009 (reviewing Ernest Freeberg, *Democ-*

racy's Prisoner: Eugene Debs, the Great War, and the Right to Dissent [2008]).

56. 165 U.S. 578 (1897).

57. Some observers regard *Chicago, Milwaukee & St. Paul Railway v. Minnesota,* 134 U.S. 418 (1890) as the first such case, but the dispute need not concern us.

58. Jesse H. Choper, et al, *Constitutional Law* (St. Paul, Minn.: Thomson/West, 2006), 311.

59. 198 U.S. 45 (1905).

60. *West Coast Hotel Co. v. Parrish,* 300 U.S. 379 (1937).

61. *NLRB v. Jones & Laughlin Steel Corp.,* 301 U.S. 1 (1937).

62. 198 U.S. at 75 (J. Holmes, dissenting).

63. Jack Balkin, "Wrong the Day It Was Decided: Lochner and Constitutional Historicism," *Boston University Law Review* 85 (2005): 720.

64. 491 U.S. 397 (1989).

65. *United States v. Eichman,* 496 U.S. 310 (1990).

66. *Planned Parenthood of Southeastern Pennsylvania v. Casey,* 505 U.S. 833, 1000–1001 (1992) (J. Scalia, concurring in the judgment in part and dissenting in part).

4. PROPOSALS THAT HAVE FAILED TO RESOLVE THE ESTABLISHMENT CLAUSE CRISIS

1. Steven G. Gey, "Life After the Establishment Clause," *West Virginia Law Review* 110 (2007): 2–3, n. 6.

2. *Hinrichs v. Bosma,* 400 F. Supp. 2d 1103, 1125 (S. D. Ind. 2005) (calling the Brennan dissent a "powerful argument"), judgment reversed by *Hinrichs v. Speaker of House of Representatives of Indiana General Assembly,* 506 F.3d 584 (7th Cir. 2007).

3. Steven G. Gey, "Rewriting the Establishment Clause for One Nation Under (A) God," *Tulsa Law Review* 41 (2006): 737.

4. Kramnick and Moore, *The Godless Constitution,* 196–97.

5. Suzanna Sherry, "Without Virtue There Can Be No Liberty," *Minnesota Law Review* 78 (1993): 82.

6. Kathleen M. Sullivan, "Religion and Liberal Democracy," *University of Chicago Law Review* 59 (1992): 207 n. 59.

7. Gey, "Under God," 1865; see also, Steven B. Epstein, "Rethinking the Constitutionality of Ceremonial Deism," *Columbia Law Review* 96 (1996): 2083.

8. Douglas Laycock, "Theology Scholarships, the Pledge of Allegiance, and Religious Liberty: Avoiding the Extremes but Missing the Liberty," *Harvard Law Review* 118 (2004): 156.

9. Arnold H. Loewy, "The Positive Reality and Normative Virtues of a 'Neutral' Establishment Clause," *Brandeis Law Journal* 41 (2003): 542-43.

10. Christopher L. Eisgruber and Lawrence G. Sager, *Religious Freedom and the Constitution* (Cambridge, Mass.: Harvard University Press, 2007), 277-78. (Pledge of Allegiance only constitutional if accompanied by secular alternative).

11. Susan Gellman and Susan Looper-Friedman, "Thou Shalt Use the Equal Protection Clause for Religion Cases (Not Just the Establishment Clause)," *University of Pennsylvania Journal of Constitutional Law* 10 (2008): 665.

12. Martha C. Nussbaum, *Liberty of Conscience* (New York: Basic Books, 2008), 308-14.

13. Loewy, "The Positive Reality," 542.

14. Steven H. Shiffrin, *The Religious Left and Church-State Relations* (Princeton, N.J.: Princeton University Press, 2009), 47.

15. Kramnick and Moore, *The Godless Constitution*, 197.

16. Sullivan, "Religion and Liberal Democracy," 207 n. 59: "Rote recitation of God's name is easily distinguished as a *de minimis* endorsement in comparison with prayer or the seasonal invocation of sacred symbols. The pledge of allegiance is a closer question."

17. Nussbaum, *Liberty of Conscience*, 314.

18. Noah Feldman, *Divided by God* (New York: Farrar, Straus, and Giroux, 2005).

19. 545 U.S. at 893 (J. Scalia dissenting).

20. 465 U.S. 668 (1984).

21. 465 U.S. at 693 (J. O'Connor, concurring).

22. 465 U.S. at 717 (J. Brennan, dissenting).

23. Ibid., 716-17 (references omitted).

24. *County of Allegheny*, 492 U.S. at 673 (1989) (J. Kennedy, concurring in the judgment and dissenting in part).

25. 542 U.S. at 45 (J. Thomas, concurring in the judgment).

26. Pa. Const., Art. I, Section 3.

27. *District of Columbia v. Heller*, 128 S. Ct. 2783 (2008).

28. 542 U.S. at 52 (J. Thomas, concurring in the judgment).

29. See *Edwards v. Aguillard*, 482 U.S. 578, 583-84 (1987) (likelihood of coercion in public schools because of mandatory attendance laws, emulation of teachers and peer pressure); see also *Lee v. Weisman*, 505 U.S. 577, 592 (1992) (particular risk of coercion in school context).

30. Thus in *Lee*, the Court found coercion at high school graduations, but also noted government's involvement in the prayers at issue. 505 U.S. at 587-88.

31. 530 U.S. 290 (2000).

32. Ibid., 309-10 (quoting *Lynch*, 465 U.S. at 688 [J. O'Connor, concurring]).

33. 370 U.S. 421, 435 n.21 (1962).

34. *Santa Fe*, 530 U.S. at 310.

35. Compare Justice Kennedy's majority opinion in *Lee*, 505 U.S. at 588 (in high school graduation context "subtle coercive pressures exist" and there are "no real

alternative[s] which would have allowed [the student] to avoid the fact or appearance of participation") with Justice Scalia's dissent, 505 U.S. at 640 ("The deeper flaw in the Court's opinion does not lie in its wrong answer to the question whether there was state-induced 'peer-pressure' coercion; it lies, rather, in the Court's making violation of the Establishment Clause hinge on such a precious question. The coercion that was a hallmark of historical establishments of religion was coercion of religious orthodoxy and of financial support *by force of law and threat of penalty.*") (italics in original).

36. 542 U.S. at 53 (J. Thomas, concurring in the judgment) (references omitted).

37. 492 U.S. at 657 and 661 (J. Kennedy, concurring in the judgment in part and dissenting in part).

38. Frederick Mark Gedicks and Roger Hendrix, "Uncivil Religion: Judeo-Christianity and the Ten Commandments," *West Virginia Law Review* 110 (2007): 276.

39. Bruce Ledewitz, *American Religious Democracy* (Westport, Conn.: Praeger Publishers, 2007).

40. Ibid., 46.

41. Gedicks and Hendrix, "Uncivil Religion," 278.

42. Steven D. Smith, "'Sectarianizing' Civil Religion? A Comment on Gedicks and Hendrix," *West Virginia Law Review* 110 (2007): 308–309.

43. Ibid.

44. Ira Lupu, "Government Messages and Government Money: Santa Fe, Mitchell v. Helms, and the Arc of the Establishment Clause," *William & Mary Law Review* 42 (2001): 771.

45. Ibid., 803–804.

46. Ibid., 803.

47. Ibid., 817.

48. Ibid. It should be noted that the Court has expressly refused to permit government to establish "an official or civic religion as a means of avoiding the establishment of a religion with more specific creeds . . ." *Lee v. Weisman,* 505 U.S. 577, 590 (1992).

49. Ibid., at 817–18.

50. These statistics are discussed in chapter 8, infra.

51. See *Van Orden v. Perry,* 545 U.S. 679 (2005) and *Pleasant Grove City, Utah v. Summum,* 129 S. Ct. 1125 (2009).

52. 545 U.S. 900 (J. Scalia, dissenting).

53. Wade Clark Roof, "The Primacy of Practice," *The Immanent Frame,* http://www.ssrc.org/blogs/immanent_frame/2009/06/08/the-primacy-of-practice/ (accessed May 6, 2010).

54. See *Lee,* 505 U.S. at 613: "Some have challenged this precedent by reading the Establishment Clause to permit "nonpreferential" state promotion of religion" (J. Souter, concurring).

55. See, e.g., Patrick M. Garry, "Religious Freedom Deserves More Than Neutrality: The Constitutional Argument for Nonpreferential Favoritism of Religion," *Florida Law Review* 57 (2005); Rodney K. Smith, "Nonpreferentialism in Establishment Clause Analysis: A Response to Professor Laycock," *St. John's Law Review* 65 (1991); and Martin Nussbaum, "A Garment for the Naked Public Square: Nurturing American Public Theology," *Cumberland Law Review* 16 (1985). An important book supporting the position is Robert L. Cord, *Separation of Church and State: Historical Fact and Current Fiction* (New York: Lambeth Press, 1982).

56. In a sense, all of the writers I identify above with separation, neutrality, and equality are opponents of nonpreferentialism. See in particular, Douglas Laycock, "'Nonpreferential' Aid to Religion: A False Claim About Original Intent," *William & Mary Law Review* 27 (1986): 875.

57. See Kelly S. Terry, "Shifting Out of Neutral: Intelligent Design and the Road to Nonpreferentialism, *Boston University Public Interest Law Journal* 18 (2008): 67.

58. 472 U.S. at 91–92 (J. Rehnquist, dissenting).

59. Ibid., 98–99.

60. This is more or less the position that Eisgruber and Sager oppose in *Religious Freedom and the Constitution*.

61. 472 U.S. at 91–92 (J. Rehnquist, dissenting).

62. See, e.g., Kelly S. Terry, "Shifting Out of Neutral: Intelligent Design and the Road to Nonpreferentialism," *Boston University Public Interest Law Journal* 18 (2008): 67.

63. 545 U.S. at 893 (J. Scalia, dissenting).

64. Ibid.

65. Ibid.

66. Ibid.

67. See Wade Clark Roof, "The Primacy of Practice," *The Immanent Frame*, http://www.ssrc.org/blogs/immanent_frame/2009/06/08/the-primacy-of-practice/ (accessed May 6, 2010).

68. 545 U.S. at 894 n. 3 (J. Scalia dissenting).

69. *Van Orden v. Perry,* 545 U.S. 677, 692 (2005) (J. Scalia, concurring).

70. 505 U.S. at 645 (J. Scalia, dissenting).

71. This point is similar to an important admonition by Michael McConnell that the absence of religion is not per se neutral: "If the public school day and all its teaching is strictly secular, the child is likely to learn the lesson that religion is irrelevant to the significant things of this world, or at least that the spiritual realm is radically separate and distinct from the temporal. However unintended, these are lessons about religion. They are not 'neutral.' Studious silence on a subject that parents may say touches all of life is an

eloquent refutation." "Neutrality Under the Religion Clauses," *Northwestern University Law Review* 81 (1986): 162.

72. 545 U.S. at 900 (J. Scalia dissenting).

73. 465 U.S. 668 (1984).

74. Ibid., 693 (J. O'Connor concurring).

75. *Elk Grove,* 542 U.S. at 40 (J. O'Connor, concurring in the judgment).

76. *Lynch,* 465 U.S. at 716 (J. Brennan, dissenting) (quoting a book review that had quoted Dean Rostow).

77. Ibid.

78. *County of Allegheny,* 492 U.S. 573 (1989).

79. Ibid., at 673 (J. Kennedy, concurring in the judgment in part).

80. 505 U.S. at 589.

81. *Santa Fe,* 530 U.S. at 307.

82. *Lee,* 505 U.S. at 641 (J. Scalia dissenting).

83. 370 U.S. 421, 435, n. 21 (1962): "There is of course nothing in the decision reached here that is inconsistent with the fact that school children and others are officially encouraged to express love for our country by reciting historical documents such as the Declaration of Independence which contain references to the Deity or by singing officially espoused anthems which include the composer's professions of faith in a Supreme Being, or with the fact that there are many manifestations in our public life of belief in God. Such patriotic or ceremonial occasions bear no true resemblance to the unquestioned religious exercise that the State of New York has sponsored in this instance."

5. THE ESTABLISHMENT OF HIGHER LAW

1. *Rosenberger v. University of Virginia,* 515 U.S. 819, 833 (1995).

2. For the relationship of government speech to public forum analysis, see

generally, Mary Jean Dolan, "The Special Public Purpose Forum and Endorsement Relationships: New Extensions of Government Speech," *Hastings Constitutional Law Quarterly* 31 (2004): 71.

3. 129 S. Ct. at 1139 (J. Stevens, concurring).

4. Ibid., 1131: "Government is not restrained by the First Amendment from controlling its own expression" (quoting Justice Stewart's concurrence in *Columbia Broadcasting System, Inc. v. Democratic National Committee*, 412 U.S. 94, 139, n. 7 [1973]).

5. Ibid. (quoting Justice Scalia's concurrence in *National Endowment for the Arts v. Finley*, 524 U.S. 569, 598 [1998]).

6. Mary Jean Dolan, "The Special Public Purpose Forum and Endorsement Relationships: New Extensions of Government Speech," *Hastings Constitutional Law Quarterly* 31 (2004): 71.

7. 523 U.S. 666 (1998).

8. 524 U.S. 569 (1998).

9. 523 U.S. at 683.

10. 500 U.S. 173 (1991).

11. Ibid., 192 (quoting brief for petitioners).

12. See e.g., *Rosenberger*, 515 U.S. at 833.

13. 531 U.S. 533 (2001).

14. 515 U.S. 819, 833 (1995).

15. 544 U.S. 550 (2005).

16. Ibid., 571 (J. Souter, dissenting).

17. 129 S. Ct. 1125 (2009).

18. 129 S. Ct., at 1139 (J. Stevens, concurring).

19. *Finley*, 524 U.S. at 599 n. 3 (1998) (J. Scalia, concurring in the judgment).

20. *Pleasant Grove*, 129 S. Ct. at 1139 (J. Stevens concurring).

21. Robert D. Kamenshire, "The First Amendment's Implied Political Establishment Clause," *California Law Review* 67 (1979): 1110.

22. Kent Greenawalt, Book Review, "How Does 'Equal Liberty' Fare in Relation to Other Approaches to the Religion Clauses?" *Texas Law Review* 85 (2007): 1233–1234.

23. *Finley*, 524 U.S. at 599 n.3 (1998) (J. Scalia, concurring in the judgment).

24. Edward S. Corwin, "The 'Higher Law' Background of American Constitutional Law," *Harvard Law Review* 42 (1928): 367.

25. See Patrick McKinley Brennan, "Persons, Participating, and 'Higher Law,'" *Pepperdine Law Review* 36 (2009): 481.

26. See Frederick Mark Gedicks, "An Originalist Defense of Substantive Due Process: Magna Carta, Higher-Law Constitutionalism, and the Fifth Amendment," *Emory Law Journal* 58 (2009): 585.

27. "The jurists who believe in natural law seem to me to be in that naïve state of mind that accepts what has been familiar and accepted by them and by their neighbors as something that must be accepted by all men everywhere." Oliver Wendell Holmes, "Natural Law," 32 *Harvard Law Review* 40, 41 (1918).

28. C. S. Lewis, *The Abolition of Man; or, Reflections on Education With Special Reference to the Teaching of English in the Upper Forms of Schools* (New York: The Macmillan Company, 1947).

29. Ibid., 2.

30. Ibid., 9.

31. "The God Debate," *Newsweek*, April 9, 2007, http://www.newsweek.com/id/35784 (accessed May 7, 2010).

32. Charles L. Black Jr., *The Humane Imagination* (Woodbridge, Conn.: Ox Bow Press, 1986), 37.

33. Lewis, *Abolition of Man*, 12.

34. Paul Bloom, "The Moral Lives of Babies," *New York Times Magazine*, May 9, 2010, 44.

35. Arthur Leff, "Unspeakable Ethics, Unnatural Law," *Duke Law Journal* 1979 (1979): 1249:

As things now stand, everything is up
for grabs.
Nevertheless:
Napalming babies is bad.
Starving the poor is wicked.
Buying and selling each other is
depraved.
Those who stood up to and died resist-
ing Hitler, Stalin, Amin, and Pol
Pot—and General Custer too—
have earned salvation.
Those who acquiesced deserve to be
damned.
There is in the world such a thing as
evil.
[All together now:] Sez who?
God help us.

36. Alfred North Whitehead, *Adventures of Ideas* (New York: The Macmillan Company, 1933), 125. My friend and colleague Robert Taylor pointed this reference out to me.

37. 370 U.S. 435, n. 21: "There is of course nothing in the decision reached here that is inconsistent with the fact that school children and others are officially encouraged to express love for our country by reciting historical documents such as the Declaration of Independence which contain references to the Deity. . . ."

38. Robert F. Cochran, "Is There a Higher Law? Does it Matter?" *Pepperdine Law Review* 36 (2009): ii.

39. Howard Lesnick, "The Rhetoric of Anti-Relativism in a Culture of Certainty," *Buffalo Law Review* 55 (2007): 899, quoting Clifford Geertz, *Islam Observed: Religious Development in Morocco and Indonesia* (New Haven, Conn.: Yale University Press, 1968), 97.

40. Pope Benedict XVI, *Charity in Truth* (San Francisco: Ignatius Press, 2009) accessed at http://www.vatican.va/holy_father/benedict_xvi/encyclicals/documents/hf_ben-xvi_enc_20090629_caritas-in-veritate_en.html (Introduction) (accessed May 8, 2010).

41. Connie S. Rosati, "Is There a 'Higher Law?' Does it Matter?" *Pepperdine Law Review* 36 (2009): 623.

42. Ibid., 624.

43. H. L. A. Hart, "Positivism and the Separation of Law and Morals," *Harvard Law Review* 71 (1958) and Lon L. Fuller, "Positivism and Fidelity to Law: A Reply to Professor Hart, *Harvard Law Review* 71 (1958).

44. Steven D. Smith, *Law's Quandary* (Cambridge, Mass.: Harvard University Press, 2004).

45. Steven D. Smith, "Higher Law Questions: A Prelude to the Symposium," *Pepperdine Law Review* 36 (2009): 473.

46. John 14:6.

47. John 18:38.

48. Joseph Cardinal Ratzinger, *Truth and Tolerance: Christian Belief and World Religions*. Translated by Henry Taylor (San Francisco: Ignatius Press, 2004), 230.

49. Charles Taylor, *A Secular Age* (Cambridge, Mass.: Belknap Press of Harvard University Press, 2007), 609.

50. 380 U.S. 163 (1965).

51. 398 U.S. 333 (1970).

52. 380 U.S. at 176.

53. 398 U.S. at 340 (J. Black, announcing the judgment of the Court).

54. Mark Juergensmeyer, "Rethinking Secularism in the Global Age," *The Immanent Frame* (September 11, 2008) http://blogs.ssrc.org/tif/2009/09/08/rethinking-secularism-and-religion-in-the-global-age/ (accessed May 8, 2010).

55. Mark Lilla, *The Stillborn God: Religion, Politics and the Modern West* (New York: Knopf, 2007).

56. Mark Lilla, "The Politics of God," *New York Times Magazine*, August 19, 2007, http://www.nytimes.com/2007/08/19/magazine/19Religion-t.html?_r=1&scp=1&sq=mark+lilla&st=nyt (accessed May 8, 2010).

57. Steven G. Gey, "Life After the Establishment Clause," *West Virginia Law Review* 110 (2007): 33.

58. 430 U.S. 705 (1977).

59. http://gretachristina.typepad
.com/greta_christinas_weblog/2009/08/
church-and-state.html (accessed November 12, 2009).

60. *Lynch v. Donnelly,* 465 U.S. 668, 688 (1984) (J. O'Connor, concurring).

61. 319 U.S. 624 (1943).

62. Ibid., 642.

63. Martin H. Redish and Kevin Finnerty, "What Did You Learn in School Today? Free Speech, Values Inculcation, and the Democratic-Educational Paradox," *Cornell Law Review* 88 (2002): 62.

64. Stephen E. Gottlieb, "In the Name of Patriotism: The Constitutionality of 'Bending' History in Public Secondary Schools," *New York University Law Review* 62 (1987): 497 and Stanley Ingber, "Socialization, Indoctrination, or the 'Pall of Orthodoxy': Value Training in the Public Schools," *University of Illinois Law Review* 1987 (1987): 15.

65. Jeremy Waldron, "Right and Wrong: Psychologists vs. Philosophers," *New York Review of Books,* October 8, 2009, http://www.nybooks.com/articles/archives/2009/oct/08/right-and-wrong-psychologists-vs-philosophers/ (accessed May 8, 2010).

6. USING RELIGIOUS SYMBOLS TO ESTABLISH HIGHER LAW

1. The endorsement test was undermined to an uncertain extent in two opinions in *Salazar v. Buono,* 130 S. Ct. 1803 (2010), which is discussed further in the text below. Justice Kennedy (for himself and Chief Justice Roberts) referred to his previous criticisms of the test, see ibid., 1819, and Justice Alito referred to the test as the "so-called 'endorsement test,'" ibid., 1824, which is not much of an endorsement. Since Justices Scalia and Thomas would certainly vote to overturn the endorsement test, its validity is in question.

2. 130 S. Ct. 1803 (2010).

3. Justice Alito actually decided for himself that implementation of the land transfer statute would not violate the Establishment Clause. Justice Kennedy and Chief Justice Roberts seemed to agree with that despite the limited relief granted by the Court. Justices Scalia and Thomas decided that the plaintiff lacked standing, but presumably also agreed that the statute is constitutional. There does not seem to be any doubt as to what will happen next in the case: the transfer will be permitted and the cross will stay.

4. For full text, see http://www
.arlingtoncemetery.net/flanders.htm
(accessed April 29, 2010).

5. 130 S. Ct. at 1820.

6. Ledewitz, *American Religious Democracy,* 203.

7. Robert N. Bellah, *Beyond Belief* (New York: Harper & Row, 1970), 168.

8. Ibid., 171.

9. 505 U.S. at 589.

10. Wilfred M. McClay, "Foreword," in Ronald Weed and John von Heyking, eds., *Civil Religion in Political Thought* (Washington, D.C.: The Catholic University of America Press, 2010), x.

11. Ratzinger, *Truth and Tolerance,* 238.

12. http://www.indiana.edu/~ivieweb/
mlkwhere.html (accessed May 8, 2010).

13. Pierre Teilhard de Chardin, *The Divine Milieu* (Brighton, England; Portland, Ore.: Sussex Academic Press, 2004), 116.

14. John Dewey, *A Common Faith* (New Haven, Conn.: Yale University Press, 1974).

15. *Lynch,* 465 U.S. at 693 (J. O'Connor, concurring).

16. Ibid., 716–17 (J. Brennan, dissenting) (references omitted).

17. *McCreary County,* 545 U.S. at 893 (J. Scalia, dissenting).

18. Ibid.

19. Steven Goldberg, *Bleached Faith* (Stanford, Calif.: Stanford Law Books, 2008).

20. Ibid., 81 and 130.

21. *Lynch,* 465 U.S. at 711–12 (J. Brennan, dissenting).

22. Shiffrin, *The Religious Left,* 44.

23. Feldman, *Divided by God,* 242.

24. Austin Dacey, *The Secular Conscience* (Amherst, N.Y.: Prometheus Books, 2008).

25. Bruce Ledewitz, *Hallowed Secularism* (New York: Palgrave Macmillan, 2009).

7. APPLYING HIGHER LAW IN CHURCH/STATE ISSUES

1. Alexander M. Bickel, *The Least Dangerous Branch,* 2nd ed. (New Haven, Conn.: Yale University Press, 1986), 111–27.

2. 393 U.S. 97 (1968).

3. 482 U.S. 578 (1987).

4. Philip Kitcher, *Living with Darwin* (Oxford; New York: Oxford University Press, 2007).

5. 400 F. Supp. 2d at 737.

6. Deborah Solomon, "Questions for Robert Wright," *New York Times Magazine,* May 31, 2009, 22.

7. Richard Dawkins, *River Out of Eden* (New York: Basic Books, 1995), 133.

8. Steven Weinberg, "Without God," *New York Review of Books,* September 25, 2008, accessed at http://www.nybooks.com/articles/21800 (accessed October 12, 2009).

9. Frans B. M. de Waal, *Primates and Philosophers* (Princeton, N.J.: Princeton University Press, 2006).

10. Simon Conway Morris, *Life's Solution* (New York: Cambridge University Press, 2003).

11. Stuart A. Kauffman, *Reinventing the Sacred* (New York: Basic Books, 2008).

12. 374 U.S. 203 (1963).

13. 449 U.S. 39 (1980).

14. 505 U.S. 577 (1992).

15. 530 U.S. 390 (2000).

16. 505 U.S., at 589.

17. Ted Peters and Martin Hewlett, *Can You Believe in God and Evolution* (Nashville, Tenn.: Abingdon Press, 2006).

18. *McCollum v. Board of Education,* 333 U.S. 203 (1948).

19. *Zorach v. Clauson,* 343 U.S. 306 (1952).

20. *Freedom From Religion Foundation, Inc. v. Obama,* --- F. Supp. 2d --- (W. D. Wis. 2010).

21. The reader should note that this discussion is entirely hypothetical with regard to the YMCA. I have no idea how and whether my branch, or any other branch, pursues these program objectives. The issues raised, however, are in no sense hypothetical. They are being raised all the time.

22. All biblical references are taken from the Revised Standard Version, 1952.

23. 551 U.S. 587 (2007).

24. Kramnick and Moore, *The Godless Constitution.*

25. Ibid., 19.

26. Ibid., 168.

27. U.S. Const. art. VI, cl. 3: "but no religious Test shall ever be required as a Qualification to any Office or public Trust under the United States."

28. 403 U.S. at 622.

29. Rebecca Sinderbrand, "New Huckabee Ad Appeals to Christian Conservatives," CNN report, http://www.cnn.com/2008/POLITICS/01/01/huckabee.christians/index.html, January 1, 2008 (accessed May 8, 2010).

30. David Edwards and Jason Rhyne, "Catholic League President Slams Huckabee for 'Subliminal' Cross Ad," *The Raw Story* report, http://rawstory.com/news/2007/Fox_rips_Huckabee_for_using_subliminal_1218.html, December 18, 2007 (accessed May 8, 2010).

8. THE FAILURE OF SECULARISM UNDER THE NEW ATHEISM

1. Ledewitz, *Hallowed Secularism.*

2. Dacey, *The Secular Conscience.*

3. Ledewitz, *American Religious Democracy,* 3.

4. Then Senator Hillary Clinton announced in January 2005 that she had "always been a praying person." Michael Jonas, "Sen. Clinton Urges Use of Faith-Based Initiatives," *Boston Globe*, January 20, 2005, B1.

5. Ledewitz, *American Religious Democracy*, 203.

6. Nancy Gibbs and Michael Duffy, "How the Democrats Got Religion," *Time Magazine*, July 12, 2007.

7. http://www.crosswalk.com/news/commentary/11543702/, June 7, 2007 (accessed October 17, 2009).

8. See e.g., Sigmund Freud, *The Future of an Illusion*, trans. W. D. Robson-Scott (New York: H. Liveright, 1928).

9. See e.g., Bryan R. Wilson, *Religion in a Secular Society: A Sociological Comment* (London: Watts, 1966).

10. John Micklethwait and Adrian Wooldridge, *God is Back* (New York: Penguin Press, 2009).

11. Ross Douthat, "Mass Market Atheism," *The Atlantic*, July/August 2008, http://www.theatlantic.com/doc/200807/atheism-douthat (accessed May 8, 2010).

12. Sam Harris, *The End of Faith* (New York: W. W. Norton & Co., 2004).

13. Daniel C. Dennett, *Breaking the Spell* (New York: Viking, 2006).

14. Richard Dawkins, *The God Delusion* (Boston: Houghton Mifflin Co., 2006).

15. Victor J. Stenger, *God: The Failed Hypothesis* (Amherst, N.Y.: Prometheus Books, 2007).

16. Christopher Hitchens, *God Is Not Great* (New York: Twelve, 2007).

17. Mark Lilla, *The Stillborn God* (New York: Knopf, 2007).

18. See, e.g., Tina Beattie, *The New Atheists* (Maryknoll, N.Y.: Orbis Books, 2007) and John F. Haught, *God and the New Atheism* (Louisville, Ky.: Westminster John Knox Press, 2008).

19. Kevin Phillips, *American Theocracy* (New York: Viking, 2006).

20. Kitcher, *Living with Darwin*.

21. Richard Dawkins, *The Blind Watchmaker* (New York: Norton, 1986).

22. Peter Hamby, "Obama: GOP Doesn't Own Faith Issue," *CNN Politics*, October 8, 2007, http://www.cnn.com/2007/POLITICS/10/08/obama.faith/ (accessed October 17, 2009).

23. *Transcripts, CNN*, http://transcripts.cnn.com/TRANSCRIPTS/0706/04/sitroom.03.html, June 4, 2007 (accessed October 17, 2009).

24. Rick Warren, *The Purpose Driven Life* (Grand Rapids, Mich.: Inspirio, 2004).

25. Cathy Lynn Grossman, "An Inaugural First: Obama Acknowledges 'Non-Believers,'" *USA Today*, January 22, 2009, http://www.usatoday.com/news/religion/2009-01-20-obama-non-believers_N.htm (accessed May 9, 2010).

26. *Pew Forum on Religion and Public Life*, "How the Faithful Voted," November 5, 2008, http://pewforum.org/docs/?DocID=367(accessed November 26, 2009).

27. Barry A. Kosmin and Ariela Keysar, "Summary Report, March 2009," *Trinity College*, http://livinginliminality.files.wordpress.com/2009/03/aris_report_2008.pdf (accessed November 10, 2009).

28. Jon Meacham, "The End of Christian America," *Newsweek*, April 4, 2009, http://www.newsweek.com/id/192583 (accessed November 14, 2009).

29. Cathy Lynn Grossman, "People with 'No Religion' Gain on Major Denominations," *USA Today*, September 22, 2009, http://www.usatoday.com/news/religion/2009-09-22-no-religion_N.htm (accessed October 20, 2009).

30. Kosmin and Keysar, http://livinginliminality.files.wordpress.com/2009/03/aris_report_2008.pdf.

31. Grossman, "People with 'No Religion' Gain on Major Denominations."

32. Sam Schulman, "Divine Comedy," *Commentary,* June 2007, http://www.commentarymagazine.com/viewarticle.cfm/god-is-not-great-by-christopher-hitchens-10890?search=1 (accessed May 9, 2010).

33. Stenger, *God.*

34. Ibid., 78.

35. Ibid., 195–96.

36. Ibid., 252.

37. Ibid.

38. Ibid., 254.

39. Ibid., 257.

40. Ibid., 258.

41. Ibid., 256.

42. Hitchens, *God Is Not Great,* 283.

43. Ibid.

44. *Pew Forum on Religion and Public Life,* "Many Americans Mix Multiple Faiths," December 9, 2009, http://pewforum.org/docs/?DocID=490 (accessed December 10, 2009).

45. Stenger, *God,* 195.

46. Genesis 18:25.

47. Dawkins, *The God Delusion,* 42.

48. Ibid., 221.

49. Ibid., 222.

50. Ibid., 233.

51. Ibid., 262.

52. Ibid.

53. Ibid., 271.

54. Ibid., 270.

55. Christopher Hitchens, "'Evil,' Scoff if you must, but you can't avoid it," *Slate,* December 31, 2002, http://www.slate.com/id/2076195 (accessed May 9, 2010).

56. Dennett, *Breaking the Spell,* 285.

57. Ibid., 305.

58. Ibid.

59. Richard John Neuhaus, *The Naked Public Square* (Grand Rapids, Mich.: W. B. Eerdmans Pub. Co., 1984), 173.

9. THE NEW NEW SECULARISM AND THE HIGHER LAW

1. Peter Steinfels, "The New Atheism, and Something More," *New York Times,* February 13, 2009, http://www.nytimes.com/2009/02/14/us/14beliefs.html (accessed October 30, 2009).

2. Ibid. (quoting Ronald Aronson).

3. Ronald Aronson, *Living Without God* (Berkeley, Calif.: Counterpoint, 2008).

4. André Comte-Sponville, *The Little Book of Atheist Spirituality,* trans. Nancy Huston (New York: Viking Press, 2007).

5. Steinfels, supra (quoting Comte-Sponville).

6. John Dewey, *A Common Faith* (New Haven, Conn.: Yale University Press, 1974 ed.), 53.

7. See e.g., Michael Hampson, *God Without God* (Winchester, UK; New York: O Books, 2008).

8. Kauffman, *Reinventing the Sacred.*

9. Ibid., 3.

10. See Walter Isaacson, *Einstein* (New York: Simon & Schuster, 2007), 335.

11. Kauffman, *Reinventing the Sacred,* 6.

12. Ibid., 9.

13. Conway Morris, *Life's Solution.*

14. Ibid., 2.

15. Ibid., 327.

16. Joseph Cardinal Ratzinger, *Truth and Tolerance,* trans. Henry Taylor (San Francisco: Ignatius Press, 2004), 141–42.

17. Dacey, *The Secular Conscience.*

18. Ibid., 23.

19. Ibid., 41.

20. Lewis, *The Abolition of Man,* 12.

21. Ronald Aronson, "The New Atheists," *The Nation,* June 7, 2007, http://www.thenation.com/doc/20070625/aronson (accessed November 21, 2009).

22. Chet Raymo, *When God is Gone Everything is Holy* (Notre Dame, Ind.: Sorin Books, 2008).

23. Susan Neiman, *Moral Clarity* (Orlando, Fla.: Harcourt, Inc., 2008).

24. James C. Edwards, *The Plain Sense of Things* (University Park: Pennsylvania State University Press, 1997).

25. Daniel Burke, "Atheism 3.0 Finds a Little More Room for Belief," *Beliefnet,* http://blog.beliefnet.com/news/2009/10/

atheism-30-finds-a-little-more.php (accessed November 4, 2009).

26. Greg M. Epstein, *Good Without God* (New York: William Morrow, 2009).

27. Burke, supra (quoting Epstein).

28. Gey, "Life After the Establishment Clause," 32–35.

29. Jack Call, *God is a Symbol of Something True* (Winchester, UK; Washington, D. C.: O Books, 2009).

30. Quoted in Justin Fox, "In the Long Run," *New York Times Book Review,* November 4, 2009, 13, http://www.nytimes.com/2009/11/01/books/review/Fox-t.html?_r=1&scp=1&sq=keynes&st=cse (accessed November 9, 2009).

31. Anthony B. Pinn, "Atheists Gather in Burbank: A Humanist's Response," *Religion Dispatches* (October 27, 2009), http://www.religiondispatches.org/archive/religionandtheology/1894/atheists_gather_in_burbank%3A_a_humanist%E2%80%99s_response/ (accessed November 6, 2009).

32. Austin Dacey, "Decomposing Humanism: Why Replace Religion?" *Religion Dispatches,* October 29, 2009, http://www.religiondispatches.org/archive/religionandtheology/1963/decomposing_humanism%3A_why_replace_religion (accessed November 6, 2009).

33. Dennett, *Breaking the Spell,* 321–28.

34. Mark Juergensmeyer, "Rethinking Secularism and Religion in the Global Age," *The Immanent Frame,* September 11, 2008, http://blogs.ssrc.org/tif/2009/09/08/rethinking-secularism-and-religion-in-the-global-age/ (accessed November 8, 2009).

35. Robert Wright, *The Evolution of God* (New York: Little, Brown, 2009).

36. Robert Wright, "A Grand Bargain Over Evolution," *New York Times,* August 22, 2009, http://www.nytimes.com/2009/08/23/opinion/23wright.html (accessed November 7, 2009).

37. Nicholas Wade, *The Faith Instinct* (New York: Penguin Press, 2009).

38. Nicholas Wade, "Evolution All Around," *New York Times Sunday Book Review,* October 11, 2009, http://www.nytimes.com/2009/10/11/books/review/Wade-t.html?pagewanted=2 (accessed November 7, 2009).

39. "Letters to the Editor," *New York Times Sunday Book Review,* October 23, 2009, http://www.nytimes.com/2009/10/25/books/review/Letters-t-THEFACTOFEVO_LETTERS.html (accessed November 7, 2009).

40. Elsa Dixler, "Letters: Scientists Respond to Our Review of Richard Dawkins' 'Greatest Show on Earth,'" *New York Times Paper Cuts,* October 23, 2009, http://papercuts.blogs.nytimes.com/2009/10/23/letters-scientists-respond-to-our-review-of-richard-dawkinss-greatest-show-on-earth/ (accessed November 7, 2009).

41. Bruce Ledewitz, "'God' Is Just Another Word: A Report from a Panel on the Role of Religious Speech in Government," *Religion Dispatches,* September 15, 2009, http://www.religiondispatches.org/archive/politics/1832/%E2%80%9Cgod%E2%80%9D_is_just_another_word%3A_a_report_from_a_panel_on_the_role_of_religious_speech_in_government. See also Linell Cady, Frederick Clarkson, and Bruce Ledewitz, "Rebuilding the Wall of Separation: A Progressive Discussion on Church & State," *Religion Dispatches,* September 15, 2009, http://www.religiondispatches.org/archive/politics/1794/rebuilding_the_wall_of_separation%3A_a_progressive_discussion_on_church_%26_state_ (accessed November 7, 2009).

10. IS GOD A UNIVERSAL SYMBOL?

1. *McCreary County,* 545 U.S. at 897 (J. Scalia, dissenting).

2. Supreme Court of the United States, Argument Transcripts, http://www.supremecourt.gov/oral_arguments/

argument_transcripts/08-472.pdf (accessed May 9, 2010).

3. 545 U.S. at 894 (J. Scalia, dissenting).

4. 545 U.S. at 720, n.18 (J. Stevens, dissenting).

5. *Van Orden,* 545 U.S. at 692 (J. Scalia, concurring).

6. *McCreary County,* 545 U.S. at 890 (J. Scalia, dissenting).

7. 505 U.S. at 642 (J. Scalia, dissenting).

8. *McCreary County,* 545 U.S. at 900 (J. Scalia, dissenting).

9. David L. Holmes, *The Faiths of the Founding Fathers* (Oxford; New York: Oxford University Press, 2006), 46.

10. *McCreary County,* 545 U.S. at 893, n. 3 (J. Scalia, dissenting).

11. Mordecai M. Kaplan, *The Meaning of God in Modern Jewish Religion* (Detroit: Wayne State University Press, 1994) (italics in original), 62.

12. Hampson, *God Without God.*

13. Ibid., 8.

14. 380 U.S. 163 (1965).

15. Ibid., 180.

16. Paul Tillich, *Systematic Theology,* 3 vols. (Chicago: University of Chicago Press, 1951–63), 205.

17. Karl Rahner, *Foundations of Christian Faith,* trans. William V. Dych (New York: Crossroad, 1982), 63.

18. Bernard J. F. Lonergan, *Method in Theology* (New York: Herder and Herder, 1972), 103.

19. Huston Smith, *Why Religion Matters* (New York: HarperCollins, 2001), 222–23.

20. Hampson, *God Without God,* 10.

21. Acts 17:22–28.

22. Sarvepalli Radhakrishnan and Charles A. Moore, eds., *A Source Book in Indian Philosophy* (Princeton, N.J.: Princeton University Press, 1957), 623.

23. Jerome A. Stone, *Religious Naturalism Today* (Albany: State University of New York Press, 2008), 6.

24. Ibid.

25. Neiman, *Moral Clarity,* 2–3.

26. Gen. 18:25.

27. Neiman, *Moral Clarity,* 3.

28. Kramnick and Moore, *The Godless Constitution.*

29. Pankaj Mishra, "The Revolt of the Monks," *New York Review of Books,* February 14, 2008, http://www.nybooks.com/articles/21032 (accessed May 9, 2010).

30. Neiman, *Moral Clarity,* 238.

31. 328 F.3d at 491 (J. Fernandez, concurring in part and dissenting in part).

32. Neiman, *Moral Clarity,* 226.

33. Weinberg, "Without God."

34. Stone, *Religious Naturalism,* 121.

35. Werner Heisenberg, *Physics and Beyond,* trans. Arnold J. Pomerans (New York: Harper & Row, 1971), 213.

36. Ratzinger, *Truth and Tolerance,* 238.

37. Westboro Baptist Church Home Page, *GodHatesFags* http://www .godhatesfags.com/ (accessed November 15, 2009).

38. Ledewitz, *Hallowed Secularism,* 198.

11. THE NEW POLITICS OF HIGHER LAW SECULARISM

1. *Pew Forum on Religion and Public Life,* "A Look at Religious Voters in the 2008 Election," February 10, 2009, http://pewresearch.org/pubs/1112/religion-vote-2008-election (accessed November 19, 2010). Statistics from the 2008 election in the following discussion are taken from this site.

2. Ledewitz, *American Religious Democracy,* 3–4.

3. Michael Sokolove, "The Outsider's Insider," *New York Times Magazine,* November 8, 2009, 24, 27.

4. Ibid., 26.

5. Bill McKibben, "The Christian Paradox: How a Faithful Nation Gets Jesus Wrong," *Harper's Magazine,* August 2005, http://www.harpers.org/archive/2005/08/0080695 (accessed November 20, 2009).

6. Edward Lee Pitts, "Patients & Partners," *World Magazine,* November 21, 2009, http://www.worldmag.com/articles/16086 (accessed November 22, 2009). Technically, this was just a story rather than an editorial, but there is not that much difference between the two at *World.*

7. Jamie Dean and Edward Lee Pitts, "Abbey's Road," *World Magazine,* November 7, 2009, http://www.worldmag.com/articles/16042 (accessed November 20, 2009).

8. Ibid.

9. 494 U.S. 872 (1990).

10. *Boerne v. Flores,* 521 U.S. 507 (1997).

11. *Gonzales v. O Centro Espirita Beneficente Uniao Do Vegetal,* 546 U.S. 418 (2006).

12. David M. Herszenhorn, "Health Bill Earns One Republican Vote," *New York Times Health Blog,* November 8, 2009, http://prescriptions.blogs.nytimes.com/2009/11/08/health-bill-earns-one-republican-vote/?scp=1&sq=steny%20h%20hoyer%20bipartisan%20vote&st=cse (accessed November 21, 2009).

13. Jay Newton-Small, "House Passes Health Care Reform," *Time Swampland Blog,* November 8, 2009, http://swampland.blogs.time.com/2009/11/08/house-passes-health-care-reform/ (accessed November 21, 2009).

14. Richard Rorty, "Religion As Conversation-Stopper," in *Philosophy and Social Hope* (New York: Penguin Books, 1999), 168.

15. Richard Rorty, "Religion in the Public Square—A Reconsideration," *Journal of Religious Ethics* 31 (2003): 141.

16. "Call to Renewal Keynote Address," *Organizing for America,* June 28, 2006, http://www.barackobama.com/2006/06/28/call_to_renewal_keynote_address.php (accessed November 21, 2009).

17. 403 U.S. 15 (1971).

18. Jürgen Habermas, *Between Naturalism and Religion,* trans. Ciaran Cronin (Cambridge, UK; Malden, Mass.: Polity Press, 2008).

19. Ibid., 130.

20. Ibid., 131.

21. Ibid., 132.

22. 492 U.S. 490, 565 (1989) (J. Stevens, dissenting).

23. Catharine MacKinnon, "Reflections on Sex Equality Under Law," *Yale Law Journal* 100 (1991): 1315.

24. Steven Malanga, "Whatever Happened to the Work Ethic?" *City Journal* 19, no. 3 (Summer 2009), http://www.city-journal.org/2009/19_3_work-ethic.html (accessed November 22, 2009).

25. Lilla, "The Politics of God" (quoted supra in chapter 5).

26. Ledewitz, *American Religious Democracy,* 157–58.

27. Reinhold Niebuhr, *The Irony of American History* (Chicago: University of Chicago Press, 2008).

28. Brian Urquhart, "What You Can Learn from Reinhold Niebuhr," *New York Review of Books,* March 26, 2009, http://www.nybooks.com/articles/22472 (accessed November 22, 2009).

29. *John Templeton Foundation,* "Does the Universe Have Purpose?" http://www.templeton.org/purpose/essay_Gingerich.html (accessed on November 22, 2009).

30. Ruth Braunstein and David Kyuman Kim, "Rethinking Secularism: The Power of Religion in the Public Sphere," *The Immanent Frame,* October 23, 2009, http://blogs.ssrc.org/tif/2009/10/23/the-power-of-religion-in-the-public-sphere-open-thread/ (accessed November 22, 2009).

CONCLUSION

1. Jeffrey Stout, "The Folly of Secularism," *Journal of the American Academy of Religion* 76, no. 3 (2008), 533–44.

SELECTED BIBLIOGRAPHY

BOOKS

Aronson, Ronald. *Living Without God: New Directions for Atheists, Agnostics, Secularists, and the Undecided*. Berkeley, Calif.: Counterpoint, 2008.

Beattie, Tina. *The New Atheists: The Twilight of Reason and the War on Religion*. Maryknoll, N.Y.: Orbis Books, 2007.

Bellah, Robert N. *Beyond Belief: Essays on Religion in a Post-Traditional World*. New York: Harper and Row, 1970.

Bickel, Alexander M. *The Least Dangerous Branch: The Supreme Court at the Bar of Politics*. 2nd ed. New Haven, Conn.: Yale University Press, 1986.

Pope Benedict XVI. *Charity in Truth*. San Francisco: Ignatius Press, 2009.

Black, Charles L., Jr. *The People and The Court: Judicial Review in a Democracy*. New York: Macmillan, 1960.

———. *The Humane Imagination*. Woodbridge, Conn.: Ox Bow Press, 1986.

Call, Jack. *God Is a Symbol of Something True: Why You Don't Have to Choose Either a Literal Creator or a Blind Indifferent Universe*. Winchester, U.K.; Washington, D.C.: O Books, 2009.

Choper, Jesse H., et al. *Constitutional Law: Cases, Comments, Questions*. St. Paul, Minn.: Thomson/West, 2006.

Comte-Sponville, André. *The Little Book of Atheist Spirituality*. Translated by Nancy Huston. New York: Viking Press, 2007.

Conway Morris, Simon. *Life's Solution: Inevitable Humans in a Lonely Universe*. Cambridge, U.K.; New York: Cambridge University Press, 2003.

Cookson, Catharine, ed. *Encyclopedia of Religious Freedom*. New York: Routledge, 2003.

Cord, Robert L. *Separation of Church and State: Historical Fact and Current Fiction*. New York: Lambeth Press, 1982.

Dacey, Austin. *The Secular Conscience: Why Belief Belongs in Public Life*. Amherst, N.Y.: Prometheus Books, 2008.

Dawkins, Richard. *The Blind Watchmaker*. New York: Norton, 1986.

———. *River Out of Eden: A Darwinian View of Life*. New York: Basic Books, 1995.

———. *The God Delusion*. Boston: Houghton Mifflin Co., 2006.

Dennett, Daniel C. *Breaking the Spell: Religion as a Natural Phenomenon*. New York: Viking, 2006.

Dewey, John. *A Common Faith*. New Haven, Conn.: Yale University Press, 1974.

Dworkin, Ronald. *Is Democracy Possible Here? Principles for a New Political Debate.* Princeton, N.J.: Princeton University Press, 2006.

Edwards, James C. *The Plain Sense of Things: The Fate of Religion in an Age of Normal Nihilism.* University Park: Pennsylvania State University Press, 1997.

Epstein, Greg M. *Good Without God: What a Billion Nonreligious People Do Believe.* New York: William Morrow, 2009.

Feldman, Noah. *Divided by God: America's Church–State Problem—and What We Should Do About It.* New York: Farrar, Straus and Giroux, 2005.

Freud, Sigmund. *The Future of an Illusion.* Translated by W. D. Robson-Scott. New York: H. Liveright, 1928.

Friedman, Barry. *The Will of the People: How Public Opinion Has Influenced the Supreme Court and Shaped the Meaning of the Constitution.* New York: Farrar, Straus, and Giroux, 2009.

Goldberg, Steven. *Bleached Faith: The Tragic Cost When Religion Is Forced Into the Public Square.* Stanford, Calif.: Stanford Law Books, 2008.

Habermas, Jürgen. *Between Naturalism and Religion: Philosophical Essays.* Translated by Ciaran Cronin. Cambridge, U.K.; Malden, Mass.: Polity Press, 2008.

Hampson, Michael. *God Without God: Western Spirituality Without the Wrathful King.* Winchester, U.K.; New York: O Books, 2008.

Harris, Sam. *The End of Faith: Religion, Terror, and the Future of Reason.* New York: W. W. Norton, 2004.

Haught, John F. *God and the New Atheism: A Critical Response to Dawkins, Harris, and Hitchens.* Louisville, Ky.: Westminster John Knox Press, 2008.

Heisenberg, Werner. *Physics and Beyond: Encounters and Conversations.* Translated by Arnold J. Pomerans. New York: Harper and Row, 1971.

Herberg, Will. *Protestant, Catholic, Jew: an Essay in American Religious Sociology.* Garden City, N.Y.: Doubleday, 1955.

Hitchens, Christopher. *God Is Not Great: How Religion Poisons Everything.* New York: Twelve, 2007.

Holmes, David L. *The Faiths of the Founding Fathers.* Oxford; New York: Oxford University Press, 2006.

Isaacson, Walter. *Einstein: His Life and Universe.* New York: Simon and Schuster, 2007.

Kaplan, Mordecai M. *The Meaning of God in Modern Jewish Religion.* Detroit: Wayne State University Press, 1994.

Kauffman, Stuart A. *Reinventing the Sacred: A New View of Science, Reason, and Religion.* New York: Basic Books, 2008.

Kitcher, Philip. *Living with Darwin: Evolution, Design, and the Future of Faith.* Oxford; New York: Oxford University Press, 2007.

Kramer, Larry D. *The People Themselves: Popular Constitutionalism and Judicial Review.* New York: Oxford University Press, 2004.

Kramnick, Isaac, and R. Laurence Moore. *The Godless Constitution: A Moral Defense of the Secular State.* 2nd ed. New York: W. W. Norton, 2005.

Ledewitz, Bruce. *American Religious Democracy: Coming to Terms with the End of Secular Politics.* Westport, Conn.: Praeger Publishers, 2007.

———. *Hallowed Secularism: Theory, Belief, Practice.* New York: Palgrave Macmillan, 2009.

Lilla, Mark. *The Stillborn God: Religion, Politics and the Modern West.* New York: Knopf, 2007.

Lewis, C. S. *They Asked for a Paper.* London: G. Bles, 1962.

———. *The Abolition of Man; or, Reflections on Education With Special Reference to the Teaching of English in the*

Upper Forms of Schools. New York: Macmillan Company, 1947.

Lonergan, Bernard J. F. *Method in Theology*. New York: Herder and Herder, 1972.

McConnell, Michael W., John H. Garvey, and Thomas C. Berg. *Religion and the Constitution*. New York: Aspen Law and Business, 2002.

Micklethwait, John, and Adrian Wooldridge. *God Is Back: How the Global Revival of Faith Is Changing the World*. New York: Penguin Press, 2009.

Neuhaus, Richard John. *The Naked Public Square: Religion and Democracy in America*. Grand Rapids, Mich.: W. B. Eerdmans Pub. Co., 1984.

Neiman, Susan. *Moral Clarity: A Guide for Grown-Up Idealists*. Orlando, Fla.: Harcourt, Inc., 2008.

Niebuhr, Reinhold. *The Irony of American History*. Chicago: University of Chicago Press, 2008.

Nussbaum, Martha C. *Liberty of Conscience: In Defense of America's Tradition of Religious Equality*. New York: Basic Books, 2008.

Peterson, Merrill D., ed. *Thomas Jefferson: Writings*. New York: The Library of America, 1984.

Phillips, Kevin. *American Theocracy: The Peril and Politics of Radical Religion, Oil, and Borrowed Money in the 21st Century*. New York: Viking, 2006.

Radhakrishnan, Sarvepalli, and Charles A. Moore, eds. *A Source Book in Indian Philosophy*. Princeton, N.J.: Princeton University Press, 1957.

Rahner, Karl. *Foundations of Christian Faith: An Introduction to the Idea of Christianity*. Translated by William V. Dych. New York: Crossroad, 1982.

Raymo, Chet. *When God Is Gone Everything Is Holy: The Making of a Religious Naturalist*. Notre Dame, Ind.: Sorin Books, 2008.

Ratzinger, Joseph Cardinal. *Truth and Tolerance: Christian Belief and World Religions*. Translated by Henry Taylor. San Francisco: Ignatius Press, 2004.

Rorty, Richard. *Philosophy and Social Hope*. New York: Penguin Books, 1999.

Shiffrin, Steven H. *The Religious Left and Church–State Relations*. Princeton, N.J.: Princeton University Press, 2009.

Smith, Huston. *Why Religion Matters: The Fate of the Human Spirit in an Age of Disbelief*. New York: HarperCollins, 2001.

Smith, Steven D. *Law's Quandary*. Cambridge, Mass.: Harvard University Press, 2004.

Stenger, Victor J. *God: The Failed Hypothesis: How Science Shows that God Does Not Exist*. Amherst, N.Y.: Prometheus Books, 2007.

Stone, Jerome A. *Religious Naturalism Today: The Rebirth of a Forgotten Alternative*. Albany, N.Y.: State University of New York Press, 2008.

Taylor, Charles. *A Secular Age*. Cambridge, Mass.: Belknap Press of Harvard University Press, 2007.

Teilhard de Chardin, Pierre. *The Divine Milieu*. Brighton, England; Portland, Ore.: Sussex Academic Press, 2004.

Tillich, Paul. *Systematic Theology*. 3 vols. Chicago: University of Chicago Press, 1951–63.

Tushnet, Mark V. *Taking the Constitution Away From the Courts*. Princeton, N.J.: Princeton University Press, 1999.

Waal, Frans B. M. de. *Primates and Philosophers: How Morality Evolved*. Princeton, N.J.: Princeton University Press, 2006.

Wade, Nicholas. *The Faith Instinct: How Religion Evolved and Why It Endures*. New York: Penguin Press, 2009.

Warren, Rick. *The Purpose Driven Life: Selected Thoughts and Scriptures for the Graduate*. Grand Rapids, Mich.: Inspirio, 2004.

Weed, Ronald, and John von Heyking, eds. *Civil Religion in Political Thought: Perennial Questions and Enduring Rel-*

evance in North America. Washington, D.C.: The Catholic University of America Press, 2010.

Whitehead, Alfred North. Adventures of Ideas. New York: Macmillan Company, 1933.

Wilson, Bryan R. Religion in a Secular Society: A Sociological Comment. London: Watts, 1966.

Wright, Robert. The Evolution of God. New York: Little, Brown, 2009.

ARTICLES

Dolan, Mary Jean. "The Special Public Purpose Forum and Endorsement Relationships: New Extensions of Government Speech." Hastings Constitutional Law Quarterly 31 (2004): 71–139.

Gey, Steven G. "Life After the Establishment Clause." West Virginia Law Review 110 (2007): 1–50.

———. "'Under God,' The Pledge of Allegiance, and Other Constitutional Trivia." North Carolina Law Review 81 (2003): 1865–1925.

Gedicks, Frederick Mark, and Roger Hendrix. "Uncivil Religion: Judeo-Christianity and the Ten Commandments." West Virginia Law Review 110 (2007): 275–304.

Loewy, Arnold H. "The Positive Reality and Normative Virtues of a 'Neutral' Establishment Clause." Brandeis Law Journal 41 (2003): 533–543.

Sullivan, Kathleen M. "Religion and Liberal Democracy." University of Chicago Law Review 59 (1992): 195–223.

INDEX

Abolition of Man (Lewis, C. S.), 104, 105, 106, 107, 108, 196, 257nn28–30, 257n33, 262n20

Abortion, 40, 47, 70, 127, 164, 166, 187, 226, 232–36, 240; and Justice Scalia, 70, 71; and President Obama, 237; and the United States Supreme Court. See also *Planned Parenthood of Southeastern Pennsylvania v. Casey; Roe v. Wade; Rust v. Sullivan*

Acts. *See under* Bible

Adams, John, 48, 57

Adler v. Duval School Board, 250n35

Adventures of Ideas (Whitehead), 258n36

Aguilar v. Felton, 9, 249n17

Alito, Samuel: majority opinion in *Pleasant Grove City, Utah v. Summum*, 38, 73, 100, 251n40, 251nn46–47, 257nn4–5, 257n17; opinion in *Salazar v. Buono*, 259n1, 259n3; as replacement of Justice Sandra Day O'Conner, xiii, 38, 39, 97

Allgeyer v. Louisiana, majority opinion by Justice Peckham, 67, 253n56

American Religious Identification Survey, 86, 176, 255n50

American Theocracy (Phillips), 175, 261n19

Arkansas Educational Television Commission v. Forbes, 100, 257n7

Armey, Dick, 232

Aronson, Ronald, 190–93, 206, 244; *Living Without God*, 190–91, 262n3; "The New Atheists," 196, 262n21

Atheism 3.0 Finds a Little More Room for Belief (Burke), 197, 262n25, 263n27

Atheists Gather in Burbank (Pinn), 201, 202, 263n31

Bellah, Robert, 130; *Beyond Belief*, 128–29, 259n7; and Mark Juergensmeyer, 113, 206; on Rousseau and "civil religion," 84, 85, 128

Belmont Abbey College, 233–34

Benedict XVI (pope), 130, 138; *Caritas in Veritate* (Charity in Truth), 108, 131, 258n40

Between Naturalism and Religion (Habermas), 238, 265n18

Beyond Belief (Bellah), 128–29, 259n7

Bible, xii, xiii, xxi, 65, 66, 93, 94, 97, 128, 138, 147, 150, 152, 186, 227; Abraham and God, 182, 221, 262n46; Acts 17:22–28, 220, 264n21; and creation/evolution, 145, 146, 148, 195, 227; Genesis 18:25, 145, 148, 227; John 3:16, 180, 182, 262n46; John 14:6, 258n46; John 18:38, 258n47

Black, Charles L., Jr., v, xvi, 108; *The Humane Imagination*, 105, 106, 257n32;

BRUCE LEDEWITZ is Professor of Law at Duquesne University School of Law and is a graduate of Yale Law School. He is author of *Hallowed Secularism: Theory, Belief, Practice* and *American Religious Democracy: Coming to Terms with the End of Secular Politics*. Ledewitz is a recognized expert in the fields of constitutional law and criminal law. He served as secretary to the National Coalition Against the Death Penalty from 1985 to 1990.

www.ingramcontent.com/pod-product-compliance
Lightning Source LLC
Chambersburg PA
CBHW050224270326
41914CB00003BA/561